More Praise for *The* **and Growing a 1**

"If you are serious about creating and building a talent and development firm, this is your go-to book. It explains the difference between success and failure in this industry. Steve Cohen is the "been there, done that" guy with wide and deep experience. He knows the TD industry like no one else. What an amazing well-researched resource."
—*Geoff Bellman, Founder, GMB Associates, Ltd.*
Author, The Consultant's Calling

"This is ostensibly a book about starting and growing a talent development firm, but it is really relevant to anyone starting any new business. I have had the privilege to work with Steve Cohen on a number of company boards over the years and I know how much value he adds to an aspiring business owner. Now we can all benefit from his experience by following the clearly laid out outline in this book. From being intentional about your mission and vision, to thinking carefully about whom you wish to serve, and then, most important, determining how you intend to add value and build competitive advantage, he leads you to success."
—*Jeff Goodman, Senior Operating Partner, The Riverside Company*

"At last a book that is different from the plethora of theoretical books on the market these days telling you how to run your business *The Complete Guide to Building and Growing a Talent Development Firm* tells it "like it is" and is clear, practical, and readable. Steve Cohen opens up and shares his immense wealth of experience and success strategies that many firms pay dearly for."
—*Ann Herrmann, CEO, Herrmann International*
Co-Author, The Whole Brain Business Book

"Do you think you want to be or develop a business that focuses on talent development? Or, to grow a business you already have? Steve knows this industry and consults with many of the best. And, because he knows what goes into making, differentiating, and selling these unique products and services, you will feel he is talking directly to you—as your trusted adviser and confidante!"
—*Patricia McLagan, Founder and CEO of McLagan International, Inc.*
Author of the forthcoming Unstoppable You:
Adopt the New Learning 4.0 Mindset and Change Your Life

"Steve Cohen has given us a priceless business consultant's GPS. He supplants jargon with clarity, theory with experience, projections with practicality, and strategy with results. This careful, smart, and easy-to-read book draws you in and enables you to put its lessons to good use."

—*Louis Patler, President, The B.I.T. Group*
Author, Make Your Own Waves *and* If It Ain't Broke . . . BREAK IT!

"An invaluable, relevant, and practical resource—that's what Steve Cohen has delivered in *The Complete Guide to Building and Growing a Talent Development Firm*. Clear, concise, and on point, the book provides a pivotal foundation for growing a thriving business in the talent development industry. It is a masterpiece for anyone dedicated to this industry, whether firing up a business or leveraging long-term success. It's a comprehensive toolkit complete with provocative questions challenging the status quo and offering new possibilities for consideration."

—*Pamela J. Schmidt, Executive Director, ISA—The Association of Learning Providers*

"An absolute must-read resource for anyone involved in or contemplating the business of talent development! From trends to day–to-day operations to clarifying the difference between building a business and creating a practice, Steve Cohen provides keen insight from his many years in the field, as well as thought-provoking questions. This is an invaluable, brilliant handbook!"

—*Susan Scott, Founder and CEO, Fierce, Inc.*
Author, Fierce Conversations

"Steve Cohen serves up the long-awaited, definitive guidebook for anyone seeking to build or grow their talent development business. This book is jam-packed with best practices—proven lessons, tools, insights, and methods—based on his decades of doing the real work, as one of the true pioneers of talent development, globally. It's a rare classic and keepsake."

—*Paul G. Stoltz, Founder and CEO, PEAK Learning*
Author, Adversity Quotient @ Work *and* GRIT

The Complete Guide to

BUILDING AND GROWING

A TALENT DEVELOPMENT FIRM

Stephen L. Cohen

PRESS

ATD Press is an internationally renowned source of insightful and practical information on
talent development, workplace learning, and professional development.

ATD Press
1640 King Street
Alexandria, VA 22314 USA

Ordering information: Books published by ATD Press can be purchased by visiting ATD's
website at www.td.org/books or by calling 800.628.2783 or 703.683.8100.

Library of Congress Control Number: 2017933601
ISBN-10: 1-56286-773-3
ISBN-13: 978-1-56286-773-7
e-ISBN: 978-1-56286-775-1

ATD Press Editorial Staff
Director: Kristine Luecker
Manager: Christian Green
Community of Practice Manager, Human Capital: Ann Parker
Developmental Editor: Jack Harlow
Cover Design: Tim Green, Faceout Studio
Text Design: Francelyn Fernandez
Printed by Versa Press, East Peoria, IL

CONTENTS

To my parents, Bea and Murray, long gone but not forgotten, for their continued encouragement and support for all my educational and professional pursuits.

To my sons, Andrew and Joshua, still here and always present, for inspiring me to continually encourage and support them through my educational and professional pursuits.

ACKNOWLEDGMENTS

In considering whom to thank for their contributions to this book, I realized the list could stand alone as its own chapter. After all, this book is a product of 40-plus years of experience during which many people helped me acquire my knowledge and hone my skills. I am sure I have inadvertently left out some, but I did my best to credit everyone to whom I am grateful.

For starters, where would I be without all the colleagues with whom I have worked and shared perspectives over the years? They include those from Assessment Designs International, my very first firm, to Harbridge House, Wilson Learning, The Learning Design Group, Dove Consulting, Carlson Marketing, Carlson Companies, Right Management, to Strategic Leadership Collaborative, my current business. My two original partners from Assessment Designs, Cabot Jaffee and Fred Frank (unfortunately deceased) and their families, have been life-long friends. David Dove, whom I first met at Harbridge House, also remains a valued and trusted colleague and friend.

During everyone's professional journey you meet people in different contexts, as either clients, co-workers, or bosses only to see the relationship grow into something more. People such as Ann Buzzotta, Andrea Deege, Audie Dunham, Chuck Gorman, Karen Grabow, Anne Grason, Jackie Greaner, Keith Halperin, Bill Hertan, Diane Hessan, Tony Jace, Karen Kendrick, Ron Kirsch, Nancy Lewis, Toni Lucia, Susan McClure, Elizabeth Moore, Dave Muxworthy, Tina Olson, Peter Pattenden, Gary Quinlan, Pam Schmidt, Jim Schroer, Jeff Sugarman, Christy Weum, and Kevin Wilde. I appreciate all of your support and count my blessings that I know you.

I also have been blessed to have a large network of wonderful author colleagues and friends in the talent development world. A few have stood the test of time and have been inspirations for how to write and present clearly and succinctly. They include Geoff Bellman, Elaine Biech, Ann Herrmann-Nehdi, Beverly Kaye, Jim Kouzes, Pat McLagan, David McNally, Louis Patler, Len Schlesinger, Susan Scott, Paul Stoltz, and Nick Tasler.

A special shout-out goes to the Riverside Company. I have been honored to serve on the boards of five of its training and education companies and conducted strategic growth planning for many others. I have learned just as much, if not more, from them as I've contributed. Thanks to Jeff Goodman, Mike Eblin, Peter Tsang, and Ann Hayes for their continuous support.

My thanks extends to the boards of other training and education suppliers that I've been fortunate to serve on and learn from. They include Better Communications, Crisis Prevention Institute, Decision Pulse, Employment Law Training/ Navex, ExperiencePoint, Fierce, Grace Hill, Herrmann International, Interaction Associates, Lexipol, NetSpeed Learning, and OnCourse Learning. The knowledge and experience I bring to this book can be directly derived from these wonderful and enriching experiences, and I deeply thank each and every one of these CEOs for their confidence in me to assist them.

One group that has been intricately involved with the writing of this book are the client organizations and their representatives with whom I have had the honor to consult. Too many to list, and yet they should not go unnoticed because they in fact have provided the background and context for what I write here.

My career, and a result this book, would not have been possible without a short but powerful list of professional associations and support groups. Certainly, my nearly 40-year participation with both ATD and the Instructional Systems Association as a board member, frequent volunteer, and beneficiary of the programming and information has benefited my development immeasurably. While less involved over the years, my association with the International Society for Performance Improvement and the Society for Industrial and Organizational Psychology have been equally helpful in shaping my career. Although I'm no longer active, one other important association was the Woodlands Group. This small quarterly gathering of 15 to 20 professionals was instrumental in my development as a relatively young practitioner. I thank all of its past and current members for their support.

Of course, a book can't be written well without the advice and consult of the professionals. ATD has been extraordinarily generous with its time and editorial competency. In the earlier years, it was Pat Galagan, Nancy Olson, and Paula Ketter who helped me hone my craft while writing my *TD* articles. More recently, it has been people such as Ryann Ellis, Ann Parker, Clara Von Ins, Julia Liapidova, and Alex Quinn who have overseen my blog posts and other contributions. But my biggest shout-out must go to my editors, Jack Harlow and Christian Green, whose patience and insight deserve their own medal of honor, for helping me add, delete, and revise so this book came together in a meaningfully relevant way. In addition, early readers such as Stacy Engle, Randy Redwitz, and Joe Trueblood have been a great resource for me. Yes, it does take a village.

Finally, and perhaps most important, I owe a great amount of gratitude to my family who have stuck together in total support through thick and thin. While I was largely off away consulting during critical years of my children's growth, they and their mother managed to keep the family together through some admittedly trying times. We have never been closer, and I chalk this up to their intestinal fortitude to put love before all else.

INTRODUCTION

*Before you start some work, always ask yourself three
questions—why am I doing it, what the results might be,
and will I be successful. Only when you think deeply and
find satisfactory answers to these questions, go ahead.*
—Chanakya

Before answering the three questions Chanakya, a philosopher from India, posed in his quote, I'll first ask you: Why are you reading this? What results might you obtain? And will you be successful? As you will soon discover, the you in this book encompasses a larger group. This introduction outlines my intent, my experience and background in the industry, my hopes for what you will get from it, and how I've organized it.

Purpose and Need

Some excellent books have already been published around the corners of this topic—for example, Elaine Biech's fabulous contributions of *The Business of Consulting* (2007), *The Consultant's Quick Start Guide* (2001), and *The Consultant's Legal Guide* (2000); Geoff Bellman's superb *The Consultant's Calling* (2002); and Peter Block's classic *Flawless Consulting* (2000). But these informative books are not what I had in mind when I set out to write mine. While many of the principles and practices outlined in these books apply to the talent development industry, there are many differences between a general consulting firm and one in the specific talent development space. Particularly, the nature of its drivers—its content, delivery, and instruction. This book is about setting up a business in the specific field of talent development, not just about being a good consultant or even creating a general consulting practice.

My primary purpose for writing this book is to give back to the profession that has been so good to me. This is a two-way street, but being able to spend my entire career in a profession I love makes me feel just a little unworthy, because it has been so much fun. More specifically, it has provided me the opportunity to give back, after learning so many lessons and making many mistakes, to both those thinking about starting a talent development firm or those already engaged in one and planning to grow it.

A large part of my current consulting practice involves sitting on boards of training and education firms and facilitating their strategic planning efforts. In addition, I have been part of at least eight different consulting enterprises in the industry over my more than 40-year career. What I have discovered is there are countless questions about how to most effectively operate a very profitable talent development business, even from those who have done reasonably well. However, I found that no one has pulled this information together as a reference for these questions and best practices. I hope this book will serve this need.

My Experience in the Talent Development Field

I am the first to admit I don't possess all the knowledge and experience in the industry. I make no claims that my points of view are better or more accurate than anyone else's. Rather, I believe I can pass on some perspectives and insights that may alter the way you look at business challenges. And yet, with the one-size-rarely-fits-all state of the modern business world, you must place the offered suggestions in the context of your own business, goals, experience, and expertise.

That said, I do bring some very unique experiences from a talent development supplier's perspective. I have spent more than 40 years in the talent development consulting world, from my first day in graduate school studying for my PhD in industrial/organizational psychology. I have founded, co-founded, or directed eight different talent development entities, the majority of which focused on assessment and development in the industry. Four of them I sold, and several others I helped to restructure within other organizations. Suffice it to say, the different missions I have served, objectives I have met, and budgets I have overseen mean I have been around the talent development block a few times.

I've gained considerable insight into navigating the industry and running consulting businesses that cater to it. I was sought out to share my experience and advice as a board member of many training and education businesses, as well as conducting strategic growth planning for them. To date, I have had both the pleasure and honor to serve on more than 15 boards, alongside some very astute people. During my tenure on these boards, I have often witnessed outstanding growth—on average about 200 percent. But the true value gained by serving in this advisory capacity has been from watching the mistakes that were made, helping to correct them, and then making sure these businesses were on solid ground.

All of this collective experience has provided a wealth of insight into the people development world, and I owe it to the industry to share what I've learned. While I don't have all the answers, let alone know all the questions to ask, I know most of the issues and challenges, and in some cases even best practices for operating and growing these businesses. No doubt, there is much to discuss. Each chapter will focus on a specific topic germane to building and growing a talent development business.

What Do I Want For You?

I have written this book for those in the business of consulting and training supplier services. You could be an internal talent development professional contemplating going out on your own or joining a consulting firm. You could already have an individual or small private consulting practice and be considering what it will take to be more successful. Or, you could be leading a larger firm committed to growth. Finally, you could be a senior-level learning leader trying to figure out how to more effectively perform your internal role.

The challenge is appealing to all these audiences simultaneously while remaining equally relevant. In the end, you will have to determine what's relevant to you and how you will apply what you are learning.

In writing this book, I've led with my opinions based on my experience, although I try more often than not to support those opinions with informed research. Therefore, the purpose of this book is to be more heuristic than definitive in an exchange of ideas on the topics presented. My goal is to stimulate thinking sometimes through provocative statements and other times through questions. I am hopeful it will create a strong dialogue between you and your partners, colleagues, and businesses, to the benefit of all.

Book Organization

Selecting topics to cover in a book like this is always difficult. I have decided to pick the topics most germane to building a growing and successful business in this industry. Although I will not cover all the bases, I will cover those I think will be most meaningful to you. If you are in the business of talent development, I am sure you will find valuable and readily applicable insights.

I organized this book around the series of events that typically take place in establishing, managing, developing, and growing any business, but in the context of the talent development supplier industry. Therefore, I have placed the chapters in the order in which you would most likely need to consider them, assuming you were starting from scratch. In a way, they represent the business value chain of what has to take place to go to market and then subsequently what is needed to survive, and hopefully thrive, in it. Because of this, the chapters can stand on their own as specific topics you might want to turn to as you're confronted with a particular issue. This book can serve as a reference through the lifecycle of your business.

This book comprises three sections. Part 1: Getting Grounded sets the foundation for building your business. To start, I address the industry as a whole: What are its dynamics, trends, and practices (chapter 1)? From there, I move on to helping you understand what you want from your business (chapter 2) and how you can begin to set the foundation for its success (chapter 3). Part of this foundation is understanding what you own as a business and how you can ultimately leverage it in the marketplace (chapter 4). Part 2: Creating Momentum provides the underpinnings of operating your business. It includes differentiating and selling your offer so it doesn't collect dust on the proverbial shelf (chapters 5 and 6). Next, I cover how to operate both the front and back of the house in a sustainably profitable manner (chapters 7 and 8). Finally, Part 3: Moving Forward is about identifying and overcoming barriers to growth (chapter 9), as well as looking ahead by exploring what's in store for your business and the industry, and how you can best prepare for the unpredictable future that lies ahead (chapters 10 and 11).

At the end of each chapter I've included reflection questions for you to think about. They refer to how you are managing the challenges mentioned in the chapter, or ask you to consider your options going forward. They encourage you to think about how you are addressing the many issues that surface when establishing, building, and growing a talent development business. At the very end of the book is an action planning appendix, with room to answer questions for each chapter, which will help you apply what you have learned. You may want to respond to these after you have read each chapter or wait until you have digested the entire book.

This isn't a tell-all book, a revelation of the industry's dirty little secrets. It also isn't intended to be a how-to book, with prescribed steps you must follow. Wouldn't it be nice if it was that easy?

Establishing and growing a business in any industry is a complicated endeavor, dependent on many interrelated factors. As I mentioned, I don't have all the answers. Despite the book's title describing it as "The Complete Guide" it could've easily been hundreds of pages longer, covering ever finer points about the industry.

By the time you are reading it, some industry information may have become dated. What won't be dated, however, are the many lessons learned and best practices observed throughout my career. So as you set out with this book in hand, you may be seeking a special formula for success. I am pleased you've turned to me to offer my advice and insight.

I hope you enjoy reading this as much as I've enjoyed writing it.

Steve Cohen
Founder and Principal
Strategic Leadership Collaborative
Minneapolis, MN
March 2017

PART 1

GETTING GROUNDED

1

UNDERSTANDING INDUSTRY DYNAMICS AND TRENDS

*The barriers are not erected which can say to aspiring
talents and industry, "Thus far and no farther."*
—*Ludwig van Beethoven*

You can get lost trying to keep pace with the changes currently taking place in talent development, not to mention the transformation of the field since I started my career 50 years ago. It wasn't long ago that the industry was defined by models and theories such as McGregor's Theory X and Theory Y, Maslow's Hierarchy of Needs, and Herzberg's Two-Factor Theory. Personal computers weren't even on the radar, unless you call a deck of punch cards that fed into a massive mainframe, personal. Add to that the radical changes in the makeup of the workforce: multiple generations, diverse cultures, and freer mobility of workers between jobs. The workplace is different today. The current pace of change far exceeds that which I experienced not too long ago. Navigating through it successfully is challenging.

There was a time when almost all talent development firms were teaching softer leadership, communications, interpersonal, and sales skills, and computer-based training was in its infancy. Today, businesses in the talent development industry set out to get organizations and their employees up to speed on the ever-changing state of federal policies, legal compliance in ethics, anti-discrimination policies, HVAC technical skills, oil and gas rig operations, mortgage lending policies, and sanitary food manufacturing techniques. Yet, while the content of the business of talent development has broadened, technology has brought even greater change to the industry in which software as a service-based subscription platforms in the cloud are common.

This chapter is designed to not only ground you in what has taken place in the industry, but also introduce you to the most recent changes. Let's start with a brief history of the field, before we dive into what we know about the industry and the major trends going forward.

A Wild and Windy Road: Historical Perspective

Any consulting firm focused on providing advisory services for improving the performance of the workforce would qualify as a talent development supplier, sometimes referred to as a vendor. These could include individual consultants, full-fledged consultancies, or simply providers of training services in areas such as skills development, coaching, change management, engagement, performance management, and technical skills—any area that can enhance the skills, knowledge, and attitudes of the workforce to ultimately improve performance. We sometimes refer generically to these programs, products, and services as an offer. In other words, what is offered to clients as solutions to their workforce development challenges.

It would be an understatement to say the talent development supplier industry has undergone considerable change. In the last 50 years, it has experienced just about every kind of consolidation and distribution play possible: roll-ups and integrations, mergers and acquisitions, franchises and distributors, partnerships and brokers. This would indicate either a maturing industry or one that has yet to fully evolve. One thing is certain, there are fewer barriers to enter the industry now. Whether those who enter the industry will be successful depends on many of the factors covered in this book.

As the global economy has changed, driving often unique but certainly different demands in the workforce, the talent development supplier industry has had to keep pace. Some firms have been relatively successful navigating this change, while others have not, and still others have outright failed. In the United States, it's now a more than $70.6 billion industry, some $8 billion of which was spent on external services (*Training* 2016), which was a 29 percent increase over the prior year. But it hasn't always been this way. Not too long ago, the human capital asset was considered more of a necessary evil than a true business game changer with relatively little money earmarked for skills training.

In addition to the many changes in the global economy affecting talent development, other forces influencing the supplier industry have been at play as well. For instance, there have been many attempts at supplier acquisition and consolidation, including some ill-fated ones. Provant attempted to roll up 21 training companies in the late 1990s, but after financially overextending itself, it started divesting in 2001 and a year later sold the remaining companies to Drake Beam Morin—Japan (J. Zenger 2013).

At about the same time, there was another short-lived attempt at a roll up of about a dozen firms by Enterprise Profit Solutions (EPS), an offshoot of a division of Deloitte & Touche. While the acquisitions included more traditional human resources firms, EPS purchased 10 talent development businesses, all for stock in the new company that planned to go public. However, EPS did not have an integration strategy, which left these companies on their own. Less than a year after its founding, EPSstarted to come apart, never went public, and its founders had to exit the company, by then so buried in debt they couldn't even issue junk bonds (Welles 2002). Unfortunately, all of these companies had to buy themselves back even though they received no cash when they were first acquired.

On the other hand, there have been some successful consolidations. Examples include the Times Mirror acquisition of Zenger-Miller, Learning International, and Kaset International from 1985 to 1992 (which were then consolidated into Achieve Global in 1998); Kenexa's acquisition by IBM; Taleo's by Oracle; Lynda. com by LinkedIn (then by Microsoft); and Success Factors by SAP.

Another successful acquisition was the Institute for International Research's (IIR) purchase in 2000 of five companies (Achieve Global, Omega, Huthwaite, Forum, and ESI International). IIR later became part of Informa, after being acquired in 2005, which itself was finally sold in July 2013 to Providence Equity Partners, one of the largest private equity businesses in the world (Informa 2013). Other private equity firms such as The Riverside Company and Renovus Capital Partners have also targeted training and education companies in building their funds by identifying strong platform companies and then growing them through frequent add-ons.

Setting the early pace was one of the first supplier industry acquisitions when John Wiley & Sons purchased Wilson Learning in the early 1980s, which was then divested in 1991 to Wilson's Japanese subsidiary. However, Wiley reentered the talent development business with the relatively recent acquisitions of Pfeiffer & Company, Profiles International, Inscape Publishing, and CrossKnowledge.

What you can conclude from all of this activity is that the talent development supplier industry has been going through its own metamorphosis, supported by the influence of technological advancements in human resource information systems, learning management systems, and online learning capability. In 2013 alone, the industry spent more than $5 billion on talent management systems software (Jones and Wang-Audia 2014).

From the outside, it appears talent development is a growth industry, creating an interesting dynamic of small businesses mixed in with the big players. You don't have to look much further than to IBM's and SAP's respective acquisitions of Kenexa and Success Factors to recognize that big business has also realized the potential for high growth in the talent development arena. Clearly, the competitive landscape is changing.

Know What You Don't Know: Industry Knowledge

Achieving success in the talent development supplier industry means you truly understand the nature of your business, its value proposition, and the business model that will ensure sustainable profitability. Not being able to grasp these factors is a formula for failure. As we consider the past, experience the present, and imagine the future, this industry can be described at any of those junctures by three drivers that have and will continue to influence its demand, structure, and market strategy.

These three drivers—content, instruction, and delivery—are independent, multifaceted constructs, but all dependent on one another (Figure 1-1). When combined, they create a customer experience. While some in the industry only focus on one of these drivers and temporarily do well in that particular sphere, they will ultimately fail because the other two define the customer experience as well. It is their unique combination and interplay that differentiates a successful supplier in the talent development industry.

Owning the intellectual property, or content, without the capability to deliver it in an instructionally sound way that achieves results, whether in a more traditional classroom facility or through technology, will not create a differentiated user experience. Nor will owning a unique delivery platform without relevant content, even if instructionally sound. What this implies is a complex industry that involves considerable knowledge, insight, and foresight of the marketplace to build and grow a successful business.

Figure 1-1. Talent Development Industry Drivers

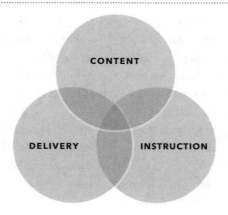

Take the aforementioned Provant, for example. The intended training business roll-up was masterminded by a company that had successfully acquired both ambulance and waste treatment businesses throughout the United States. And yet, the business models for successful ambulance or waste treatment companies have far greater similarities than those in the training field. Provant's leaders thought the same could be done with training businesses, but they didn't understand that each of those businesses had unique content and value propositions and delivered their offering differently, in many cases to international audiences. Attaining economies of scale by integrating back-office functions such as human resources and technology were strong motivating forces to bring costs down, but integrating other operations such as product development, marketing and sales, and training delivery was much more difficult, because each company had its own distinct offer and delivery methods. In fact, while the intent was to have these companies cross-sell each other's offer, they were simultaneously incentivized to make their company's numbers, ultimately keeping them from total collaboration.

Contrast Provant with IIR and Informa. In their acquisition strategies they recognized the unique differences in their training businesses. While they took advantage of integrating some back-office functions, they kept the firms separate, maintaining their own brands. More recently, Providence Equity Partners built a portfolio of 12 talent development firms under the umbrella of TwentyEighty, many of which were sold to it by Informa.

Also consider John Wiley & Sons' purchase of Wilson Learning in the late 1970s. Wiley assumed Wilson was also in the publishing business because it printed training binders and thus could leverage Wiley's in-house printing, warehousing, and production capabilities. However, Wilson was no more a publisher than Wiley was a training business. The intended synergies never took place. Fortunately, a generation later, Wiley recognized what business it is in with its acquisition of Pfeiffer & Associates, Profiles International, Inscape Publishing, and CrossKnowledge. While these businesses provide assessment and training materials and programs, most use resellers and distributors, rather than directly delivering their own materials.

Numerous other examples support this premise, but what is most important is that to be successful, the architects and leaders of these mergers and acquisitions must truly understand their business model, as well as those they acquire.

One of the more interesting events in the talent development supplier acquisition world involves tangential businesses that see this as a growth industry worth investing in. Korn-Ferry, a leading executive recruiting firm, has been very active over the past few years accumulating talent development companies: Lominger; Lore International; Novations; and PDI-Ninthhouse, Pivot, and Hay (Burnison 2013, 45-48). Like many other companies, Korn-Ferry sees the talent development

7

industry as a hedge around their original head-hunting business, which is subject to economic peaks and valleys. Time will tell whether they made a wise decision.

Similarly, Right Management, a career outplacement business, also subject to the vagaries of economic stability, flourished during bad economic times when people were let go and needed outplacement services, yet suffered when times were good with fewer people leaving and unemployment relatively low. Right Management bought a dozen or so organizational and talent development companies over several years in the mid-1990s to early 2000s to help flatten out its financial performance. In 2004, it was bought by the huge temporary staffing company Manpower, as its hedge against the frequent fluctuations in the staffing economy.

As the talent development industry continues to evolve and expand, integration, whether through acquisitions of new businesses or mergers with existing ones, will continue to define the competitive landscape. As you build and grow your business, the lessons from these integrations, many of which have unraveled in one way or another, will be critical to ensuring your future success.

Here Today, Gone Tomorrow?: Current Fads and Lasting Trends

Trends in one industry guide the trends in others; although determining which causes which is always difficult to assess. But some emerging trends clearly affect almost every industry, including talent development. Consider four trends McKinsey & Company recently identified (Dobbs, Manyika, and Woetzel 2015):

1. **Beyond Shanghai:** The age of urbanization, involving a shifting of the center of economic activity and dynamics to emerging markets and the cities within these.
2. **The Tip of the Iceberg:** Accelerating technical change, involving the sheer ubiquity of technology in our lives in its scope, scale, and economic impact.
3. **Getting Old Isn't What It Used to Be:** Responding to the challenges of an aging world, which means a stronger burden on a reduced workforce to drive growth, as well as the severe strain put on government finances to care for the aging.
4. **Trade, People, Finance, and Data:** Greater global connection, which means more interconnectedness and dependencies across industries, countries, and people than ever before.

I will not try to dissect the influence of every trend on the talent development industry. I'll leave that to the economists and futurists. So with the four trends in mind, here are a few impactful trends for those focused on building a talent development supplier business.

It is hard to argue that the most significant industry trend of the last couple of decades has been anything but the influence of technology on the delivery of content. This ranges from the ever-evolving online learning programming to human resources information systems and platforms that house and distribute that programming and other content.

Significant advancements continue in the area of technology-enabled talent development. Blended learning, the merging of technology-enabled with face-to-face delivery methods, has almost become an expectation, not the exception it was 10 years ago. In addition, we are just scratching the surface in gamification and only starting to explore virtual learning as the apparatus for creating virtual worlds. These advancements are largely about how to reach the learner more efficiently.

Other advancements continue to emerge for how to reach the learner more effectively; that is, learning more readily just in time, applying it more immediately, and then remembering it longer. There seems to be a resurgence in brain anatomy in understanding how learning takes place. As a result, we are seeing more and more bite-sized learning applications in smaller timeframes with focused information. Consider that Ned Herrmann brought us Whole Brain Thinking 50 years ago, which continues today through Herrmann International. Starting with how people process their approaches to learning differently and how learning curricula must consider this in their design and development, there is likely to be much more exploration in the area of neurological underpinnings of learning, and a good deal more to learn that hasn't yet been specifically applied to the talent development industry.

While technology's influence remains on the minds of organizations, they realize their most important asset is their human capital. The costs of recruiting and hiring new talent in the face of a relative skill set paucity, particularly in the United States, has caused significant concern. Finding, developing, and retaining more qualified human capital has become so economically advantageous that corporations finally recognize its hidden value. One would have hoped this would have been recognized without the force of an economic driver, but regardless of what caused this surge in behavior, it's real and undoubtedly long lasting.

The very human assets mentioned are also changing dramatically. Comparing the characteristics of the Baby Boomer workforce with that of a future in which Millennials and Gen Zers are leading the charge, Bruce Tulgan (2016) identifies 19 factors that will distinguish these two types of workforces. Examples include what the younger generations want in a job (flexibility versus security); what they want in their manager (support, guidance, and feedback versus autonomy); what they want in their leaders (coaching, teaching, and mentoring versus authoritarian and directive); and what their attitudes are toward their career (build a career around the desired life versus build a life around the desired career), among others.

The numbers alone are staggering. Tulgan's study estimates that by 2020 the Western workforce will comprise less than 20 percent of Baby Boomers, who in 2016 made up about 30 percent, while first-wave and post-Millennials will make up 30 percent, compared with 14 percent in 2016. The worldwide workforce is experiencing a significant age shift accompanied by different wants and needs from employment. As a result, the goals and expectations of these newer workforce entrants will change the landscape of how work is accomplished in the future and therefore the skills and capabilities needed to successfully navigate the world of work.

This is not to say there aren't more significant trends beginning to emerge that will continue to influence the industry. Pat Galagan (2015, 28-33) does an excellent job identifying six: the boundary-less career; employee satisfaction's bleeding edge; sort-of-new performance management; new learning movements; simple and slow; and mobile learning. She makes a very strong case for how each of these trends already influences the talent development industry, and there's no reason to believe they won't continue.

The influence of a domino effect is easier to accept than to understand and interpret. Global trends trickle down to affect organizations and the workforce, and eventually define the industries serving it, such as talent development. In 2015, ATD conducted a study with Rothwell & Associates and Penn State University to better understand the trends and challenges faced by the talent development field. In the study 31 industry thought leaders from global organizations were interviewed, and they identified 15 trends that would affect talent development between 2015 and 2020, including the need for a more innovative workforce, high turnover rates, world economic interdependence, and company and education provider partnerships. It was concluded that learning technology will continue to rise, strong talent pipelines need to be built, talent development professionals need to engage as strategic business partners, global organizations need to be able to solve problems and innovate, and value-added partnerships need to be developed. In short, these challenges require clear talent development goals, effective delivery methods, and measurable results. The talent development supplier industry is in the perfect position to assist organizations in serving all three of these needs.

Among the most significant changes and trends occurring in all industries, including talent development, is how firms reach prospects and customers. Technology enables you to reach more people in less time for less cost, but sorting through the vast number of prospects and converting them into customers requires even more sorting.

What is unknown at this point are events which will continue to disrupt how we look at the talent development industry. There's no question that capabilities such as agility, adaptability, and flexibility in how we see and reflect on what presents itself in the business environment are, and likely will be, in greater demand.

Dream On: Entrepreneurship

The talent development supplier industry is still largely made up of one- or two-person entrepreneurships, with the exception of large companies such as Accenture, McKinsey, Xerox Learning Services, and Deloitte, not to mention technology and content platform companies such as Udemy, IBM's Kenexa, Microsoft's Lynda.com, SAP's Success Factors, and Skillsoft. What makes the industry difficult to define is that businesses are consolidating into even larger companies, while smaller consulting practices, freelance independent contractors, authors, and speakers exist as their own entities.

Consider the membership of the Instructional Systems Association, a group of about 80 learning provider organizations. Over its 40 years, 65 to 70 percent of ISA's membership has been considered small (that is, under $5 million in revenue), 20 to 25 percent medium ($5-$25 million), 10 to 15 percent large (more than $25 million), and 3 to 5 percent quite large (more than $100 million) (Schmidt 2016). If these statistics are representative of the industry—and there is no reason to believe they aren't—it's clear that talent development is an entrepreneurial industry. In fact, because interest in growing is an important qualifier to being a member of ISA, many more small practices that earn less than $5 million in revenue probably skew the relative percentages even more toward the small side.

As a result, you must consider whether you can operate as an entrepreneur. In 2012, a study was conducted to determine the personal skills unique and predictive of those people who would become serial entrepreneurs. When compared with a control group of 17,000 working adults, the group classified as entrepreneurs self-assessed above the control group average in the skills of persuasion, leadership, personal accountability, goal orientation, and interpersonal skills (Bonnstetter 2012).

A Pioneer in the Talent Development Supplier Industry

My favorite story of an entrepreneur in the industry is of Larry Wilson (now deceased), one of the very first people to enter the training and development space with Wilson Learning Corporation, which he founded in the late 1960s. Larry was an insurance salesman, but not just any salesman. He was one of the youngest to reach the million dollar plateau when that was a significant achievement. He believed selling did not require a manipulative or adversarial approach; instead, he used a counselor approach to meet customer needs and produce more effective results. At the time, this was a groundbreaking concept that created a new generation of salespeople who recognized the value of establishing relationships based on trust and win-win problem solving. So Larry took what he had learned as a successful salesman and trained others to be as successful. He created the training program Counselor Salesperson, which, nearly 50 years later, is the basis for most sales training programs.

Larry knew he wasn't equipped or even interested in building a business. He just wanted to create great programs that could help people "become all they could be." So he hired operators to do the dirty work, such as tend to the finances, processes, people, and the like, while he pursued the next big thing. He demonstrated a willingness to take risks, one of which was introducing video to training. He used VHS or Beta tapes, the latest technology at that time, to better engage learners, as we do today with online programming. Next, he become one of the very first to bring computer-based video learning to the industry. After his company was acquired by John Wiley & Sons in 1981, Larry built a subsidiary business to house Wilson's Interactive Technology Group, a conglomeration of software engineers, video writers and producers, instructional developers, and graphic designers all working to create state of the art videodisc self-instructed programs, the forerunner of online learning today.

As a model for entrepreneurship in the talent development industry, Larry can best be described as optimistic, passionate, undeterred, relentless, enthusiastic, and energetic. Like Larry, great entrepreneurs are also visionaries who see what others can't. They are excellent communicators who can articulate their vision in a way that captivates and excites others. But they are also humble and grateful for their successes.

What is most interesting is that many of the characteristics that make an effective entrepreneur are not the same as those needed to build a well-organized profitable business. Often, true entrepreneurs are so focused on chasing their visions they don't think about the implications of costs, time, and energy on the rest of their business. Unless they have an unlimited budget or are surrounded by business builders, their vision can interfere with establishing and growing the business.

Also, if you are expecting a reasonable work-life balance as an entrepreneur, you should probably rethink starting a business of any kind. It's typically all-consuming with a reasonable amount of self-imposed stress and anxiety, in large part due to the responsibility for meeting payroll. This is why it is important to only take on business that you love.

After reading this book, you should determine whether you are equipped to be an effective entrepreneur. Remember, you will also be competing against many people who are characterized by this archetype.

The Entrepreneurial Spirit

Entrepreneurs are often driven by their commitment to succeed. While they may sometimes appear to be disorganized, they take time to prepare their next steps. They fall down and get up again. They anticipate what the future will hold. They take appropriate risks. In sum, they are passionate, persistent, and persevere at all costs. These characteristics, and others, are masterfully described in Louis Patler's 2016 book, *Make Your Own Waves*, in which he uses 10 surfer's rules as a meaningful metaphor for entrepreneurs and innovators: Learn to Swim; Get Wet; Decide to Ride; Always Look "Outside"; Commit, Charge, Shred!; Paddle Back Out; Never Turn Your Back on the OceanDare Big; Never Surf Alone; and Stay Stoked! A very delightful, influential, and relevant read for all current and future entrepreneurs.

Conclusion

Undoubtedly, the talent development industry has become very important to overall organizational performance. Done right, starting a talent development supplier firm can also be seen as a good investment opportunity. This is largely because of the elevated prominence talent development has garnered due to its importance to business performance. As a result, there has been considerable activity in the investment community during the last 25 years and it doesn't look as though things will change anytime soon, as noted in chapter 11. While it was typically considered only a necessary cost in the past, leveraging human capital is now a major concern to boards of directors today.

Looking forward, technology and demographic shifts have brought significant changes to the talent development role in organization performance and productivity. This has inspired an entrepreneurial consulting industry to support these changes. To survive and thrive you must take these factors into consideration if you decide to start your own talent development firm.

Reflection Questions

A Wild and Windy Road: Historical Perspective

- What do you think made some talent development supplier firms successful and others not?
- Are there patterns that can explain those that have and continue to be strong industry contributors from those that don't?
- Are there critical factors that separate what's useful from what's not?

Know What You Don't Know: Industry Knowledge

- What are some examples of talent development supplier firms, or their acquirers, that failed due to a lack of basic understanding of how the industry goes to market and operates?
- What examples demonstrate how understanding the talent development industry facilitated a firm's success and growth?

Here Today, Gone Tomorrow?: Current Fads and Lasting Trends

- What trends are having the greatest impact on your business?
- How would you reshape what you are doing to embrace these trends?
- Are there other trends that could have a more significant influence on your business model in the future?

Dream On: Entrepreneurship

- How would you characterize your propensity to demonstrate entrepreneurial characteristics?
- How important is it for you to envision your business?
- What have you done to compensate for some of your entrepreneurial characteristics by surrounding yourself with people who are business operators?

2

DECIDING WHAT YOU WANT AND NEED

Do you want to know who you are? Don't ask. Act!
Action will delineate and define you.
—Thomas Jefferson

When you were a kid, you may have been asked, "what do you want to be when you grow up?" Most likely, you had no idea, so you responded with professions such as firefighter, baseball player, nurse, teacher, doctor, ballerina, and so on. You probably didn't say that you wanted to own and build a business in the talent development industry. Unless, of course, you were very, very precocious. Fast forward several years. Once you've entered the talent development field and have some predisposition for creating your firm, you will have to decide whether you want to build a small practice, a larger business, or perhaps lead a corporate talent development function. Only when you have answered this question can you determine your approach and where to devote your attention. This chapter addresses which path you will follow.

Know Thyself: Build a Business or Create a Practice?

Over the years, I've had a lot of industry friends, colleagues, and professional contacts ask me about how to start a talent development consulting business. Most people think it's an easy jump from an internal job or even one in consulting because they have a lot of experience, a wide network of contacts, and are pretty talented. Indeed, consulting sounds intriguing. What could be better than working from home or a shared office, doing work you love with people you like, and making a lot of money?

Unfortunately, many people make the jump, only to realize they are not very successful or happy. The primary reason for the lack of success is that most new consultants haven't figured out whether they want to establish a small one- to two-person practice, create a small firm, or build a larger business. Starting a one-person practice or a small consulting group that may sometimes rely on other independent contractors to assist with client work is different than building a full-fledged business or company. They require different approaches and experience levels.

Indeed, the differences are quite large. It's critical to know this before setting out on your journey. Here are some important questions to address as you think about the business you want to establish.

How Do You Acquire Business?

Perhaps this goes without saying, but you won't get any business if you don't seek it out, regardless of whether you have visions of creating a one-person consulting practice or establishing and growing a larger business. If you're not a strong promoter, which is true of many consultants, what's your course of action after all your friends, colleagues, family, and initial contacts dry up? The long-term advantage of forming a larger firm is that you will ultimately need to create a business development engine with other people who can market and sell your offering. But this is much more difficult to do as a private consultant, given that your focus will be working on projects, rather than drumming up new business.

Your best sales tool is doing a great job for your clients in the hope of attracting additional business. But clients don't necessarily have you in mind when they're developing their annual budgets, unless you are working on a long-term retainer. In a private consulting practice, you are basically on your own and rely on creating a presence (through a website, social media, or other networking tool) to attract new leads. Creating an organization with a separate sales and marketing team, with lead generators, sales reps, and account managers, is one key difference between setting up a private consulting practice and building a full-fledged talent development firm.

You also need to be clear about the clients and type of business you take on. You want to focus on your areas of interest and on your passions. If not, you could end up doing less than quality work and undermining your brand. Also, don't take work for someone else's benefit, and know when it is OK to say "no, thank you." These are difficult decisions you will need to make when acquiring business.

Do You Want to Manage Others?

Do you want to hire people or contract with others and become responsible for everything they say and do on your behalf? Is being on your own what attracted you to starting a business? Or are you drawn to building a legacy business? Even if you love managing people and are good at it, it can be a drain on the time and resources you need to build the business. Instead, you will likely need to hire people to manage your staff while you establish an infrastructure that can support the business in its current and future forms.

Not surprisingly, many consultants start out on their own and subsequently build bigger businesses only to learn that managing them is the last thing they want to do. In many cases, they aren't very good at doing it. If you're in this situation, you have two choices: either fold back the company to a more manageable venture or hire someone who is operationally competent to grow the business while you continue to consult with clients. This often becomes the tipping point for firms in the talent development supplier industry and makes quality hiring decisions crucial to long-term success.

Are You Prepared to Understand and Manage Financials?

If you are not good at both understanding and overseeing the numbers, you are going to have to rely on someone else to do this for you. Although small business software packages are readily available, they don't magically fill themselves with data. You, or someone else, must do that. We all know of businesses that appear to be very successful on the outside but are hemorrhaging financially on the inside because they don't really understand the dynamics of running a sustainably profitable firm.

The problem might be amplified if you are a capable consultant in your particular area of expertise, but don't have a knack for pricing out work and staying on budget. Before long, you end up working more hours than justify your financial return. This is why it is critical for you to fully comprehend how your business is going to make money. For example, as an independent consultant, how much will you pay yourself, and how will you go about doing it? How will you plan around an often inconsistent cash flow? How will you accrue for taxes you owe, because most of your work will be through 1099 contracting that pays gross fees and doesn't account for deductions? If you stay independent, you will have to figure this out because you may not be able to afford the type of financial help you really need.

Certainly, financial issues become more complicated the more you grow your business. You can rely on competent external resources to assist you with the financial expertise and systems you need until you can hire the appropriate internal staff. If you want to build a business, you will need certified financial professionals to help you navigate these issues, maybe even as full-time employees. In either case, not understanding how the business makes—and loses—money is perhaps the most fundamental mistake any entrepreneur makes.

How Do You Plan to Stay Relevant?

Another critical success factor for any business is keeping abreast of the latest industry trends and key players. Even though much of the industry's content has been recycled over the years, you need to consider what edge or improvement you can add. What is your firm's core competency? Maybe content isn't your competitive advantage. Perhaps it's the way you interact with clients, the accuracy of your observations, or your experienced interpretations that distinguish your business. Do you possess any new methods or tools to accomplish these tasks? Over the last 40 years, technological developments have played a big part in learning, and these advances certainly require you to stay up-to-date. Staying relevant could also mean simply focusing on what you are very good at and continually getting better at it.

Today, there are easy ways to keep abreast of industry advancements to maintain relevance. You can attend professional conferences, network with colleagues, surf the Internet, or write about or speak on topics with which you have deep expertise and significant experience. As an individual practitioner, you will have to rely much more on these activities to not only stay relevant, but also demonstrate your continued presence in the marketplace. After all, you are selling yourself as much as your business. If your expertise and capabilities aren't significantly distinguishable from competing practitioners or firms, you don't hold an advantage unless you simply price yourself below your competition, which is rarely a good long-term strategy.

How Will You Maintain Discipline?

It can get very lonely as an independent practitioner, or tiny firm, working out of your home office or a contracted external office. More important, despite the lure of a relatively flexible lifestyle, if you aren't busy managing people or the growth of a business, how do you ensure you're staying busy? In a home office, how do you avoid the multitude of distractions from family, the temptations of nearby pantry snacks, the desire to watch television, or the need to finish uncompleted chores? Many people set up shop outside their home because of potential distractions at home.

The truth of the matter is that there is always more downtime when working alone, because projects rarely start when others come to an end. It takes a good amount of discipline to minimize this dead time. Time management becomes a major factor that independent practitioners must learn to master if they are going to establish a profitable long-term business model. You are on your own, or at the most have a colleague or two, to take up the slack or attend to the myriad of administrivia that challenge the independent consultant. On the other hand, while it is nice to have colleagues close by with whom to interact, the downside is you have colleagues close by with whom to interact. Discipline is also required in a large office setting, given the demands of email, conference calls, meetings, and personal interactions.

How Important Is Work-Life Balance to You?

The extent to which one wants and needs work-life balance differs from person to person. Maintaining a relatively simple one- or two-person practice could enable greater balance than being part of a larger organization with a multitude of challenges and employees requiring your time. But having fewer people and less structure to worry about does not mean you can necessarily manage yourself. It comes down to committing to a lifestyle that meets your needs. Will you be able to ignore the weekend requests for your time to finish that proposal by Monday? You might face these same pressures if you are a small firm or large company.

Many firms have successfully committed to a "lifestyle" business and are doing quite well. These firms are less interested in making money than they are in providing service to others, at any cost. Some businesses have figured out how to do well by doing good, recognizing that to continue to do good, they had to continually do well. Others have found this commitment difficult to maintain especially in the face of accelerated growth goals.

Travel commitments to grow your business may also affect your work-life balance. Spending a lot of time on the road can be tiring. The consulting business, regardless of size, is extremely time consuming and demanding of your vigilance. Whether you are delivering a program or consulting service you may not always understand your clients' needs.

The Bottom Line

At the end of the day, the full-fledged business or smaller consulting practice approach has its pros and cons, depending on what you are looking for and your desired lifestyle. Table 2-1 offers a partial breakdown of some of the main differences.

Table 2-1. Differences Between a Business and a Practice

Variable	Building a Business	Creating a Practice
Equity	Corporate entity for potential cash-out exit	Investments from profits
Offer	Replicable products or services	Your personal expertise and experience
Delivery	Dependent on self and largely others	Dependent on self only
Selling	Formal sales and marketing engine	Mining and expanding your personal network
Brand	Positioning a business brand	Creating a personal brand
Hierarchy	Answer to and support many	Answer to and support yourself
Overhead	Plant, people, infrastructure	Home office or minimal outside space
Management	Overseeing others	Overseeing yourself
Work Time	Traditional 8-5+	Anytime you want
Labor Rates	Need to cover overhead	Need to cover yourself
Lifestyle Business	Others' choice	Your choice
Structure	Systems and processes required	Minimal requirements
Networking	Work colleagues and multiple professional connections	Staying connected beyond your "little island"
Intellectual Property	Typically owned by the business	Typically owned by you
Competitive Advantage	Replicability and scale	Personal touch

This is not to say you can't have a little of both. In fact, if you build even a small practice, many of the items in the left-hand column might apply. And, if you are an internal learning leader managing a training and education profit center, you will also probably identify more with the left side of the table. Knowing and exploring these differences before deciding which path to take will save you time, money, and frustration. Understanding what will work for you, given your interests, talents, and current situation will allow you to make an informed decision that's much more likely to yield success.

Inc. It or Limit It?: Business Structure

Regardless of whether you are interested in establishing or growing a business or practice, you will have to consider how you want to legally structure the entity. You have several options, but the guiding framework depends entirely on your personal situation and your short- and long-term business interests.

There are six types of business structures you can use for your firm: sole proprietorship, general partnership, limited partnership, limited liability corporation (LLC or PLLC for professional), S corporation, and C corporation. Sole proprietorships and general partnerships are fine but generally have unlimited liability for business debt. The rules of structure are provided by the agreements the parties establish, but if either of these business structures is sued for any reason, yours and your partners' personal assets, not just those of the business, are open to scrutiny for payment of potential claims. A limited partnership is a little different, in that only assets of the general partner are at risk, while those of the limited partners are not. One of the advantages in creating an LLC is that it provides some limitation on your liability by protecting your personal assets in the event of a judgment against your business. Both an S corporation and C corporation offer limited liability as well, but have different taxation rules. Single-member LLCs are taxed just like sole proprietorships; multiple-owner LLCs and S corporations are taxed just like partnerships. While completing your federal tax returns won't be affected if you have a single-member LLC, both multi-owner LLCs and S corporations require filing separate income tax returns.

A C corporation structure could be subject to double taxation, with corporate taxes on its income and on any money distributed to its owners or shareholders in the form of dividends. It is a taxable entity in that it is taxed on its total net income. But a C corporation can also distribute its profits by paying some as salary and retaining the balance in the corporation, which may reduce the tax bracket for both the corporation and the shareholders. In an S corporation it is possible to pay the shareholders a small salary and pay the balance to them as a dividend, reducing the impact of Social Security and Medicare taxes. Keep in mind that S corporation and C corporation structures are much more complicated from a tax, legal, and accounting perspective than a relatively simple LLC. This usually means professional fees will be higher to address these complications. There are other differences between LLCs and corporations on the type and amount of documentation and reporting requirements, with the latter typically requiring more.

While you review your options, understand that I am not a tax attorney or CPA. The information here comes from my own experience and is included for your convenience and consideration. I urge you to get professional advice before moving forward with structuring or restructuring your business.

Can You Have Your Cake and Eat It Too?: Business Models

Once you figure out whether you want to establish a small practice or build a full-fledged business, you must plan how to move forward. It is advisable that you organize your thoughts with a documented business plan. You don't have to share it with anyone, but thinking it through will help you crystalize how to build your business.

Appendix A offers a sample table of contents representing what you should include in your plan. While largely used for establishing new businesses, I have found that a business plan can be very helpful during critical junctures in the growth of the business. Most important, it will provide you with a road map for the key elements of your business.

Part of the formula for growth depends on the specific business model to which the business adheres. A business model describes how you will create and capture value. It describes the customer value proposition, pricing approach, and overall organization. At the highest level, two broad business model categories stand out in the talent development supplier industry: products and consulting services. You will need to figure out whether you want to offer off-the-shelf products, tailored products, customized programs, consulting solutions, SaaS-based platforms, implementation and subscription services, or some combination of these. What will each deliver to your customers? How?

The products business largely consists of off-the-shelf ready-made programs or courses that are either paper- or software-based. The deliverable is some type of training and instructional program or software platform that the client implements within its corporate environment. While you can tailor these programs to fit the buyer's specific needs, you are limited in how much you can alter them without affecting the underlying business model of selling a product. Your goal is to maximize your gross margin (revenue minus cost of sales) from the scale created by repeatedly selling the same product without doing too much to it. Any time taken to customize the product affects the margin because of the labor it takes. This can be very costly unless you can figure out a way for your clients to self-customize without relinquishing your intellectual property or jeopardizing the underlying instructional integrity of your offer. Self-customization can be more easily controlled with online courseware that allows for certain course adjustments. Regardless, the product business model is based largely on moving inventory despite the fact just-in-time production and SaaS-based platforms are today's reality.

At the other extreme, consulting services business theoretically starts with blank pieces of paper that evolve into a new and unique solution for each client. This business model is labor intensive, for which daily fees are established and billable hours logged. Revenue is limited by the number of people who can bill their labor and the number of hours in each available working day. If a consulting firm wants to double its revenue, it has to double its staff of consultants because consultant fees are its only source of revenue (Sawhney 2016, 84). The time billed must aggregate to pay for the consultant's salary and benefits, cost of sales, and overhead, hopefully leaving some profit. Often, consultancies apply previously used methods, tools, and processes for each client so as not to reinvent the wheel for each engagement. Nonetheless, the time it takes to customize these for each client can still be significant.

In this case, consulting services do not refer to services designed to support the business' products, such as train the trainer programs, certifications, printing and production, customized binders, tailored case studies, curriculum design, and implementation services. The distinction is that consulting involves providing hands-on expertise in addressing organizational challenges whose solutions may go way beyond that of a product-based training program.

There is a third possible business model: a hybrid of products and services, but it is difficult to achieve. Consulting services and product companies view products very differently in creating, monetizing, and managing them. The challenge becomes how you embed products into service offerings (Sawhney 2016, 88).

In a nutshell, these talent development business models represent adjusting an existing offer rather than creating a new one. In between, of course, are gradations and blends that take a little from each approach. However, what makes these models so different are the type of people and processes firms need to have in place to operate effectively and profitably.

Let's start by looking at the ends of the continuum. What follows are a few large business model categories to help you sort this out.

The Offer

Unless a firm can be profitable it really doesn't matter how it configures its offer. In the end, it must provide compelling, relevant, and results-based solutions. You can best accomplish this by focusing on one type of offer rather than several. In reality, few firms effectively sell both off-the-shelf products and consulting solutions simultaneously. This should come as no surprise because the go-to-market business strategies are completely different. When this has been attempted one of the business approaches usually ends up subsidizing the other, resulting in bottom-line profit erosion.

Deciding how to configure an offer must be determined to sustain long-term client trust and loyalty. Understanding the different business models required for providing a consistently desired offer will inform this decision.

Financial Management

The financial models of a product versus a consulting services-based business also differ in that such line items as capitalization expense, inventory, and amortization fit the products business, while labor rates, utilization, and employee capability and competency fit the consulting business. It seems clear that off-the-shelf products can be much more profitable than any other type of offer; you can absorb the development costs over time by a large quantity of relatively high margin sales. While these product development costs can typically be amortized over a number of years, there are still significant costs to creating them because the personnel and timeframe required to do so can add up. Once people start tailoring and reconfiguring these products, they begin losing their potential profitability because expenses typically rise.

The largest costs of consulting services are those attributed to the people involved in selling and delivering them. There is no real inventory, per se, just intellectual property in models and processes that can be pieced together to provide clients with desired solutions. The more complex the solution, the more experienced the consultants must be, which equates to higher salaries. Most of the time in practice, margins are considerably lower for consulting businesses than they are for those delivering basic pre-developed program packages. For consulting firms, the financial model depends on the utilization or application of consulting days multiplied by day rates, minus their costs, which are largely compensation related, and the costs of general overhead and administration.

Inventory Control

Another major difference between the product and consulting models is how you manage inventory. Products need to be produced; consultants need to show up. And while advances in digitization allow for just-in-time production, some form of inventory control is inherent in the production, revision, distribution, and accounting of products. Even licensing deals allowing clients to reproduce the digital material files require some kind of tracking process.

However, a consulting business only requires the consultant to be present when interfacing with a client. The only real inventory is the number of consultants on the bench. As such, these people can be contractors, creating a more variable cost model in that you deploy them only when needed and ensure their compensation through a contract with the client. To the extent fully employed bench consultants are not out with a client, they are a drain on financial resources.

Selling Capability

What are the main challenges with committing a firm to sell more standardized off-the-shelf programs or consulting services? They certainly require somewhat different selling approaches.

One could argue that selling off-the-shelf programs is no different than selling consulting engagements. While some salespeople can be successful in both situations, my experience has been the opposite. In fact, some very effective product salespeople have a difficult time selling custom solutions and consulting solutions. While the skill set may generally be the same, the deep expertise required to sell consulting services is quite different from the level required to sell a product with existing features and benefits, which at the least can be memorized. Salespeople can readily articulate and repeat a sales pitch from client to client with only minimal alteration, although considerable skill is still required to assess, understand, and recommend how the product addresses a solution for the client.

While the offer may look the same, in a consulting services sale , the configuration required to meet the specific needs of different clients usually varies considerably. In fact, this total customization process is one of its inherent benefits to certain customers. The patience and time required of the business to work through a true consultative solution is often greater than that required to sell a product with a specific applicability. The sales cycle for a relatively large consulting project will take much longer to scope, explain, clarify, and ultimately sell than simpler but widely distributed product sales.

Scale Building

It's much easier and cheaper to scale a product business than a consulting practice. A product ready for distribution represents sunk costs, either all at once or over several years of an amortization schedule. The deeper and wider the sales engine, the more you can reduce the costs per sale.

Cost-effectively scaling a consulting business is more difficult because the unit of currency is hours utilized and billed. The only way to grow this type of business is to hire more consultants, who often are expensive to employ. Yet, many very large consulting firms have scaled their businesses by employing junior-level consultants to do much of the heavy lifting, charging relatively senior-level fees, while the senior- level consultants and partners develop new business and oversee projects and client relationships. Additionally, true labor-intense consulting firms can often leverage their research, process tools, and models used and validated over time to engage clients without constantly reinventing the wheel.

Personnel Skills

While back-office operations can employ the same kind of people for either type of business, they must be experienced in such functions as finance and accounting, human resources, IT, and operations. Aside from these functions, you need different people to effectively run and grow these two types of businesses. A consulting services firm depends mostly on the experience and skills of its consultants, while a products business depends mostly on product development, innovation, and marketing management capabilities. Consulting firms require individuals who have deep industry expertise, as well as very strong communications, project management, and mastery facilitation skills.

Here is where the level of depth required differs from a product business. Certainly, you need effective training skills for those delivering off-the-shelf programs. Indeed, these trainers can make or break a program's success. But a deeper mastery of facilitation and process skills are a necessity for productive consulting relationships. (See chapter 5 for further discussion on the topic.) Furthermore, excellent analysis skills are disproportionately required for consultants who must assess the client's needs and recommend the most appropriate solutions, many of which are not readily apparent.

***

The above differences are the most critical to achieving success in either of these business models. They demonstrate why it is difficult to combine the two so that both flourish without one borrowing from the other's success. In fact, unless you cordon off the product and service businesses, it is very difficult to grow a combined business, except when the services offered are for implementing the products and thus embedded into the original product sale.

More typical, you end up deploying one side to support the other, depending on which is doing better at the time. This lose-lose formula affects the business, and masks the performance of the group doing poorly. Consider the example of a career outplacement firm, which depends on labor to deliver its services, albeit using some standardized systems, processes, and even packaged programs. While the outplacement services largely rely on people to sell and deliver, the true value and margin of the business is in the products it creates as stand-alone entities, such as workbooks. They can then be delivered in-house by the client, ultimately relying less and less on the firm providing the products and programs. The structure of these two business models would look very different.

A Rolling Stone Gathers No Moss: Focus, Focus, Focus

How can you adjust your growth strategies to ensure the long-term sustainability of your business? Past and recent strategic growth experts point to a few consistent themes: focus, differentiation, delivery, and industry knowledge. One of the leading experts on strategy, Michael Porter (1985), research competitive advantage and addressed cost, differentiation, and focus as the threede generic strategies. Building on Porter, Gary Hamel and C.K. Prahalad (1994) suggested competing by reinventing industries and regenerating strategies through shaping the future industry structure and competing for core competence leadership. This would effectively ensure industry foresight and intellectual leadership, the management of migration paths, and competition for market position and share. Even further, Michael Treacy and Fred Wiersema (1997) identified three disciplines of market leaders—customer intimacy, operational excellence, and product leadership—and are quick to mention organizations need to focus on one to differentiate themselves from the competition. They note that very few successful enterprises have been able to implement even two of these strategies simultaneously.

Much like Hamel and Prahalad before them, W. Chan Kim and Renée Mauborgne's *Blue Ocean Strategy* (2005) focuses on value innovation by creating uncontested market space, making competition irrelevant, creating and capturing new demand, breaking the value-cost trade-off, and pursuing differentiation and low cost. In addition, A.G. Lafley and his colleagues (2012) address how to narrow down novel strategic options to the one choice most likely to ensure success through a focused seven-step scientifically rigorous process. The commonalities among strategic growth patterns are greater than the differences. And the most common element is focus as a growth strategy for any business.

More recently, Michael E. Raynor and Mumtaz Ahmed (2013) made a strong case for strategic focus in their book, *The Three Rules*. They researched 25,000 companies over a 45-year span to assess the return on assets for these businesses. Using a consistent set of criteria, they placed the companies into three groups: "miracle workers" in the 90th percentile for return on assets, "long runners" in the 60th to 80th, and "average Joes" below the 50th. They found that the miracle worker companies had all chosen a strategy that put them in one of three categories—high price/low performance, mid-price/mid-performance, or high performance/low price—and stuck to that strategy to compete. This was true regardless of industry. They concluded that exceptional companies follow one of two guiding principles: better before cheaper or revenue before cost. Their third rule was that there are no other rules. Firms must define their relative position versus their relevant competition and not try to be all things to all people.

In any entrepreneurial-led industry, it is very easy for business leaders to lose focus and chase the next big thing. Indeed, what makes entrepreneurial ventures successful is a vision for the future, which sometimes takes them away from their focus. Yet, too many firms that do so either fail or experience stunted growth.

Several years ago, Harbridge House, a relatively large traditional business strategy consulting firm (once owned by Allstate Insurance and now part of Coopers & Lybrand, which acquired it in 1993), thought it could ride out the peaks and valleys of its consulting business by developing and delivering pre-packaged executive-level training programs. However, the company was already invested in creating highly customized management development programming. To make the training angle work, it hired very capable and experienced people to create a new group and expected its high-level client contacts would provide an easy path to purchase decisions. The result was a very effective and beautifully packaged executive development program.

Unfortunately, Harbridge House was never able to make this a successful venture and folded it shortly after. It didn't fully understand the respective true value propositions of its consulting and training businesses. Nor did it realize the costs of producing, inventorying, and marketing its training materials. The new group's cost structure didn't fit the firm's consulting labor model, so when people in this group didn't show billable hours, they were immediately branded as sloughing off. As expected, the training group had a short life span. Around the same time, the firm got involved with management assessment. It partnered with Assessment Designs to create a very specific assessment center package to evaluate for executive potential, but this was another short-lived venture. And it was unsuccessful for the exact same reason as the executive training program.

Similarly in 1984, when Wilson Learning bought Assessment Designs, the intention was quite logical. Wilson thought developing a capability to assess the strengths and weaknesses of sales and management employees would lead clients to its own learning and development solutions. But the Wilson Learning salespeople didn't understand how the assessment results, which weren't specifically reconfigured to match the skills taught in Wilson's training programs, could be tied back to those programs. Likewise, Assessment Designs' consultants had no idea how to relate their assessment results to the Wilson training programs. While the two companies managed to co-exist for several years, the businesses never fully leveraged what could have been a very powerful integration. It was a clear case of each taking their eye off what they should have individually been focusing on.

Again, many years later, Dove Consulting, a small but leading strategy business focused largely in the financial services and food and beverage industries, merged with the Learning Design Group, a traditional custom training business. The merger assumed Dove's more than 60 consultants would be readily able to sell the training programs around leadership, sales, and service. However, the consultants weren't motivated to sell training because it cut into their billable hours. They weren't interested in understanding how their clients would benefit from these new services. As it turned out, their clients weren't the actual buyers of training. Eventually Dove realized the combined firms created little to no value and severed its ties by spinning off the Learning Design Group to Carlson Marketing Group.

Carlson Marketing, a leading loyalty marketing consulting firm, and division of Carlson Companies, a multi-billion-dollar global leader in the hospitality and travel business, decided to buy the custom learning company to add a training and education capability to its offer. Custom learning would enable its clients' employees and customers to be better educated on the loyalty programs they established. With a large worldwide sales force, Carlson Marketing thought it could easily open the necessary doors for this additional offer. Four years later, after realizing how this strategy took it away from its focus, Carlson Marketing divested the training business.

In these cases, the firms failed because they lost focus on what they did best. Sure, there are examples of firms that have successfully managed competing business models with somewhat disparate offers. But typically firms will not succeed when they lose focus, unless they have figured out how to separate the respective businesses. Success is more likely to stem from doing one thing really well rather than doing many things not so well.

Conclusion

Understanding the type of business you want to build and where your competencies lie are critical to determining how you proceed in the talent development supplier industry. Whether it's a small private practice, medium-size firm, or large company, you have to be clear on not only what you want but what you need to live the lifestyle you most prefer. Whether you are starting out, interested in managing your current business more effectively, or growing your firm, knowing this information will help you choose the path that's right for you and set you up for success.

Reflection Questions

Know Thyself: Build a Business or Create a Practice?

- Which makes the most sense for you, establishing a practice or building a business? Why?
- How are you taking advantage of what you want and like to do as a consultant?
- What are some challenges you have unexpectedly faced after starting a business or practice? How are you addressing these?

Inc. It or Limit It?: Business Structure

- What are the pros and cons of the various business structures, as they relate to your situation?
- What have you done to ensure that the legal entity under which your business falls is the most appropriate for your personal and professional goals?
- How can you be sure you are receiving the best legal and tax advice you can get?

Can You Have Your Cake and Eat It Too?: Business Models

- What has been your experience with businesses that have tried to sell both products and services? Where have they been successful and where have they failed?
- As you think about your practice or business, what have you done, or will you do, to either separate or integrate these two different types of offers?
- How will you plan to make these two different operational systems work together to yield success for both sides of the business?
- What are the pros and cons of a product versus consulting services offer as you think about starting your business or growing your current operation?
- What are the differences you expect, or have already noticed, in your business between your products and consulting offers?

A Rolling Stone Gathers No Moss: Focus, Focus, Focus

- What examples can you offer in which focus was an extraordinarily successful strategy for a talent development firm; yours or others?

- What examples can you offer in which lack of focus was responsible for a firm's lack of growth or failure? What specifically went wrong?
- What can you do in your business to ensure a myopic focus that is narrow and deep versus thick and shallow?
- What price-performance business model are you focusing on to compete in the industry?

3

SETTING THE FOUNDATION FOR SUCCESS–OR FAILURE

There are no secrets to success. It is the result of
preparation, hard work, and learning from failure.
—Colin Powell

Once you have established a sense of what you want your business to look like and focus on, you should set a clear path to achieving that. This is largely accomplished by first determining a strategy and then creating a plan to execute it.

This chapter focuses on how you envision your business, some models for articulating it, and tips and techniques to make it happen. It also discusses the importance of establishing a mission and vision for your business, the need to plan how you want to achieve them, and the critical importance of carrying out that plan, both efficiently and effectively.

Culture Always Trumps Strategy: Mission, Vision, Values

It's been said that culture beats strategy, that the bedrock for any strategy is alignment with the overall purpose and vision. No matter how well developed your strategy, your business has one purpose, and if your strategy doesn't support this purpose, you are bound to achieve little success or even fail. Typically, mission and vision are the strongest influencers for any company's culture. This doesn't mean your mission can't change over time, but when it does so should your strategy to support achieving it. Often, however, mission, vision, and values are confused, so let's define each of these concepts so you can use them to drive your business to succeed.

First, let's be clear about the elements that make up culture. The mission and vision of a business can set the stage for establishing a focused and passionate environment. The values ascribed to, and hopefully practiced every day, also provide

33

the tone and expectations for how people behave and relate to one another within this culture. While it may seem pedantic to even mention this to businesses in the talent development industry, which often help their clients establish this culture, it is by no means easy to achieve. Culture is multifaceted, from its intellectual to its emotional elements (Barsade and O'Neill 2016). And it touches all aspects of employees' work involvement, such as their commitment, creativity, decision making, work quality, and retention, not to mention its effect on bottom-line performance.

Even the relatively cut-throat private equity world recognizes the influence of culture on performance. In one study reported in *CLO* magazine by Denison Consulting, 38 private equity portfolio companies, totaling 32,000 employees, examined the effect of organizational culture on financial performance, including EBITDA (earnings before interest, tax, depreciation, and amortization) and sales revenue. The study used the Denison Organizational Culture Survey (DOCS), which measures 12 combined factors that form four cultural elements: adaptability, mission, involvement, and consistency. Higher scores reflect greater clarity and alignment to these elements. The results showed a positive link between organizational culture and financial performance. More specifically, the combination of the four cultural elements predicted 19 percent of the difference in sales growth and 4 percent in EBITDA growth across portfolio companies. Companies with top scoring culture had 8 percentage points greater EBITDA and sales growth over a three-year period (Ko, et al. 2016, 18-20).

Simon Sinek's very popular and pragmatic TED Talk on three concentric circles of What, How, and Why (with Why in the center) further explain the critical importance of understanding the business you are in and its purpose before a strategy can be articulated to support it. The *why* is what inspires people to come to work to figure out how they will go about contributing to *what* their company offers its buyers. As he says, people don't buy what you do, but why you do it. Strong cultures supporting highly effective businesses act, think, and interact from the inside-out (2009). How then can you apply the *what* and the *why* to your businesses' vision and mission?

Vision Versus Mission

Vision and mission; mission and vision. The two sound similar but they lay the groundwork for your business in different ways. A business's vision statement focuses on its future potential or what it intends to be. As such, your vision statement should be future-based and meant to inspire and give direction to you and your employees, not your clients or customers. It is a description of what your company intends to become. It answers the question, "Where do I see my business going?"

While a vision statement might contain references to how your business intends to make that future a reality, the how should be part of your mission statement. Your mission statement should be designed to convey a sense of your business's purpose to both internal employees and the external community. It answers the question, "Why does my business exist?" That is, what are you offering and whom do you serve? Sometimes these are used as tag lines to a corporate name, but usually they are the impetus for why people come to work every day, whether it is to save lives, provide clean water throughout the world, or even to enable a workforce to reach its potential.

As your business grows, its objectives and goals may change. Therefore, you should revise your vision statement as needed to reflect the changing business culture as your goals are met. Tiffany Silverberg (2015), a business writer and editor, has noted that vision statements should go beyond profit margins and internal benefits and look toward the long-term effect a company wants to have on its customer base, its industry, the economy, and the environment. Similarly, a mission statement is not evergreen. As your business evolves, its mission and intent may also change. A mission statement will keep your business on track, but it shouldn't become stale or irrelevant, so revisit it every few years to fine-tune it as necessary.

Writing a Mission Statement

What are the opportunities or needs your company addresses? What is the business of your organization? How are these needs addressed? What level of service is provided? What principles or beliefs guide your organization?

An effective mission statement answers these key questions about your business. It should be short, yet resonate with both employees and those outside the business. It should express your purpose in a way that embodies support and ongoing commitment. It sets the tone for your business and outlines concrete goals. It should be aspirational enough to give employees something to reach for and unify their day-to-day efforts. It also should be specific enough to create a brand that will be embraced by those who buy the organization's products and services.

As you read these statements, look for the common elements. They don't specifically set out a long-term end state but rather focus on why they are in business and whom they serve.

Examples of Mission Statements

- **Patagonia:** Build the best product, cause no unnecessary harm, use business to inspire and implement solutions to the environmental crisis.
- **IKEA:** To create a better everyday life for the many people. Our business idea supports this vision by offering a wide range of well-designed, functional home furnishing products at prices so low that as many people as possible will be able to afford them.
- **Medtronic:** To contribute to human welfare by application of biomedical engineering in the research, design, manufacture, and sale of instruments or appliances that alleviate pain, restore health, and extend life.

From Mission to Vision

Once you establish a mission, you can develop a vision for how that mission will be obtained. But keep in mind the Japanese proverb that "Vision without action is a daydream. Action without vision is a nightmare." That is, a vision alone won't accomplish very much other than to help articulate the desired end state. Take a look at the examples of well-known visions statements, past and present. As you can see, they are quite different from mission statements. A vision is a vivid image of what you want your business to be in the future, based on your goals and aspirations. Having a vision will give your business a clear focus and can ensure that you won't head in the wrong direction.

Examples of Vision Statements

- **Amazon:** Our vision is to be Earth's most customer centric company; to build a place where people can come to find and discover anything they might want to buy online.
- **Honda:** Six Hondas in every garage.
- **Microsoft:** A personal computer on every desk.
- **NASA:** A man on the moon in 10 years.
- **PepsiCo:** PepsiCo's responsibility is to continually improve all aspects of the world in which we operate—environment, social, and economic—creating a better tomorrow than today. Our vision is put into action through programs and a focus on environmental stewardship, activities to benefit society, and a commitment to build shareholder value by making PepsiCo a truly sustainable company.

What do these statements have in common? Basically, they all describe a future state, one that communicates aspirations of where the business wants to be.

Moving to Values

The third leg of the stool describes a company's values. They illustrate how your business will act as it works to achieve its mission and vision. Some have even said that having a set of values is at the heart of a company. More often than not, these values are what stakeholders see, because they show up in the behavior of the company's employees. Values often define a company's passions and commitments to carry out its business goals. They anchor every aspect of the business with a set of commonly held beliefs and commitments. They become the deeply ingrained principles and guide employee behavior and company decisions. They serve as the behaviors the company and employees expect of each other.

Examples of Company Values

- **Build-A-Bear Workshop:** Reach, Learn, Di-bear-sity, Colla-bear-ate, Give, Cele-bear-ate.
- **L.L. Bean:** Sell good merchandise at a reasonable profit, treat your customers like human beings, and they will always come back for more.
- **Wegmans Food Markets:** Our "Who We Are" Values: Caring, High Standards, Making a Difference, Respect, and Empowerment.
- **Bright Horizons Family Solutions:** The HEART Principles: Honesty, Excellence, Accountability, Respect, Teamwork.

Putting It All Together

Despite their importance, mission, vision, and values are often confused and can become overly complicated as a company builds and grows. Table 3-1 summarizes some of the key elements that will help guide you in drafting them.

To help demonstrate how mission, vision, and values come together to represent a unified company, let's take a look at several successful companies. I selected Park Nicollet Health Systems in Minnesota, my go-to health provider for more than 25 years. Park Nicollet has guided me through triple bypass heart surgery, several knee surgeries, and a few other emergency calls for my kids as they were growing up. I can say with total confidence that their mission, vision, and values are readily observable in their promise and their outward behaviors to their patients and employees.

Table 3-1. Mission-Vision-Values

Element	Mission	Vision	Values
Answers	Why?	What?	How?
Definition	Statement	Snapshot	Words
Length	Short	Long	Evergreen
Purpose	Informs	Inspires	Instills
Activity	Doing	Seeing	Believing
Source	Heart	Head	Soul
Order	First	Second	Third
Effect	Clarifies	Challenges	Manifests

Adapted from Smith (2016).

- **Mission:** Our mission is to improve health and well-being in partnership with our members, patients and community.
- **Vision:** Health as it could be, affordability as it must be, through relationships built on trust.
- **Values:**
  - **Excellence:** We strive for the best results and always look for ways to improve. I do my best and always look for ways to improve.
  - **Compassion:** We care and show empathy and respect for each person. I care and show empathy and respect for each person.
  - **Partnership:** We are strongest when we work together and with those we serve. I am most effective when I work together with my colleagues and with those we serve.
  - **Integrity:** We are open and honest, and we keep our commitments. I am open and honest and I keep my commitments.

When mission, vision, and values are well thought through and manifested every day in how the business operates, they serve to as a foundation for the business. Below are just a few good examples of talent development companies who have nicely articulated their vision, mission, and values.

ExperiencePoint (A Toronto-based company that provides training simulations around innovation and change.)

- **Mission:** To make experience a better teacher by making it faster, safer, and sharply focused.
- **Vision:** We imagine a world in which people can engage in complex challenges with confidence and competence.

- **Values:** 1) We learn by doing. (Experiment to explore and understand. Make mistakes and fail better. Have the humility to listen, ask for help, and try again.); 2) We serve our clients and one another with authenticity and excellence (Give more than we take. Under promise and over deliver. Follow up fast.); 3) We build products, relationships, and the business (Start with desirability. Playing offense. Believing anything is possible.); 4) We own our work and the way we get it done. (Put first things first. Do the right thing. Do what it takes.); 5) At the end of the day, family comes first.

Center for Creative Leadership (A Greensboro, North Carolina, nonprofit organization that conducts research, programs, and consulting in all areas of leadership development.)

- **Mission:** To advance the understanding, practice, and development of leadership for the benefit of society worldwide.
- **Vision:** To fully realize our mission, the Center will create new knowledge that advances our field and that positively transforms the way leaders, their organizations and their societies confront the most difficult challenges of the 21st century.
- **Values:** Creating new knowledge, being a great place to work, supporting local and global communities, managing our operations responsibly, and engaging our stakeholders.

GP Strategies (A company based in Columbia, Maryland, that focuses on improving performance through technical and management training.)

- **Mission:** To solve business challenges by providing the expertise and solutions needed to attain ultimate performance results.
- **Vision:** To equip and enable people and businesses to perform at their highest potential.
- **Values:** Making a meaningful impact, acting with integrity, communicating directly and honestly, delivering quality services and products, developing innovative solutions based on need, striving for continuous improvement, demonstrating teamwork, respecting others, and optimizing shareholder value.

Stop and Smell the Roses: Strategic Planning Versus Scenario Planning

As a board member at my alma mater, Hobart and William Smith Colleges, I faced, along with my fellow trustees, the challenge of helping to map the college's future in the wake of potentially huge industry disruptions, such as cost of a college education. As a strong advocate of a strategic planning approach to determine how to address future growth, I suggested we take part in a visioning exercise that would help us navigate the disruptions that could occur. However, we were only able to speculate about the magnitude and impact of the disruptions based on past and current trends. So the first step was to identify the various scenarios that could exist, based on these trends, and then figure out the most important elements that need to be incorporated into the strategic plan. As I was participating in this activity, I realized that in many cases strategic planning is not the right approach to mapping the future of a firm. Instead, scenario planning made more sense.

Strategic planning and scenario planning both look to the future to anticipate the variables that may stunt an organization's growth, and in some cases threaten its very survival. Identifying and examining the differences between the two will help you choose the right course of action for your talent development business. To do this, let's look at the respective purpose, process, and payoff of each of these approaches.

Strategic Planning

The primary objective of strategic planning is to ensure short- and long-term business growth at the top and bottom lines. It should focus on determining your primary customers and how they relate to all your stakeholders, including employees. Typically, strategic planning involves establishing and tracking specific measureable targets. In forming such a plan, you can employ traditional analysis, such as SWOT (strengths, weaknesses, opportunities, threats) or ABCDE (assessment of current situation; baseline the gap; components of strategy; delivery of component; evaluation of progress) or other approaches, such as the Inspiration Model and the Alignment Model.

These basic strategic planning models are often effective for new organizations that do not have much prior experience with strategic planning or have much time to spend on it. Your business can start with this approach and then expand on it as you become more comfortable with its mechanics and become more established.

By identifying your strengths, weaknesses, opportunities, and threats, you can use them to inform the decision-making process when choosing an approach. But the process actually begins by developing a strategic plan based on who you are, why you exist, whom you serve, and how you act in accord with your mission, vision, and values.

In general, the components of the basic strategic planning process include:
1. identifying the purpose of your organization and developing a mission statement

2. creating general goals, or vision, for your organization to accomplish the mission

3. identifying specific action steps to implement each goal

4. evaluating and updating the plan over time.

One advantage of this approach is that the outcome assigns accountabilities to senior-level personnel who are then expected to carry out the plan. In addition, it allows for frequent tracking, follow-up, and revisions.

For firms focused on growth, a critical aspect of strategic planning is to develop a set of growth metrics. These are markedly different than the aforementioned traditional one-line vision statements, such as Honda's "Six Hondas in every garage." Growth metrics are typically bold statements bound by a timeline. They tend to rally employees around common business goals. In addition to the timeline for accomplishing these goals, growth metrics include quantitative measures to assess when they will be attained, thus providing the foundation for an execution plan. These metrics most likely include revenue and EBITDA goals, gross margins, customer retention figures, Net Promoter Scores, and time to market. Typically, given the pace of change today, growth metrics are projected for three to five years.

By conducting strategic planning, you develop a detailed execution plan based on analysis of the current state of your business. The plan will not only identify strategic imperatives or success criteria for your business, it will also identify those who will be responsible for each imperative, when achievement will take place, the milestones accomplished along the way, and the resources necessary to execute the plan.

Structuralist Versus Reconstructionist

While you can choose from many strategic planning models, there are really only two overarching approaches to consider. Structuralist involves doing what you are currently doing better than any other business in your space. This, of course, requires vigilance and continuous improvement so that you are always one step ahead of the competition. But your basic offer doesn't change that much over time, only the quality of its content and delivery.

Reconstructionist involves building a business in your industry that has not been envisioned, or at a minimum creating an offer that is not just new and improved but transformational.

Chapters 5 and 10 will address the topics of innovation and disruption, respectively. But for now think of these two strategic approaches this way: Instead of letting your environment define your strategy (structuralist), craft a strategy that defines your environment (reconstructionist). Neither method is necessarily right or wrong, better or worse, but the growth plans you would put in place for each would be significantly different.

Scenario Planning

Scenario planning, which is sometimes considered a part of strategic planning, can help you lay the groundwork for developing a strategy. Its main objective is to identify what lies ahead and the barriers that must be overcome to move forward. In many ways, it is designed to help navigate potential disruptions. While strategic and scenario planning can deliver the same end product, scenario planning might be better executed prior to a fully established strategic plan. Although scenario planning is viewed by some as more of a technique than a model, it can be used in conjunction with other models such as SWOT or ABCDE to ensure strategic thinking is incorporated into the process. Scenario planning allows you to prepare for different situations that may occur because of a change in the environment and other external forces.

Strategic planning usually starts with an agreement on the mission, vision, and values of a firm, and then shows you how to achieve each. Scenario planning ends with your vision because it is a function of the factors most likely to occur that could interfere with them. One way to develop future scenarios is to assess trends that are most likely to occur and most important to the success of your business. Another way is to explore the likely impact they can have on the future of the business compared with the certainty inherent in predicting their occurrence. A simple 2 x 2 matrix can be used to evaluate these trends. Trends likely to have the most impact with the greatest certainty would need to be addressed before those likely to have the least impact and most uncertainty. However, you should not ignore these low-impact, low-certainty trends; the matrix contents may shift depending on changes in the environment.

Consider the industry trend of e-learning in the context of scenario planning. In the past, companies would have identified it as a key trend with varying evaluations of its certainty. Firms that saw both high impact and certainty should have incorporated more e-learning into their offer or put in place measures to prevent it from eroding their current business approach. The initial trend analysis helps you figure out which scenarios you need to plan for. A vision is then created, which is aligned with the most likely scenarios, and then altered accordingly. If, for example, the firm's vision is to be the leader in instructor-led classroom learning, but then virtual massive open online courses become more prevalent, either its vision may change or steps will have to be put in place to adapt to this alternative delivery methodology.

For planning purposes, stakeholders project different scenarios that could occur and which might influence the organization. Some examples include changes in policies or regulations, funding, demographics, or technology. The stakeholders discuss these likely scenarios, including the best case, worst case, and a reasonable case for each external force. A review of the worst case is especially useful to highlight the importance of preparing for such a scenario. Then, brainstorming takes place to show how the business can effectively respond to the various scenarios or what it can do to strengthen itself so it's not influenced by external forces. Calm and rational thinking helps all stakeholders consider various scenarios, instead of reacting in crisis mode without pre-planning.

An example from my alma mater and most colleges and universities is the trend of rising tuition. This trend is going to continue and will have a big influence on the very survival of the college. If it can't contain the costs or raise its revenue to combat them, it will surely suffer in its attempt to deliver the level of quality education to which it is committed. Planning for this scenario might include identifying alternative sources of revenue for the college to help defray some tuition and room and board costs for students; conducting a capital campaign to raise more endowment money; or working on the value proposition and benefit to students for paying this amount of tuition. Once the major trends are identified with their accompanying implied issues, an action plan can be formulated for each to address them. These high-level action plans would then be integrated into one large strategic plan to address all their interconnections.

In the end, while scenario planning may inform your strategic plan, its main purpose is to identify what the future might look like based on possible situations emerging from past and current trends. The factors likely to contribute to these future scenarios, along with their expected impact and certainty, can serve as the basis for creating a successful business plan.

Summary

Strategic and scenario planning can be valuable for building and growing your business, allowing you to analyze it from different perspectives. Strategic planning focuses on three to five years; however, with the rapid pace of change, many organizations focus more on three years than five. In contrast, scenario planning focuses on a longer timeframe, perhaps as many as 10 years.

Table 3-2 provides an overview of the similarities and differences between these two approaches.

Table 3-2. Comparison of Strategic and Scenario Planning

Item	Strategic Planning	Scenario Planning
Purpose	Business growth	Future situation assessment
Process	From vision to plan execution: vision, mission, values growth metrics strategic imperatives critical actions milestones, resources, accountabilities, timelines endings	From industry trend analysis to key factor agreement: trend identification scenarios development what if statements impact analysis vision strategic plan
Payoff	Short term: 3-5 years	Long term: 10+ years

What Got You Here May Not Get You There: Strategic Growth Planning

With the differences between scenario and strategic planning approaches in mind, let's move on to a specific process you can use to plan your strategic growth, whether you are a one-person organization, a company with hundreds of employees, or even an internal learning organization. This process takes careful consideration. Hope is not a strategy, and trying harder is not an action plan.

Execution is paramount. Indeed, we've all heard or read the claim that a majority of strategic growth plans fail to be executed. In fact, all too often these plans fail to describe how to navigate to successful execution. At the other end of the spectrum, some businesses develop a plan so complex and overwhelming that it paralyzes those responsible for moving the business forward. Or, they adhere to a plan so rigid that compliance becomes the goal rather than using it as a guidepost flexible enough to be altered.

The most important part of a strategic growth plan is how it describes what your organization needs to initially accomplish to achieve its goals. Basically, an effective growth planning process involves six simple phases:

1. mission, vision, values
2. growth metrics
3. strategic imperatives
4. key initiatives
5. critical actions
6. endings.

Mission, Vision, Values

As previously mentioned, any size organization needs to fully understand:
- the guiding purpose for doing what it does (mission)
- what it wants to achieve at the end of the day (vision)
- the parameters that describe how it behaves (values).

If you do not clearly establish your mission, vision, and values, you will struggle, and more likely fail, to move forward with a strategic growth plan. They serve as the foundation of your plan, hence their need to be definitive.

Growth Metrics

What is your business trying to achieve? While a vision will certainly describe where you might want to end up, it does so in a more amorphous high-level manner. As such it is highly aspirational; for example, "Six Hondas in every garage." After all it is only a narrative, no matter how compelling. Instead, the growth metrics should translate your grander vision into measurable milestones and metrics.

Strategic Imperatives

Strategic imperatives need to describe the most critical elements a business must accomplish to achieve its growth goals. These imperatives are the value-added directives that will lead to success. They describe the what of the business. Leaders should follow a less-is-more mandate when determining these imperatives, wherein perhaps only three to five make the list.

Key Initiatives

For each strategic imperative, you should outline three to five key initiatives (specific projects or assignments) that define the achievement of that imperative. These initiatives describe how your business will achieve these imperatives, so they must also be measureable and action-oriented.

Critical Actions

Simply determining what and how you will achieve your growth goals doesn't take the planning process far enough. In fact, this is where many strategic growth plans fail in their execution. You should attach three to five critical actions to each key initiative for the organization's leaders and teams to carry out. Generally, these actions provide the who, when, and where milestones that assign accountability for managing the initiatives.

Endings

Any organization has many, sometimes conflicting, actions it wants to complete; often, it has too many. Different departments and their leaders often consider their projects most important, but sometimes they don't add true value to the business. Thus, these actions actually work against the strategic imperatives necessary for growing the business. You need to curtail or put an end to these actions, so that you can reallocate or even terminate the resources attached to them. This is where true discipline comes in. To properly build and grow your business, you need to focus on endings; those actions that could prevent you from executing your strategic growth plan.

The strategic growth planning process might take two to three days to map out, preferably with senior-level team members charting the course. However, one can argue for the critical action phase to include a level or two below the senior team, where the work really gets done. At the very least, the critical action milestones must be shared with those responsible for carrying them out before they are finalized. Finally, it's vital to put in place a process that communicates the plan to the entire organization and realigns key roles and activities to the strategic imperatives critical to the business's long-term success. Of course, if you are a one- or two-person organization, your communication task is simpler, yet no less critical to ensuring you effectively execute the plan.

Summary

To put it in perspective, here's a real-world example of the six phases from a talent development firm, the Crisis Prevention Institute. CPI provides Non-Violent Crisis Intervention training for duty-to-care professionals such as teachers and nurses; it offers proven strategies for safely defusing anxious, hostile, or violent behavior at the earliest possible stage (Jace 2016; Note: The example does not illustrate a complete strategic growth plan, but rather one strategic imperative from a five-year strategic planning process conducted several years ago. The specific numbers noted have been altered to maintain confidentiality.)

- **Mission:** We believe in providing organizations and their employees with the tools required to effectively assess and manage difficult and challenging situations in the workplace to enhance the quality of life for staff and those in their care.
- **Five-Year Growth Metrics:** See a 15 percent increase in year-over-year annual revenue and EBITDA; reach $30 million in revenue in fiscal 2015; reach 7,500 new program participants; certify 1,500 new practitioners; and establish a global reach on three new continents.

- **Strategic Imperative:** Create a profitable international business by 2014, spinning out $2 million in revenue. (This is one of four imperatives developed for the growth vision.)
- **Key Initiatives:** Net new geographical presence established regionally— for example, Asia, Middle East, and Latin America. (This is one of three initiatives for the strategic imperative.)
- **Critical Actions:** Complete two business plans. (This is one of three critical actions for the above key initiative; each had an accompanying timeline, milestones, resources, owner, and supporters.)
- **Endings:** Halt current international country-by-country expansion.

The Odd Couple?: Strategy and Execution

Despite being key to the future of a business, strategic plans are rarely fully executed. A lot of the failure can be chalked up to the exponential rate of change today. As companies seek to keep up with change, they are quick to adjust their strategies, but are not as nimble in adjusting how they plan to execute the change. To be frank, we are poor predictors of the future —no wonder businesses fail in execution.

That said, a strategy without execution is misaligned, and execution without a strategy is misdirected. Ideas are cheap; their execution is what pays off. As entrepreneur and philanthropist Naveen Jain once said, "success doesn't necessarily come from breakthrough innovation but from flawless execution. A great strategy alone won't win a game or a battle; the win comes from basic blocking and tackling." The challenge in marrying strategy and execution is that many who are good at strategy formulation are ill-equipped to execute said strategy. To use a whole-brain reference, big right-brain thinkers often have trouble with more precise thinking left-brain activities, and vice-versa. So, in many ways discovering them working together is an oddity, however desirable.

Let's take a closer look at strategy execution lessons that can be applied to any organization. No matter the size of your business, you will have some sort of strategy to guide you. Hopefully it has been documented and is the outgrowth of input from key people in your organization. If the strategy is only in your mind, it needs to be executed.

Failure to execute the strategy is often impeded by normal changes to a business model, or when leadership demands a different direction than originally proposed, making the original strategy no longer applicable. More important, in the ever-evolving talent development industry, one could argue that sticking to a specific time-bound growth strategy could be counter-productive. But what about strategic plans not subject to major interferences in the business model or from the competitive landscape? Why aren't they implemented?

Execution Lessons

What matters most when it comes to strategy execution? In surveying thousands of employees, Neilson, Martin, and Powers (2008) found that five factors characterized companies that were effective at executing strategy:

1. Employees knew what decisions and actions for which they were responsible.
2. Key competitive information got to headquarters more quickly.
3. Decisions were rarely second-guessed, once made.
4. Information flowed freely across organizational boundaries.
5. Employees typically had the information needed to understand the bottom-line impact of their day-to-day choices. Of course, getting to this place requires installing the appropriate structure to drive effectiveness in making decisions and allowing information to flow through the business.

By understanding how decisions are made and who is empowered to make them, bottlenecks disappear and results occur faster. Giving people the right and authority to make decisions accelerates the process. In fact, according to one study, decision effectiveness was correlated to corporate financial performance 95 percent of the time. Of nearly 800 organizations surveyed, those most effective at decision making generated total stakeholder returns 6 percentage points higher than less effective firms (Bina 2016).

As the founder of or key player within your business, you should be aware of the ways many senior leaders go wrong when striving for execution excellence. In surveying 400 CEOs and managers, Sull, Homkes, and Sull (2015) identified five myths business leaders adhere to and the reasons why these impede effective strategy execution:

1. **Execution equals alignment.** Reason: Cross-business alignment is very difficult and time consuming to achieve.
2. **Execution means sticking to the plan.** Reason: Sticking to a heads-down plan blinds visibility to changing conditions.
3. **Communication means understanding.** Reason: Communicating, even clearly, doesn't ensure understanding.
4. **A performance culture drives execution.** Reason: A performance culture can often focus just on achieving set goals rather than stretching outside the box, as is often needed.

5. **Execution should be driven from the top.** Reason: Waiting for the on-high command disempowers the rank and file from getting things done in the trenches.

You can't necessarily expect everyone in your business to carry out a strategy just because you came up with one, even if it was collectively agreed upon. Executing said strategy and overcoming the many unseen cultural, hierarchical, collaborative, and communication barriers along the way is where it's put to the test.

Bottom Line

You can learn a great deal from these execution lessons. Although they become more complicated in their actual application. Perhaps, this is simply the nature of growing a business: With growth comes frequent change and even alterations to strategic direction. One way to fix the disconnect between strategy and execution is to introduce an execution planning step between the completion of the strategy and when you attempt to put it into action (Lippett 2007). More often than not, the expectation is that execution is simply a matter of taking the strategy at face value rather than fully understanding what is necessary to execute it. Planning the execution process, while seemingly easy to do and simple to understand, needs to be part of the solution.

Maintaining flexibility around strategy is a double-edged sword because sometimes flexibility can become an easy excuse for not following the original well-thought-out plan. Other times, maintaining flexibility makes sense and is necessary for the business to move forward. In either case, executing a strategic growth plan is a critical element of both the short- and long-term success of your businesses in the talent development space.

Conclusion

This chapter focused on how you can establish a strategy for planning the future of your business by understanding who you are, what you want, where you are going, what you do, and how you will go about doing it. The steps to creating a solid strategic planning process are logical and practical, but often difficult to carry out. Integrating your strategic plan with your execution plan is necessary in building a solid foundation for your business. Once you've done that, it will guide you along the path of least resistance and effectiveness.

Reflection Questions

CULTURE ALWAYS TRUMPS STRATEGY: MISSION, VISION, VALUES

- Do you have a mission, vision, and values statement? If not, why not?
- If so, how do they define why you are in business, what you hope to achieve, and how you demonstrate these through the everyday behavior of your employees?
- Where does each need to be improved to more clearly articulate what your business is all about?

STOP AND SMELL THE ROSES: STRATEGIC PLANNING VERSUS SCENARIO PLANNING

- How have you thought about your future as a business, from both the strategic planning and scenario planning perspectives?
- What are the elements of both that are most likely to affect the future of your business?
- Why would one or the other make the most sense for you to engage in at this point in the development of your business?

WHAT GOT YOU HERE MAY NOT GET YOU THERE: STRATEGIC GROWTH PLANNING

- As you review the strategic growth plan of your business, which of the noted elements are, or are not, covered in enough depth that employees understand their respective roles in helping the organization achieve business growth?
- If not, what should you do to ensure they do?
- What growth metrics have you determined are critical to the future success of your business?

THE ODD COUPLE?: STRATEGY AND EXECUTION

- When have you experienced poor execution of your own (or others') strategic plan? What were the reasons for this?
- What were the real business consequences of the failed execution?
- What traps of strategy execution have you fallen into? How could you have avoided them?
- How could your execution activities specifically improve?
- How can you bridge the gap between strategy and execution for your business?

4

KNOWING WHAT YOU OWN—AND DON'T

*Intellectual capital will
always trump financial capital.*
—*Paul Tudor Jones*

Any consulting business involved in developing programs, products, or services continually faces intellectual capital issues. This chapter aims to help you gain greater understanding of intellectual capital by answering:

- What makes up your business's intellectual capital?
- What rights to intellectual property do you own, and how do you use them?
- How can you develop and leverage intellectual property for the benefit of your business?
- What are the legal issues you need to understand to effectively manage your intellectual property?

For too long, the talent development supplier industry has relied on its ability to leverage its intellectual property. Now, these businesses may be at a crossroads in determining how much their intellectual property can differentiate them in a go-to-market strategy. As you look to build and grow your business, here are some questions to ask yourself: What if content is no longer king? If so, how will you make your offer distinct? Does widespread distribution or quality of the customer experience then become your difference maker? Does your intellectual capital become more valuable than your intellectual property? To address these questions, you need to fully understand what you own, how critical it is to your success, and how you can protect it as necessary.

Knowing What Cards to Play: Intellectual Capital Versus Intellectual Property

Let's take a look at intellectual capital. First, more often than not, new businesses wrongly conflate intellectual capital with intellectual property. However, the two are separate concepts. The easiest way to explain it is that all IP is IC, but not all IC is IP. In other words, intellectual property is a subset of intellectual capital.

One way to describe intellectual capital in a business context is that it is the difference between book value and market value. That is, it's everything that creates value but cannot be captured by traditional accounting. The book value is a function of a calculation based on assets and liabilities, and to some extent historical industry guidelines; whereas market value is what consumers are willing to pay for a business. In some cases, the book and market values might be reasonably close, yet in others there might be a great disparity depending on the simple principle of supply and demand.

This is similar to the difference between the blue book value of a car and its market value. The blue book value is computed from benchmarking other cars and inserting various factors such as age, mileage, and condition. However, if it is a high-demand car with little availability, the market may be willing to pay quite a bit above the book value to purchase it. The car possesses intangible value not captured in the book value. In valuing a business some relatively intangible factors represent its intellectual capital, such as talent capability, processes, and systems that while present don't lend themselves to a formal accounting.

Intellectual property has been the focus of the talent development industry over the years. It is what often distinguishes one supplier from another. But the umbrella under which it falls, intellectual capital, is worth exploring because it provides significant value for every firm. There are five types of intellectual capital:

- intellectual property
- organizational capital
- human capital
- relationship capital
- business model.

All together, these types represent the total wisdom of an organization. Table 4-1 provides examples of each type (Devine 2009, 1; Maddocks and Beaney 2002, 16).

Intellectual property is the easiest type of intellectual capital to conceptualize, and in many ways it represents what the talent development supplier industry offers externally to clients. Your business's intellectual property typically comprises the deliverables you sell to your clients. Your offerings might come in multiple forms, in either hard copy or digitized formats, including:

- off-the-shelf, tailored, or totally custom programs
- facilitator guides
- software programs
- application tools
- assessment inventories
- models
- participant workbooks
- videos
- web-based programs
- presentations.

Intellectual property falls into four broad categories: patents, copyrights, trademarks, and trade secrets. As a business, your challenge is to determine who owns each form, as well as their respective usage rights.

Table 4-1. Types and Examples of Intellectual Capital

Intellectual Property	Organizational Capital	Human Capital	Relationship Capital	Business Model
Patents	Information systems and technology	Employee engagement	Company brand	Strategy and competitive environment
Copyrights and trade-marks	Sales and service processes and practices	Selection and training	Client relationship management approaches	Go-to-market approach and industry focus
Program deliverables	Product development methodology	Succession planning	Supplier or partner networks	Operational excellence
Trade secrets	Project management processes	Performance management	Client and vendor contracts	Product or service leadership

Meanwhile, the other four types of intellectual capital—organizational capital, human capital, relationship capital, and business models—are somewhat more difficult to replicate. Even so, some will argue that an organization's real competitive advantage revolves around how it leverages these components—its structure, systems, and processes; the relationships it develops; the people it nurtures; and the business model it takes to market. In fact, these components are regularly what allows an organization to utilize its intellectual property in addressing its customers' business needs.

What Makes Up Intellectual Property?

Intellectual property law refers to the kind of property that results from the fruits of mental labor. It includes four primary areas: copyrights, trademarks, patents, and trade secrets, as well as industrial design and geographical indications or appellations:

- Patents protect inventions of tangible things.
- Copyrights protect various forms of written and artistic expression.
- Trademarks protect a name or symbol identifying the source of goods or services.
- Trade secrets protect secret processes, distribution methods, and other confidential information.
- Industrial design constitutes the ornamental or aesthetic aspect of an article.
- Geographical indications represent the specific geographical origin and possess qualities attributable to that place of origin.

While it may be the hardest type to quantify, human capital is the most precious and fragile of all. It represents the people who make up your business; people who invariably need attention, training, and development. They are not only responsible for developing and administering your firm's customer experience, they are also the face of delivering your services to your clients' businesses. However, it's important to know how much of your business's human capital you actually own. Assuming you are the founder, the ownership extends to you alone. In fact, the vast majority of your human capital are your employees. This human capital is subject to the events that can affect how you optimize its value. Your business should not take its human capital for granted; rather, you should ensure that it is nurtured and preserved.

Take a moment to evaluate your intellectual capital. How are you using it to improve your business and compete in the marketplace? Do you have systems and processes that lend themselves to creating a positive—and even extraordinary—end-user (learner) experience? What's more, what about your staff? Are you applying best practices when selecting, developing, evaluating, and engaging your own employees?

How have you branded your business and its offer? How are you reaching out to your marketplace? What is your core capability and how are you leveraging it? How effective are your relationships with your clients and your own external suppliers? Finally, how well is your business model aligned with your overall strategy? These are but a few of the issues and challenges talent development businesses face.

Taking It to the Bank: Developing and Leveraging Intellectual Property

While all types of intellectual capital are critical to a company's success, the most challenging type in the talent development industry is intellectual property and its use to drive business. This is largely because so much content is available for free on the Internet, presenting a sometimes uninformed question on what can and cannot be used without permission. Furthermore, because so much consulting takes place within a client organization behind closed doors rather than in public, many might feel there is little chance they'll ever be caught using "just a little" from here and "just a little" from there. Therefore, when setting out to build or grow a business that involves training clients, you must address some questions related to your intellectual property:

- How do you develop it?
- How do you create value with it?
- How do you leverage it?
- How do you evaluate it?

Developing Your Intellectual Property

A relatively simple process for pursuing the development of your programs involves three stages. Figure 4-1 offers a visual of these stages.

Stage 1: Inquire and Infer

To begin, you should explore why you need to develop intellectual property in a particular area. This involves inquiring about causes, effects, relationships, and results, as well as inferring their implications. It requires collecting data from both internal and external sources through interviews, observations, and experiences. These data enable you to build a business case for change by becoming curious about the issues at hand—instead of simply accepting the first line of thought or the present conditions.

Stage 2: Invent and Inspire

Next, embark on the process of invention—creating possible solutions through brainstorming, researching existing models and practices, designing blueprints for developing products and processes, and conducting cost-benefit analyses. It involves coming up with creative solutions focused on explicit and implicit issues, and inspiring others with a compelling case for change. This stage addresses what you are going to address by clearly defining the end in mind.

Stage 3: Install and Inspect

Wrapping up, you need to address how things get done and the challenges of implementing your IP. This involves installing and evaluating solutions in partnership with your clients and figuring out what's working and what isn't. This entails testing the solutions, revising them appropriately, and then putting them to work with workers. As such, you need to create milestones, proof points, and benchmarks—all evaluated against established metrics for success.

Figure 4-1. Creating Intellectual Capital

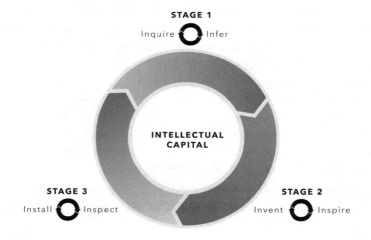

Source: Cohen and Backer (1999).

Creating Value With Your Intellectual Property

Your goal should not simply be to develop the proper IP to run your business. Instead, you should determine how to create the most value from what you develop. You need to decide what impact you can—and will—have on your clients. What are the potential outcomes of your intellectual property that you are striving to achieve? Is it about saving time and money, reducing stress, enhancing efficiency, stimulating creativity, improving understanding between people, facilitating teamwork, improving leader effectiveness, growing revenue and profit, increasing customer retention, or even all of these issues?

If your organizational capital, human capital, relationship capital, and business model can enable the effectiveness of your intellectual property, it will be easier to run your business with greater predictability and scalability. You simply need to determine:

- Which outcomes are most important to your clients' organizations?
- How are you measuring the results?
- How can you determine the linkages between IP and your customers' outcomes?
- What experiments can you try that will help you determine the value you are creating?

Leveraging Your Intellectual Property

When leveraging your intellectual property, you need to determine what IP you have that differentiates your business from your relevant competition. What's the "secret sauce" that makes your organization competitive in the market? How well are you developing, integrating, applying, and implementing this intellectual property in your talent development practice? How much true differentiated value have you created with your intellectual property?

Here are some actions to help you best leverage your intellectual property:

- Organize your talent development business around both your organization's intellectual property and the needs of your customers. Some of these relationships are easy to understand. For example, if your business model requires certain types of core capabilities and competencies to deliver its products and services, then it behooves you to create learning systems that equip your customers' personnel with them.
- Determine what is worth protecting or documenting. Your organization may own any number of copyrights, patents, and trademarks. How can you integrate and use these in your programs to create more value?
- View your organization's intellectual property as a strategic asset. That is, tightly align it with the strategic imperatives of your business.
- Understand the secret sauce that constitutes your IP—know what's unique about your business that differentiates it in the market.
- Treat intellectual property, rather than physical assets, as the principal wellspring of stakeholder value and competitive advantage in this knowledge economy.

What's critical in owning, using, and leveraging content is having a curation process that preserves it and allows for relatively easy access and alteration. In general, curation refers to tending, collecting, and managing the physical assets of content such as participant and facilitator materials. Today's digital world has made this process much easier, especially when it comes to storing and accessing information. However, it has become more complicated to maintain version control and manage appropriate access by others to pass on information. Today, firms must limit the amount of content open to re-evaluation, revision, and remixing to ensure that the wrong version is not distributed (Betts and Anderson 2016).

Evaluating Your Intellectual Property

It isn't necessarily easy for your clients to evaluate the value of your IP, although you may have established criteria to make these assessments. But do you really know its value? There are a number of relevant factors, but it is likely that the initial screening criterion is all about the content you possess. After all, if you have done your homework, you should know the business issues your clients, current or prospective, are trying to solve—and whether you possess the most relevant content (knowledge, skills, or attitudes) needed to effectively address these. Yet, possessing the relevant content is simply the bare minimum required for an organization considering working with an external supplier.

Next, prospective purchasers of your programs probably don't, but definitely should, pursue due diligence in exploring whether you own the content or are licensed to distribute it, have borrowed or customized it without permission, or in the absolute worst case, taken from someone else's work. Most people would not do this intentionally, but how sure can you be that what you have created is actually yours? Sometimes these lines are blurred. For your and your clients' sake, you need to be sure you can clearly defend what you do and do not own. Furthermore, your clients might start asking about the research base of your programs and services. How do they know your effectiveness claims are actually true? (See chapter 5 for more on this question.)

If you think this isn't an issue, I know of a talent management consulting firm that was unknowingly distributing an interviewing program that was almost an exact replica of another firm's program. (I say "unknowingly" given that the person or people largely responsible had long left the company.) My job was to review all off-the-shelf materials being sold so that I could put together an overall curriculum. When I came across this interviewing program, it looked oddly familiar. I then checked with a colleague from the other supplier and indeed it was plagiarized almost word for word. For the client organizations using it, we had to apologize and recall whatever they had left in their inventory. What would have happened if this had not been noticed, and instead brought to the business's attention with a cease-and-desist letter from the other firm years later? Of course, the supplier is legally culpable, but unless the purchase contract granted indemnification, the business might also be accountable if it continued to use the program.

Beyond Morals and Ethics: Legal Challenges

The nuances in protecting the legal rights to your work and in navigating intellectual property law extend beyond the scope of this book, and I encourage you to consult legal counsel if you have any questions. Instead, this section offers a brief overview of the challenges and issues you might face as a talent development business. What makes this topic complex is that while there are guidelines to follow, their interpretation is relatively subjective, and therefore left up to the courts to resolve any disputes. Furthermore, there are many misconceptions about the topic that I hope to raise, although in no way solve.

Intellectual property law is serious business and any blatant infringement of it will result in significant consequences, largely financial, reputational, and in some rare cases even incarceration. It applies to the development of your own programs, products, and models, as well as those your clients might be using internally. As such, as you seek to build and grow your talent development firm, you need to understand the basic guidelines and act conservatively when making decisions about the creation and use of IP. Cat Russo, president and founder of Russo Rights, says it this way: "If you didn't write something as your own original content and if it's not your original idea and you are using that material in any kind of published work that someone else will be reading (for internal or external organizational use), it's best to always request permission from the copyright holder to use that material and, in addition, to then include an attribution 'Used with permission from the COPYRIGHT HOLDER NAME'" (Russo 2015).

Of course, the issues are quite different if you use any of your client's original materials, rather than those you directly offer. Keep in mind when a client asks you to integrate its materials into yours, you may have the same legal responsibilities as the client. Over time materials from different sources are often combined so they appear to be from one source. It is essential that you protect your business with clear contracts and agreements when working with content provided by a client or third party.

The most nebulous aspect of U.S. copyright law is the fair use doctrine. It permits limited use of copyrighted material without permission from the rights holders, for purposes such as criticism and comment, news reporting, research and scholarship, non-profit educational use, and parody. The courts use four factors to test a fair use case:

1. **The purpose and character of the use:** This refers to whether the use in question helps fulfill the intention of copyright law to stimulate creativity for the enrichment of the general public, or whether it aims to only supersede the objects of the original for reasons of personal profit.

2. **The nature of the copyrighted work:** This refers to preventing ownership of work that rightfully belongs in the public domain by separating facts and ideas from copyright, but rather that only their particular expression of fixation merits such protection.

3. **The amount and substance:** This refers to the assessment of the quantity or percentage of the original copyrighted work that has been imported into the new work. In this case, often a "de minimis" defense is offered on the basis that the amount of material copied is so small that a fair use analysis isn't even conducted.

4. **The effect upon one's value:** This refers to measuring the effect that the allegedly infringing use has had on the copyright owner's ability to exploit his or her original work.

These four factors are the sole guidance the courts have to determine fair use, and as a result they are interpreted differently across districts. Here are a few other basic rules to help you determine fair use:

- **Copying something is different from creating something.** That is, are you merely copying someone else's work verbatim or using it to help create something new?

- **You can't compete with the source from which you are copying.** Without permission, you can't use another person's protected expression in any way that limits or potentially impairs the market for his or her work.

- **Giving the author credit doesn't let you off the hook.** Giving credit and adhering to fair use are completely separate concepts. You either have the right to use someone else's materials or you don't. The fact that you attribute the materials doesn't change this.

- **The more you take, the less likely it is to be fair use.** As a general rule, never quote more than a few successive paragraphs from a book or article, take more than one chart of a diagram, include an illustration or other artwork in a book or newsletter without the author's permission, or quote more than one or two lines from a poem. However, it's important to remember, and contrary to what many believe, there is no absolute word count on fair use.

- **The quality of the material used is as important as the quantity.** The more important the material is to the original work, the less likely your use of it will be considered fair.

The practicality of the fair use doctrine is that a number of conventional uses of copyrighted works are not necessarily considered infringements. For example, quoting from a copyrighted work to criticize or comment upon it, or teach students about it, is considered fair use. A teacher or instructor who prints a few copies of an article to illustrate an approach or methodology will probably have no problem when considering the four factors, other than possibly the amount and substance. All cases are not cut and dry, and in most situations all four factors are considered together to decide whether copyright was violated.

For example, a program quoting another source will probably fall under fair use even though the program may be sold to others. But, a nonprofit educational website reproducing entire articles from a magazine will probably be found to infringe if the magazine publisher can demonstrate that the website affects the market for the magazine, even though the website is noncommercial. Presenting someone else's research to support your points of view would certainly be fair use, but using their model as the basis of your own program probably would not be. In this case, you would be taking the core content of someone else's work, and on which their livelihood may be based, and using it for your own gain. Its fair use would seem questionable.

Keep in mind that other countries often have drastically different fair use criteria. Even within Europe, rules vary greatly across countries. When in doubt, always ask for permission. In fact, even when not in doubt, ask for permission. It is the only truly safe approach.

Establishing and Protecting Your Rights

The challenge as a practitioner is protecting your intellectual property when transferring it to your clients. Putting the copyright symbol (©) followed by a year and your individual or business name does lay claim to the content, as long as you first ensure that what you are copyrighting is indeed yours. For prepackaged off-the-shelf training programs, you would be remiss to not protect yourself and your content.

While there are no foolproof ways to avoid someone else using your material, you can discourage copying by printing on darker pages or using watermarked paper, which would clearly reveal that someone has illegally copied your material.

When working with clients, you should be up front about what's yours and what's rightfully your clients. For example, if you provide an unlimited license agreement for which you are allowing your clients to produce as many copies of your materials as agreed to, you still need to make sure that you include the copyright information on them. If you are handling any proprietary client information, you are not necessarily given blanket rights to reproduce it even if it's sandwiched in between your own materials.

When creating custom programs for clients with your own material, some of which you have previously created, but are tailoring it to meet their needs, you can copyright it yourself for XYZ company. It might look something like this: "© 2016 Stephen L. Cohen for XYZ Company." This designation makes it clear that they have the rights to use your materials while you are restricted in replicating any part of those that reveal client proprietary information. Thus, you can use the same models, framework, exercises, and assessments for another client, as long as you remove anything that reveals the previous client's proprietary information.

In legal copyrighting, what's most important is that you have a legitimate contract in place with your client that clearly spells out the extent to which they can use your material even if they have paid for it.

Conclusion

The talent development industry thrives on intellectual capital, and more specifically the intellectual property it has developed and continues to create. How you optimize and leverage your IP to generate profit is critical to your survival. In an age when information is at the tip of a finger's mouse click, you need to set out to not only protect your company's IP but also to differentiate your business on it. Perhaps more important to your success is how you package and deliver your IP to your customers, which the next chapter addresses.

Reflection Questions

KNOWING WHAT CARDS TO PLAY: INTELLECTUAL CAPITAL VERSUS INTELLECTUAL PROPERTY

- As you review the Table 4-1, where are your strengths?
- What areas can you use more help in developing?
- How will you go about leveraging your strengths and building up your areas of relative deficiency?
- How would you go about proving to a prospective client that you own what you are selling?

TAKING IT TO THE BANK: DEVELOPING AND LEVERAGING INTELLECTUAL PROPERTY

- What are you doing to ensure your content can't be replicated easily?
- How have you protected your intellectual property?
- How does the delivery of your content make a difference to your customers?
- Which factors—content, delivery, or instruction—differentiate your firm. How do you know?
- How does this question apply to the offerings you develop internally versus solutions from outside partner resources?

BEYOND MORALS AND ETHICS: LEGAL CHALLENGES

- What legal liabilities might you face in defending any IP laws?
- Where are you potentially susceptible to violating the fair use doctrine?
- How can you ensure your clients are using your copyrighted materials legally?

PART 2

CREATING
MOMENTUM

5

DIFFERENTIATING YOUR OFFER FROM OTHERS

*You need to understand the market, know how you
can differentiate yourself in it, and grasp the price and
the functional differentiation competitive points that
are going to allow you to be disruptive.*
—Audrey MacLean

Most businesses can determine their focus—from their people to their strategies and ideas. But not nearly as many can figure out how and why they are different from other businesses. They struggle to identify their competitive advantage. This is especially true in the crowded and competitive talent development supplier industry in which there aren't many barriers to entry, offerings look very much the same, and claims for effectiveness are often questionable. Differentiating your business and sustaining its uniqueness by frequently reconfiguring it is the key to maintaining superiority.

This chapter addresses these challenges by exploring how you should approach developing an offer and then differentiating it as part of your business. How do you convert brilliant ideas to viable and marketable products and services? What makes you unique and competitive? How do you know that what you're offering works? What claims can you make about the results you either explicitly state or implicitly imply?

These questions are critical to answer before and during the building and growing of your business. Your answers will represent your product or program development strategy. In today's environment, you need to lend this formality to your process. There are relatively few winning solutions out there. If and when you have one, embrace it; it may be difficult to come up with another one.

Developing a truly market-driven product development strategy didn't exist when the industry began. Most of the pioneers coalesced around an idea, convinced themselves of the logic and need for it, and then embarked on the long and circuitous journey of profiting from the idea. They did not start out by creating a product development map for new programming.

Here is an illustration of what I mean. In 2015, I conducted an informal survey with a number of long-standing firms in the talent development industry. They ranged in age from 14 to 51 years and in revenue from $3 to $175 million, creating a representative sample of firms in the industry. I asked them the following questions: When did you start your business? What's your current revenue? And what percentage of your current revenue is accounted for by your very first program or product, or core content with which you started your business?

The average firm was nearly 30 years old, had $32.6 million in revenue, and 70.4 percent of its current revenue came from its very first program and core content. Table 5-1 provides the full results.

What's particularly interesting is that size doesn't seem to matter. Using the median company by current revenue, the 11 companies have 68.6 percent and the 11 companies below have 72.3 percent of current sales attributed to their first program or core content. Even for the top seven companies in revenue—after which there is a significant gap from seventh at $50 million to eighth at only $18 million—their initial core content and programs still account for an average of 65.7 percent of their current revenue.

Also interesting is that when the median age of the companies is taken into account, the percentages are roughly the same, with 69.2 percent for the 11 oldest and 71.4 percent for the 11 youngest. This doesn't mean they didn't develop offshoots or extensions of their original program, rather that mostly incremental changes were made over the years, all based on their original concepts. One could argue that these products were so well developed that they stood the test of time. But why weren't these firms able to develop other successful programs? Perhaps when they started out they didn't have the right process in place. How can you crank out multiple highly valued, well-received, outcome-based programs relatively quickly and inexpensively that deliver business results for both you and your customers? This chapter helps you address this challenge.

Table 5-1. Percentage of First Product Current Revenue*

Company	Approximate Age of Company	Approximate Current Revenue (millions)	Current Percent of Revenue From Original Program
1	51	$10	90
2	51	$50	55
3	50	$11	50
4	46	$175	50
5	42	$111	40
6	40	$3	85
7	37	$90	75
8	36	$58	90
9	35	$5	95
10	30	$5	33
11	30	$8	98
12	30	$8	66
13	27	$7	38
14	25	$90	70
15	25	$12	70
16	22	$10	65
17	20	$5	75
18	20	$8	50
19	20	$5	90
20	15	$8	75
21	15	$60	80
22	14	$18	85
23	14	$8	90
Average	30	$33	70

*These numbers are rough estimates as of 2015, but are reasonably close to actuals.

Table Stakes or All In?: Is Content Still King?

Most talent development consultants believe their entire existence and livelihood is wrapped up in the notion that content is king. It is an industry largely built on the contents of books published by authors who then converted that information into training programs—or vice versa.

However, the industry has evolved over the last 50 years not only in the proliferation of its content, but also the ease with which it has become accessible. At some point, this proliferation and ease of access will reduce the significance of any one piece of content. Where does that leave you as a supplier of talent development content; the very foundation on which you are basing your capability to go to market?

In any highly competitive market it's not only important to be unique in some way, but also differentiate yourself from your competitors. This is easier said than done, particularly where the value proposition has traditionally been difficult to articulate and calculate. And this is certainly the case in the "soft" business of talent development. For instance, the industry has started to introduce finite ROI formulas for developing and retaining talent. Unfortunately, these calculations do not always have full statistical validation. Programs and projects often involve too many relatively intangible costs, which are difficult, if not impossible, to capture and assess. Consequently, there are really only a few ways to differentiate the business of learning, talent development, and performance improvement: content, instruction, or delivery.

A Closer Look at Content

In the information age, content is relatively easy to create, imitate, access, and obtain. How many 2 x 2 frameworks are there that assess relatively the same dimensions, but are just labeled differently? How many assessment tools purport to measure the same leadership or sales capabilities, but do so with different questions? How many leadership theories, approaches, and competency models can there be? Ultimately, the theories and models are rooted in the same idea—despite what their architects would have you believe. They are versions of a similar theme.

While some intellectual property is protected if original, particularly with ample research to support it, it doesn't take long for another firm to create a "similar but different" version. After all, except for a few industry stalwarts such as situational leadership, managing interpersonal relations, facilitative leadership, whole brain thinking, and counselor selling, the shelf life of most content is short. These models and programs have not only stood the test of time, but also have served as the foundational content on which subsequent programs were based. Today, many look-alikes, or even direct offshoots, compete for market share.

For example, let's look at formal presentation and speaking training programs. Although I am sure differences between them exist, how different can they be from the basic principles and process for communicating effectively? Certainly not enough for buyers and their learners to initially decipher. Or consider interpersonal style programs, all of which have a unique model and accompanying assessment tool. They pretty much boil down to a 2 x 2 framework with four similar looking quadrants labeled differently. In the end, interpersonal style is interpersonal style. How are prospective clients supposed to differentiate your offering from the vast array of programs and services available?

Certainly it would help to fully understand what is meant by content. It can take many forms—for example, raw information, implicit, or explicit knowledge. Content can be the specific sequence in which information is presented, the packaging in which it is wrapped, and the brand around which it is cloaked. The question is whether the information is an undifferentiated commodity, or is it the organization and presentation of that knowledge that makes it relevant and differentiated?

You can also distinguish your content through delivery or instruction: the experience you create to distribute and offer content, goods, and services for your client and its employee learners. Delivery is not just the presentation of the training, whether online or in a classroom. Rather, it is all that is involved in conveying information: the sequencing of the content, the frameworks that explain it, and even its packaging. Your business may deliver quality customer experiences that produces real performance improvement results. In the end, you are responsible for the entire learner experience—whether pre-work applications, classroom, online, post-work resources, or a combination—that must fulfill your client's needs.

Enter Experience and Expertise

It would be foolhardy not to mention the impact of experience and expertise on the three industry drivers. World-class content, delivery, and instruction are not enough to differentiate most talent development solutions. Rather, your experience and expertise serve as the engine that drives all three.

For example, training and consulting firms that have been in business longer and possess more experience helping clients effectively use their content are more likely to demonstrate how their content and delivery can address pressing business challenges. There is little substitute for expertise, and this is how many top consultancies differentiate themselves. However, even gurus, with bestselling books often lose their prominence because they can't be everywhere at once and must off-load their work—but not intellectual prowess—to others. In fact, there are legions of examples in which one-trick ponies don't last very long, bestselling programs have a short shelflife, or guru-founded businesses are sold to larger companies only to have the guru depart as soon as her employment contract is completed. Clearly, many talent consulting firms can fulfill a specific bill of goods, and the top ones tend to stand out because they likely focus more on conducting research, staying up-to-date on current trends, and continually perfecting their craft.

It is becoming increasingly difficult to differentiate a talent development solution on the basis of content alone without a strong focus on delivering a truly compelling instructionally sound learning experience forged by deep expertise, regardless of format. In other words, content will continue to be challenged for its throne in this industry. Hopefully, you are now better prepared to navigate the slippery legal slope in identifying, selecting, and using various learning and development concepts, models, programs, and tools. What's more, as you move forward in creating talent development offerings, consider two questions:

- What true differentiation strategies have been successful in your business?
- How have these sustained themselves over the years and effectively combatted the competition?

Surely, content can be king if you are leading the pack, and it's truly unique and can't be imitated. But just how long will this last in this ever-changing environment? Given the above, perhaps a more meaningful answer to the question of whether content is king is that it may be necessary at some level, but not sufficient at others.

Art, Science, and Business: Program Design and Development

Creating a program, product, or service in today's talent development industry requires specific knowledge, a number of skill sets, and plenty of experience. During the early stages of the industry, program design and development wasn't very sophisticated. Many of the initial programs came from people outside the talent development industry—for example, a top insurance salesperson, an owner of a several manufacturing businesses, an author, a school teacher—who built their businesses around selling their programs as solutions to problems clients had on the people development side. This is not to say their ideas and programs weren't useful; in fact, many were exceptional and have stood the test of time. But their approach resembled more of an art and less of a science. The business part just happened, or it didn't, as it tended to be more random and entrepreneurial.

Indeed, combining the art, science, and business elements of program development to consistently create successful offerings is a very difficult and challenging task. As noted, few firms in the industry have replicated the success of their very first offering, beyond updating or expanding on it. Whatever was included in these initial programs in how they came together is hard to capture again in a new program.

So what is it about program development that makes it so difficult to create something that's not only unique to the marketplace but commercially viable too? Let's look at the three pillars of program development to learn more about how best to bring them together for long-term results (Cohen 1993, 49-58).

Art refers to a specific skill, or set of skills, requiring use of intuitive faculties. These skills cannot be learned solely from studying them.

Science refers to any knowledge, activity, discipline, or study broadly accepted as having a demonstrable, objective, factual, systematic, or methodological basis.

Business refers to any form of commercial policy, practice, or activity with the objective of manufacturing, distributing, or exchanging commodities or services for financial gain.

Program Development Process

To bring order to these apparent disparate capabilities, you need a system for conceiving, developing, and delivering your programs. The most widely known is the stage-gate system (Cooper 1990, 44-55), commonly attributed to the consultancy Booz Allen Hamilton in the early 1980s. It includes eight steps:

1. idea generation
2. idea screening
3. idea development and testing
4. business analysis
5. beta and market testing
6. technical implementation
7. commercialization
8. new product pricing.

For your purpose, it's important to adhere to the discipline required to transfer an idea to a concrete program that can be marketed and implemented successfully. When I started my second company, The Learning Design Group, I followed a process that has been around for about 25 years. Without going into much detail, there were nine disciplines equally divided into three overarching phases, which are represented in Table 5-2. These nine disciplines are intended to be followed sequentially—from analysis of the market's need and reception to conception of what the program will need to look like to meet the market's need, and then finally to implementation to bring it to the market and evaluate its success.

The point is that consistently effective programs or product development results evolve from a well-documented road map, overseen by a specific product management role that adheres to milestones, timelines, and costs, while obtaining frequent client feedback.

Table 5-2. Program Development Disciplines

Analysis	Conception	Implementation
Direction	Diagnosis	Delivery
Differentiation	Design	Documentation
Discovery	Development	Deduction

Source: Cohen (1993).

Learning From a Masterpiece: Both Science and Art

Using your program development process, you can create a program or service that will frequently be sought after in the market. Some firms do this better than others, typically those that have been around for a long time and continue to show steady growth. Whatever they have done or are doing works. But this goes beyond just the process, whether it's my analysis-conception-implementation, ADDIE (analysis, design, development, implementation, evaluation), or SAM (successive approximation model, Allen 2012). You also have to develop the spirit of the offer and consider the craft of program development. Some call this inside-out learning, which assumes learning will be acquired and retained when the motivation to learn comes from within a person as opposed to being instructed to do so from the outside.

Many books have been written on this subject, with interesting and straightforward formulas that can be universally applied. I have had the good fortune of developing more than 50 off-the-shelf products and I've been responsible for directing the development of nearly 1,000 custom learning programs during my career. I have learned quite a lot about how to create compelling programming based on the principles of adult learning. Adults want learning to be more autonomous, self-directed, relevant, and pragmatic to their needs, in an engaged and reinforced environment that is task and goal oriented and respectful of their past experience and knowledge. Scientific principles of adult learning, such as those of Malcolm Knowles and others (1984), can serve as a basis, but without the art element, adult learners won't be brought into an experience that moves them to apply what they are learning outside the instructional environment.

A simpler way to view program development is to ensure programming creates a learner experience that applies the 5M formula of motivational, magical, memorable, meaningful, and measurable (Cohen, L'Allier, and Stewart 1987, 31-38). This entails including surprise, fun, and drama in the program's design in the right doses (Table 5-3).

Table 5-3. Tips for Creating an Engaging Learner Experience

Surprise, Surprise	Are We Having Fun Yet?	The Power of Drama
Do an about face	Play the game	Put on a good show
Get out of order	Toy with success	Create shock value
Break the rhythm	Run with your imagination	Compose a soundtrack
Combine apples and oranges	Lighten up	Tell a story

Source: Cohen and Jurkovic (1997).

Somewhere in between the science and art of program development is the way you incorporate the appropriate instructional method into your message. Assume for a moment there are four basic instructional approaches: information, education, training, and learning. Each one has different learner roles, learning objectives, intended outcomes, and expected behaviors. Consequently, different instructional methods are more appropriate for each of these approaches. Figure 5-1 reflects these differences. Part of its contents is based on experience, another part on conjecture, and a third on scientific underpinnings. It will provide a guideline for you to think about how to effectively communicate what you want your clients to learn.

It's critical to figure out how you might chunk your offering into bite-size units. This is true whether in a more traditional classroom or online setting. The adult learner's attention span and expected time for immediate feedback seems to have declined over the years, and will only continue to as Millennials continue entering the workplace. By focusing on smaller lessons, you can allow your client and its learners to more readily grasp and then apply the content, thus making it easier to retain information. This approach is separate from providing time for reflection and ample breaks during the learning experience, which are both key to keeping learners fresh and motivated to continue their learning. Performance tracking and assessment at these breaks adds additional focus to the learning paradigm.

The last component of program development is its business aspect. Clearly, it really doesn't matter how well you analyze, conceptualize, or implement your offering if you don't inject business principles across the disciplines. For example, the analysis phase includes strategic visioning, product alignment, pricing strategy, and market analysis. Likewise, the conception phase includes business practices of cost modeling, investment planning, and life-cycle analysis. Finally, the implementation phase includes the business practices of inventory and project management, cost-benefit analysis, total quality management, and internal ROI. Best practice program development involves appropriate doses of all three components to ensure success (Cohen 1993, 49-58). Each of the nine disciplines mentioned in Table 5-2 involve varying degrees of art, science, and business. The goal is to ensure there is a reasonable balance across the three to produce optimal results.

Figure 5-1. Matching the Method to the Message

	Information	Education	Training	Learning
Instructional Approach	Information	Education	Training	Learning
Learner Role	Active	Reactive	Interactive	Proactive
Learning Objective	Awareness	Knowledge	Capability	Application
Intended Outcome	◄------ UNDERSTANDING --- COMPETENCY --- PERFORMANCE ------►			
Expected Behavior	Believe It!	Know It!	Do It!	Use It!
Learning Method	Brochures overviews	Feedback reports	Ongoing coaching	Testing certification
	Videos audios	Debriefs	Role plays	Reality-based simulations
	Self-assessments	360-degree assessments	Small group discussions	On-the-job training
	Articles	Guided learning journals	Fish bowls	Action learning
	Business cases	Case studies	Adaptive testing	Action plans
	Briefings	Games	Group exercises	Job aids
	Journaling	Ropes courses	Case simulations	Performance support systems
	Presentations	Conferences events	Process mapping	M-learning
	Meetings	Lecturettes	Online modules	
	Web-sites portals	Brainstorming	Virtual learning	
		Storyboards		
		Chat rooms		

Source: Cohen (2002).

The Role of Innovation

It is difficult to mention new program development without some follow-up on innovation and how to continually stretch the boundaries of old and new products to meet market demands. One could argue that advances in innovation and the creative process might allow for a more iterative approach without so many steps. For example, consider IDEO's design thinking approach: inspiration, ideation, and implementation (Brown 2008, 84-92). Design thinking attempts to inspire the essential element of creativity: the ability to take an abstract idea and create something with it. It's based upon the fundamental belief that an unexecuted idea, one that is never realized, is useless. The concept involves embracing empathy for your clients.

Of course, the big question is how much innovation is enough? Based on Table 5-1, innovation and its value to long-term success is difficult to calculate. Nevertheless, innovation is a strategic choice. Whereas strategy is about embracing constraints and making trade-offs, innovation is about breaking through constraints and making trade-offs. Breakthrough innovation means embracing the future more than your competition (Raynor and Ahmed 2013). Here's an example of an innovation model that may help you determine how much innovation your programs and products need to survive and flourish (StratGo Marketing 2013).

Incremental Innovation

This consists of small, yet meaningful improvements in your products, services, and other ways you do business. They tend to be the "new and improved" innovations we are bombarded with every day: new flavors, shifts to better or all-natural ingredients, packaging improvements, faster or slower functioning, just-in-time supply chain enhancements, and cost reductions. But the basic product is the original. These can be seen every day and help extend the product, service, and business life cycles and improve profitability. They can easily be visualized and quickly communicated, and provide something new with which to grab your customer's attention in an increasingly competitive marketplace.

Think about the eye care industry for a moment. How many different sizes, colors, and shapes of eyeglasses are there? Each one of these represents an incremental change. More specifically, think about the evolution from breakable glass to nonbreakable plastic lenses, or the advent of interchangeable rims.

Substantial Innovation

This is a meaningful change in the way you do business that provides your customers with something demonstrably different (beyond "new and improved").

Breakthrough innovation produces a substantial competitive edge for a while, although the length of time anyone can maintain such an advantage is growing increasingly shorter given the widespread capabilities that are readily available and imitable. It can be an entirely new category or subcategory; that is, an offering enhancement that stands above the rest, ensuring that a group of customers will not consider a product that isn't comparable.

Staying with the eye care example, the invention of contact lenses was a substantial innovation. They changed the way people regarded eyewear. Of course, it was relatively easy to copy this idea if that was the market you were interested in pursuing. But even with this substantial innovation from traditional eye glasses, incremental improvements such as flexible, long-lasting, overnight, and even colored contact lenses emerged.

Transformational Innovation

This is usually (but not always) the introduction of a technology that creates a new industry and transforms the way we live and work. Exceedingly rare, transformational innovation often eliminates existing industries or, at a minimum, totally changes them. For this reason, transformational innovation tends to be championed by those who aren't wedded to an existing infrastructure.

In eye care, the transformational innovation was Lasik surgery and how it disrupted the eyewear industry. People who needed eye care no longer had to concern themselves with wearing glasses or putting in contact lenses. Instead, they could opt for surgery—a game changer—that left existing eyeglass and contact manufacturers scrambling.

Interestingly, transformational innovation can often be easier to pursue. Given that it purposely strays from the current product to create something very different, you don't have to rely on traditional ways of development and delivery. That said, it often requires reestablishing systems and processes, and increasing capital expense for retooling operations. For a business entrenched in a particular industry that's wedded to a profit-generating program or product, transformational innovation can be daunting. No wonder most transformational innovation comes from start-up companies.

Industry Examples of the Three Levels of Innovation

The easiest industry examples to describe involve the technological advances in production to delivery during recent years. Early on, presentations were given through the use of a chalkboard, eventually evolving to the tried-and-true flip-chart. If your business has been around long enough, you might have presented to customers using overhead projectors with acetates. You then likely moved to what was a substantial, though cumbersome, innovation: 35mm slides carried around in a Kodak carousel. Once that became antiquated, you moved on to the next transformational technology: PowerPoint slides. What is next? I can see the use of interactive clear boards permitting movement of objects by a swipe of the hand, as in the movie *Minority Report*. This will be truly transformational and isn't that far away.

Let's consider another example, this time in the environment you deliver learning. There were many ways to incrementally innovate starting with the classroom experience—from altering the length of the experience to customizing materials for a client to creating different versions for specific industries.

The substantial innovation in delivery came with the advent of e-learning and how that changed the dynamics of the learner experience. Today, e-learning looks like a pretty basic approach, and it too has been enhanced through incremental innovations. Somewhere in the middle of this continuum is the hybrid or blended experience, which alters the learning experience.

It is hard to envision a future transformational innovation in the delivery of learning. Potential candidates for this might be an intricate gamification platform or virtual reality environment. Although you could argue that these are just incremental innovations of technology, immersive virtual reality will truly transform the learning experience. Another candidate for transformation in learning delivery is a brain-embedded learning microchip that transfers information on an as-needed basis through search engine technology.

With a basic model of three innovation levels in mind, let's now turn to where innovation comes from. IDEO looks at innovation through the culmination of three factors (Lamp 2014):

- *Viability,* or the business case. Will the design solution align with the business goals? Does this solution honor the client's budget? What will the return on investment look like?
- *Feasibility*, or the technical demands. Is the technology needed to power the design solution available or within reach? How long will it take? Can the organization actually make it happen?
- *Desirability*, or the needs of the people. Will the solution fill a need that fits people's lives? Will it appeal to them? Will they actually want it?

Figure 5-2 illustrates the thinking that innovation is derived from an analysis at the intersection of all three of these factors. To increase the value of the design solution, the key is to balance desirability, feasibility, and viability.

The bedrock of the talent development supplier market lies almost solely in the products, programs, and services it offers. Regardless of what your offer is, even if it's been your moneymaker for the past decade, it will always be subject to and pressed for innovation. In large part, the extent to which you can innovate your offer will determine how you can continually differentiate your business in the marketplace. Having said this, innovation success rates are shockingly low worldwide, largely because we focus too much on customer profiles, rather than on what our customers are trying to achieve. Truly successful innovation comes from designing products, experiences, and processes that make the effectiveness of those jobs easier to achieve (Christensen, et al. 2016, 57).

Figure 5-2. IDEO's Innovation Factors

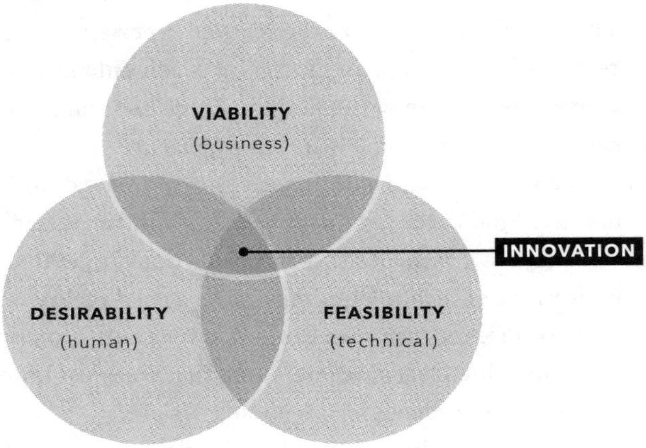

Source: IDEO (2016).

Value Creation: Short and Long Term

No matter how impressive your product, program, or service, if it doesn't create value for your clients, you won't get your business off the ground. But value creation is often a slippery slope. If you can find a unique value proposition for your clients, you will likely create more financial value for your business in both the short and long term. The two go hand in hand. Whether you are building or growing your business, it is essential to consider what rewards your clients in return for the cost, time, and effort they need to put forth to obtain it. Let's start with what it means for your offer to create financial value.

Perhaps you develop high-quality, outcome-based programs that mitigate the customer's financial risk, contain costs, improve productivity, and increase talent retention. This will set you apart and should lead to a continuous revenue stream. Assuming you continue to innovate around your offer, this could stabilize your business. If you create true value for your customers, they will be more likely to continue purchasing what you offer. However, value has different meanings depending on the client. In fact, Eric Almquist, John Senior, and Nicolas Bloch (2016) identified 30 value elements in their value pyramid, which consists of four classification levels: social impact, life changing, emotional, and functional. Understanding the value needs of your customers and how you will satisfy them is critical to your success.

The key is to decide what value your firm's products and services bring, and then execute on those by incorporating foresight about the industry's future, insight into which internal capabilities can optimize that future, and cross-sight into which assets can be configured to create value (T. Zenger 2013, 75). This starts with meaningful value proposition you offer your clients. Why should they do business with you? What value will you bring to them? Will you be able to increase their productivity, mitigate their risks, and reduce their operating costs? Once you have established your value proposition, communicated it to your clients, and delivered on it, you will be creating short- and long-term value for your customers and become a valued asset to their business.

Nowhere was this more evident than with the value Steve Jobs believed Apple could bring to its customers. Jobs thought consumers would pay a premium for ease of use, reliability, and elegance in computing and other digital devices, and that the best means for delivering these was relatively closed systems, significant vertical integration, and tight control over design (T. Zenger 2013, 76-77). The ability to create sustainable value is part and parcel to growth and growth potential because it is likely to not only attract, but continue to retain customers. As such, it continues to increase the financial value of the business.

For example, in the talent development industry many companies have created integrated technology suites addressing many of the requisite human resources elements, including job descriptions, competency assessment inventories, online learning curriculum, performance management tools, and succession management techniques. By integrating these into one platform, which is designed in an open system to incorporate external modules, they add value as a one-stop shop for all of an organization's talent development needs. Other firms rely on their unique content, which can't be obtained elsewhere. Still others create value by focusing on providing an unmatched customer and end-user experience. These approaches can all work.

Equiteq (2013), a global consultancy that advises and then brokers buy-sell deals in the consulting industry, provides a nice summary of what it sees as the real drivers to business growth and equity value in its Equity Growth Wheel.

The firm helps businesses assess the extent to which they are performing in each of eight drivers. This book, in some fashion, touches on all eight: market proposition (chapters 5 and 6), sales and profit growth (chapter 6), client relationships (chapters 6 and 8), quality of fee income (chapters 6 and 7), intellectual property (chapter 4), sales and marketing process (chapter 6), and consultant loyalty and management quality (chapter 7). Equiteq further explains that of these eight, the three most important in creating shareholder value are market proposition, sales and profit growth, and management quality.

What's Your Secret Sauce? The Importance of Creating a Distinct Brand or Product

There are a number of elements that define success in this industry. As mentioned, value creation is one example. Subsequent chapters will cover others including financial stability, a strong management team, and a well-oiled business development machine. Yet another ingredient to success is the ever-elusive secret sauce, or uniqueness, of a business. You know it when you see it, but it's difficult to describe and even more difficult to emulate. It's the critical barrier to entry that may keep your business afloat when competitors continue to pour into the market.

A distinct brand or product can serve as the quality that makes your business extremely difficult to imitate. Apple's iOS operating system, which was until recently a closed system, was a distinctive product, as is perhaps its passion for user interface elegance in design. Coca-Cola's literal secret formula has helped it maintain its leadership in soft drinks for more than 100 years. And let's not forget those companies built to last on a foundation of a purpose-driven culture that withstands the test of time. Among many obvious examples is the Walt Disney Company, whose commitment to bringing happiness to every family was why Walt Disney created the organization, and the company's unyielding passion for executing this mantra remains the bedrock on which it operates.

Examples extend to the talent development supplier industry as well. The Ken Blanchard Companies and Development Dimensions International are strong, purpose-driven cultures that have withstood the test of time. Indeed, they also possess very strong offerings, but so do many of their competitors. Their content has always been at the forefront of the industry, and their customer service records continue to be exemplary. Blanchard has a very spiritually driven business, while DDI's is very scholarly. These strong cultures give both firms a centering point that serves, in part, to make them unique.

As chapter 4 explained, protected intellectual property can also set your business apart. For example, Herrmann International has more than 30 years of research to draw from in creating and interpreting its Hermann Brain Dominance Instrument assessment tool. The Myers-Briggs Type Indicator (MBTI) has an even longer history. In addition, LMS platforms and algorithms for computing scores for assessment inventories can also count, but only if truly differentiated from competitive offers.

Still another opportunity to set yourself apart in the industry is the way you distribute and deliver your offer. Inscape Publishing, now part of the John Wiley & Sons training business, created a unique distribution model with its approximately 2,000 licensed resellers throughout the world. Delivery can be an important driver in the industry, although distinguishing your delivery can be difficult when it is relatively easy to copy just about anything. I have observed companies deliver what appears to be indistinguishable content in the talent development industry, despite their argument otherwise, in a way that transcends the competition just because of their distribution framework. Yet another way to differentiate yourself is through the delivery of your classroom experience from an inside-out rather than outside-in method. To compete effectively today with pure online learning, many firms are creating unique, enduring, and differentiated classroom experiences delivered by extraordinarily committed, passionate, and competent facilitators. It's what sets them apart in earning repeat business.

Can You Really Say That? Claims of Effectiveness

Today, more talent development clients are demanding evidence that your offer actually works the way you claim it does. Consequently, touting the effectiveness of your programs or services can be a powerful means of differentiating your offerings from the rest of the industry. However, effectiveness can be difficult to measure, and many vendors willingly or unwillingly misrepresent what their offerings achieve, which can damage their business and reputation.

Claims of effectiveness can end up as empty promises if your results are not updated continually or are invalid. For example, most vendors equate a positive change from a pre- to a post-test evaluation approach around their offer with its effectiveness. But without a proper control group, it is hard to draw definitive results from prepost testing alone. There's also the potential for the randomization of events to suggest a relationship exists between two variables when it was only a matter of circumstances not likely to be repeatable.

Evaluation frameworks such as the Kirkpatrick's Four Levels of Evaluation and the Phillips' ROI Method have given the profession very well-defined frameworks for evaluating training and development experiences on varying levels. The

Phillips have even shown how internal learning practitioners can actually put a dollar value on their training's return on investment.

To truly differentiate your development experiences on the basis of effectiveness, you must invest the resources needed to produce and deliver high-quality evaluation assessments. (Bunker and Cohen 1978; Cohen 2005; Sheppeck and Cohen, 1985). Undoubtedly, it can get overly complicated to control all the potentially intervening variables when doing real-world research. However, this isn't a suitable excuse for not conducting research or conducting it poorly.

Understanding some relatively simple statistical concepts will ensure your claims of effectiveness are accurate. One refers to the often baseless assumption that correlation implies causation. In the training and development world, say your client's employees took a course on improving their interpersonal and communications skills and then performed significantly better on a follow-up test two months after the course. However, you may not have realized the test of their competence was a self-report of how much better they thought they were doing. In this case, you wouldn't know if their heightened sensitivity to these skills from participating in the course was the real cause of the self-perceived improvement. Or perhaps this particular group received skill training or coaching on these competencies prior to or after the course. Because of some nonrandom selection, you may have ended up with a group of people who had already been through considerable training in this regard. Thus, the improved results may have simply been a coincidence based on this uneven class distribution.

When working with your current clients and approaching prospective ones, you should be willing to show them exactly how your offer—whether a selection instrument, a training program, or a developmental inventory—does what you say it does and have data to back up that claim. You owe it to yourself and those customers to conduct the appropriate research to validate your claims. In fact, if such research has not been conducted, it is certainly better to admit that and let the client purchase your product base on face value than it is to make false or uneducated claims of effectiveness.

A final issue in claiming effectiveness is being able to debunk the commonly held myths that are accepted, despite relatively little support for their effectiveness (Nowack 2015, 37, 47). As a trusted client adviser, you should be able to identify and question these myths, so that you can protect your customers from making mistakes and help differentiate your own offerings. One example would be the overly attributed 70-20-10 classification of how learning really happens. The thinking goes that 70 percent of learning happens on the job; 20 percent through informal conversations with peers, bosses, mentors, and coaches; and 10 percent from formal training courses and programs. Without getting into detail, even the authors of this research from the Center for Creative Leadership openly admit its results have been vastly misinterpreted. Very simply, the results were formed from what managers thought was the best way they learned, not whether it was actually most effective (see McCall, Lombardo, and Morrison 1988; Lindsey, Homes, and McCall 1987; McCall 2010, 4). The takeaway is not to cast dispersions on the architects of the 70-20-10 model or those who have inadvertently misinterpreted its application, but rather to alert you to the responsibility you have to your clients to understand what works and what doesn't in the industry.

To E or Not to E?: That Is the Question!

It wasn't long ago that online learning, or e-learning, burst on to the talent development scene. The industry, as well as CEOs and CFOs who were focused on the bottom line, became enamored with how the savings in travel dollars alone made it worth its weight in gold—a win-win for business. Its potential to expose many more employees to training at significantly less cost meant countless companies, and opportunistic consultants, eagerly pursued this new form of training. Despite its meteoric rise; however, its adoption slowed when companies found it difficult to implement. But times have changed with recent technological advances: mobile phones and tablets, cloud-based software, interactive applications. Today, as a talent development supplier, you are expected to incorporate technology-enabled learning into your offer if you want to be competitive.

You might look into weaving blended, flipped, or asynchronous learning into your offer to complement the in-person aspects. Your clients get the best of both worlds with the benefit of knowledge acquisition at the cheapest and fastest level, combined with real in-person practice and application. Or you might provide synchronous or prescheduled live collaborative and interactive webinar-based programming (Cohen, Deege, and Brewer-Frazier 2006, 36-41, 53). A nice example of this is an online personal improvement program conducted by Karen Kendrick in her "Brilliance" series of modules. Kendrick has a long career in learning and development having served as the chief learning officer of several large businesses. Her self-study units are guided by prerecorded scripted presentations, while participants complete workbooks downloaded from her site. Kendrick paces the sessions by stopping to give further directions for working through the workbooks. Online forums are set up for participants to connect with one another to share what they've learned. In addition, they can asynchronously chat with her as issues and challenges arise.

Of course, by using online or hybrid formats, you will need to address an important question. What is the relative effectiveness of strictly online or hybrid formats versus the traditional classroom experience when it comes to measuring learning? Some years ago, research indicated that e-learning as then defined was in fact less effective than instructor-based learning, as well as less preferred for more interpersonal and leadership skills training (Cohen and Payiatakis 2002). Granted, the industry has come a long way in both technology and instructional design, but the question of effectiveness remains. Instructional design has evolved to keep pace with advances in technology, and digital learning is more exciting, interesting, and meaningful than it has ever been. As technology improves so will the capacity to learn more efficiently and effectively. Classrooms may indeed be replaced by online learning, but you'd be wise to not completely phase out your in-person instructional presence with your clients.

The major question you have to answer is not how you are going to incorporate online learning into your business offer, but rather do you want to be a supplier providing technology, or content-based solutions? Will you establish and manage your own platform, as many suppliers in the industry have done? Or will you outsource the technology as a delivery vehicle for your content? The former is very tempting but can inadvertently change the nature of your business model; it can also be very expensive and time consuming. For instance, customers might want to purchase your LMS or LCMS platform and dump their own content into it. This is fine if that's your business model for growth. But if you are just using your own proprietary platform as a value-added feature to deliver your content, then you probably don't want to get in the business of selling and maintaining the platform without your own content. You might even question whether you want to be involved with your platform at all or simply outsource it.

Two subscription and SaaS-based organizations with whom I have worked recently have gone to market with their own proprietary learning management systems and built up significant internal software engineering capabilities to manage them. However, their brand promoted industry specific content (in law enforcement and multifamily housing) that they were delivering to their customers. To grow they could not keep up with the time-consuming updates in technology platforms and the costs of keeping a full cadre of internal technology-skilled personnel. After years in their businesses, they both decided to outsource their platforms to technology firms specializing in building tailored and custom LMSs, but also in establishing formats and processes for their clients' content creation. Even though they mentioned a skeleton software engineering crew, they realized they weren't technology companies at all, but rather focused on delivering relevant information and training to their respective industries. They decided it was more judicious to spend their time and money developing the information their customers needed, rather than the technology needed to support its delivery. The good news is the platform they now use looks and feels just like their own and retained all the features their clients want and need to achieve their own business outcomes.

Regardless of your predisposition, or even current position toward online learning, you don't have to focus on replacing the classroom, but rather "freeing it to play a new and exciting role" (Mosher 2016).

Great Consultants: Oxymoron or Difference Makers?

Another way to differentiate your business is through the capability of those responsible for delivering your offer: your consultants. Chapter 2 addressed the difference in the personnel experience and expertise needed between pure product and consulting firm business models. Let's take a deeper dive into what makes an effective consultant.

A pure consulting model involves attracting, selecting, developing, and retaining top talent in the area for which your business provides services. This talent is responsible for delivering services to existing clients and developing new clients. In bigger firms, research and delivery is often handled by junior level employees, while client development rests with the more senior level employees.

Developing an effective consultant pool involves nurturing several capabilities that fall into three categories: consulting skills, technical skills, and business skills (Nichols and Bergholz 2013). If your business revolves around a consulting services model, you should expect your senior consultants to demonstrate 10 competencies and expect your junior consultants to develop these competencies with experience and guidance within your business. These competencies are not necessarily listed in order of importance, as their priority will depend on the size and scope of your business.

Facilitation (Consulting)

Your consultants should be proficient in facilitating formal and informal settings with your client. This does not necessarily mean delivering formal training, but rather being able to observe, process, and offer input that deftly overcomes barriers, moving the group ahead on both an interpersonal and process level to achieve the desired results. More and more, these skills should be transferable to virtual settings. Sure, the engaging face-to-face, high-energy touch in the classroom is a very different skill set from the more organized, pragmatic, and perhaps even focused virtual approach. Still, one could argue virtual facilitation skills require even more one-to-one attentiveness because of the remote setting than those needed in a face-to-face environment.

Collaboration (Consulting)

Your consultants should work effectively with and around others by utilizing strong collaborations skills. This includes a willingness to work with others for mutual gain, as well s the ability to share information, provide additional insights, trust others, and relate openly and honestly to both colleagues and client personnel.

Teaching and Mentoring (Consulting)

Your consultants should be able to transfer information and instruct co-workers and even client colleagues, especially younger ones. Teaching and mentoring is different from simply coaching, as the latter typically involves an attempt to improve someone's performance. Certainly, this is a valuable capability for consultants to possess, especially if they are leading a project team. But more important is their ability to provide their team with the requisite knowledge and skills to effectively deliver services to the client.

Client Management (Consulting and Business)

Your consultants should manage client relationships through excellent interpersonal skills and work through conflict effectively as needed. They should feel comfortable and capable, ensuring that clients do what they say they will do and making sure they show up. This skill set often requires advanced flexibility to manage a vast array of different client personalities.

Adaptability (Consulting and Business)

Finally, your consultants should be able to roll with the punches while maintaining a strong center that moves the project and team in the right direction. There are always unanticipated turns and curves that demand adjustments during any engagement. Maintaining a calm and cool demeanor without demonstrating outward frustration is a critical skill set to possess.

Perception and Analysis (Business)

Your consultants should assess the client's business and provide insights the client may be too close to the situation to see clearly.

Decision Making (Business)

Your consultants should take the right action by not only being appropriately decisive but also understanding how recommendations will affect the client's business at both the micro and macro levels. This requires navigating and mitigating risks attached to making or not making a decision. Decision making involves taking frequent action to move projects along.

Organizing and Planning (Business)

Your consultants should meet deadlines, put project plans together, and manage them to completion. For the client, there's nothing worse than when the project team continually misses deadlines, especially when there are no apparent barriers to derail the delivery milestones and solutions.

Deep Expertise (Technical)

Your consultants should be well versed in your business's products and should be able to transfer that into appropriate client solutions. This could include specific expertise and experience gained through involvement in similar businesses and projects. Similarly, they should openly acknowledge any lack of expertise and be committed to acquiring that expertise if they don't have it.

Business Development (Technical)

Depending on the structure and size of the firm, your consultants should generate new business with both new and current clients. They should beat the bushes to bring in business with new clients while promoting new projects to current clients.

***

Is it possible that there really are consultants who demonstrate all these characteristics at the highest levels? Probably not, but each should be considered and honed. Great consultants can make or break your business.

Conclusion

If you can't distinguish your offer from the competition's, it doesn't matter how unique, creative, or even effective it is. Innovation for innovation's sake is not the path to ultimate success. Rather, you should innovate for results. You can rise above the competitive landscape if you can differentiate your offer on the basis of real and proven effectiveness. The ultimate measure of your success is in the value you create for both your customers and your business. From the first comes the second. Knowing what it takes to create this value is the magic formula for cultivating a long-lasting business proposition.

Reflection Questions

Table Stakes or All In?: Is Content Still King?

- What differentiation strategies have been successful for your business?
- How important in your sales process is the content you offer?
- How sure are you that your content is distinctive from other offers that appear to be similar to what you are providing?
- What other offerings can support your content?

Art, Science, and Business: Program Design and Development

- What does your program or product development process look like?
- Where could you improve it? How have you innovated with your offer?
- What remains to be done to meet the needs of your market and clients?
- How have you balanced the art, science, and business of program development?

Value Creation: Short and Long Term

- What value creation strategies do you have in place to not only grow your firm but significantly differentiate it in the marketplace?
- What can you do that you aren't doing now to further and sustain this value?

What's Your Secret Sauce? The Importance of Creating a Distinct Brand or Product

- As you think about the ideas expressed in this chapter, what differentiates your offer, whether you are a large talent development management firm or a sole proprietor?

Can You Really Say That?: Claims of Effectiveness

- How have you thoroughly validated claims of your offer's effectiveness in obtaining results?
- What experiments, including those with control groups, have you put in place to more clearly demonstrate their effectiveness?
- More important, how would you uphold your claims in courts should you be sued for false representation?

To E or Not to E?: That Is the Question!

- What have you done to evaluate the effectiveness of your e-learning offerings?
- If you don't have one, do you know how your offer stands up to comparable online programs?
- What can you do to improve your offer by incorporating e-learning elements into it?

Great Consultants: Oxymoron or Difference Makers?

- Which competencies do you possess and which do you need to spend time developing? What about your colleagues?
- Where do your competencies excel or come up short?
- Who are your role model consultants for most effectively demonstrating these competencies?

MOVING YOUR OFFER
OFF THE SHELF

*The aim of marketing is to know and understand the
customer so well the product or service ... sells itself.*
—Peter Drucker

So you've developed an offering, hopefully with the intention of addressing a unique market need that differentiates it from the competition. Now you can sit back and listen to the phone ring or wait for your inbox to flood with requests from companies clamoring for your product or service. Right? If only it were that easy.

Moving your offer off the shelf is all about being deliberate in marketing and selling, so that you can gain the right to win over customers. Unfortunately, it's not easy to break into the marketplace. Often, this is not because a firm cannot help an organization resolve a major business issue, but more likely because that organization never heard of it. Other times, the offer simply ends up looking much like everyone else's or fails to deliver the goods.

This chapter attempts to explain in part why so many talent development supplier businesses fail to get off the ground, as well as how marketing and selling often have just as much to do with your offer's success as its effectiveness relative to the competition. I'll address how you go about getting your solution in front of potential clients and then moving it into their hands, with the hopes of building long-term, fruitful relationships.

Building a Well-Oiled Machine:
Your Business Development Engine

While the Internet—and the wide network of possible customers it offers—might make selling appear to be easier and less costly, selling is still a complicated process, given all the steps between initiating prospect contact and closing the sale. Selling remains complicated because you need to simultaneously attract three different types of buyers, with each necessitating a different strategy. First, there are new prospects who try you out by buying one product or service. Second, there are customers who purchase multiple times, although within a short time-frame. Third, there are clients who purchase multiple times over many years. On top of this, you cannot forget to engage the major influencer of all these buyers: the end-user. Without satisfying the needs and winning the subsequent endorsement of the people who use your product or service, not just the company that purchases it, you are unlikely to see many follow-up purchases.

Business-to-business selling has become more difficult because purchasing departments are now more involved in the buying process. You might have to interact with representatives who do not understand what they are buying, and instead are more focused on getting the best price for their organization. Thus, when you are competing with other businesses to serve an organization's needs, you might find yourself struggling to price your offer at face value when you know the lowest bidder typically gets the sale. Even if you win the bid, you might be left with the "poison pill" of agreeing to a low-ball offer and not make any money on the sale.

The flip side of the Internet's benefits to marketing and selling is that the proposal writing and demonstration process are more competitive than ever. Proposals and demos are now only a click away. But who has time for this and how many can you actually win? You may think that the Request for Proposal (RFP) process is rigged anyway, as the proposal is specifically written for a favorite insider. I know of one talent development firm that won't submit a written proposal unless it has had a prior relationship and interaction with the potential purchaser. Avoiding the RFP process might end up saving you a lot of time and energy on diminishing returns. While winning a third of the time is a pretty decent percentage, the two-thirds of projects you lose take up time better spent working with higher-valued prospects and clients.

In the talent development supplier industry, the effectiveness and efficiency of your business development engine plays a large role in your success. Fortunately, as you look to build and grow your business, not having a long-term marketing and selling presence does not preclude you from reaching the right clients. The widespread use of social media, with its ability to target more people at significantly less cost, is challenging the traditional sales and marketing channels. Incorporating social media into your traditional direct selling methods can be a huge benefit.

Talent development firms with a long history of direct selling approaches, whether through their own or partner channels, are on the fringe of virtual distribution techniques. New firms, most likely not hampered by a labor intensive business development engine, are better positioned to incorporate social media in direct selling. While older firms may argue their complex products and services require direct face-to-face selling, it is also clear that today's more sophisticated buyer is more willing and able to purchase through alternative virtual methods.

The Buying Cycle

Just as your car can't operate without fuel, your business development engine can't operate without its fuel, the buyer. Buyers are fickle until you have secured their trust, and the buying process has changed considerably in recent years. My experience is that many buyers do not engage with a direct salesperson until they have carefully reviewed the company's website. In fact, 57 percent of buyers make their buying decisions before engaging with sellers (Dillow and Nusca 2016).

Today's decision process has slowed significantly due to the increased number of people involved in making the decision. On average, large corporations involve more than five people in every buying decision; that number increases the larger and more complex the solution. For example, if you are selling an online program to the learning and development manager, someone from IT will also have input, not to mention the legal, finance, and purchasing representatives of the buying company. Add to this cadre any contracted business consultants on the payroll and you will face a large team of decision makers, many of whom aren't even familiar with your program or service. Yet your salespeople are only likely to speak with two of them (Sanders 2016).

In addition, buyers are often overwhelmed by the many choices of products and services. Standing out from the competition is critical to making an impression. That's why you must master how you plan to differentiate your offer before entering the market (see chapter 5). You must convince potential buyers that they are getting value for their purchase and can afford that value—that they are making the correct decision. To do so, you must fully understand where the buyer is in the buying cycle, thus recognizing when to approach or pull back from the buyer.

Timing is everything. For example, if you are selling to the government, you need to understand that if agencies don't spend their budget by the end of October, they will lose that money for the next year. If you approach a government agency too early (for example, in July), it might not be ready to talk seriously. At that time, it may not know what it's spent in the current year and the implications for the following year's budget. Approaching potential buyers at the right time will help you at least get their attention.

You also have to ascertain when a buyer is simply exploring, seriously considering, or fully committed to making a purchase. Every buyer has objections. Your primary duty is to anticipate those objections and address them as quickly as possible. You've likely already lost the sale if you're scrambling to overcome their objections once the buyers put them forward. One strategy is to raise possible objections yourself before the potential buyer does. This will allow you to demonstrate how you will resolve them and get clarification from the buyer that you have satisfied any concerns.

The Selling Cycle

Selling is a multifaceted and ongoing opportunity, and closing a sale usually doesn't happen overnight or after just one call. Keeping the sales cycle continuously moving is key to delivering your sales goals. It may start with finding, attracting, and landing a customer, but every post-sale interaction is not only another opportunity to sell but a realistic opportunity to lose that business. The buying cycle is no longer separate from the selling cycle. They run parallel.

In some ways, sales is a numbers game: The more people you engage, the better chance you have of landing a sale. On the flip side, if you engage the wrong type of buyers, you inevitably waste precious time, money, and energy. Spray-or-pray, or nontargeted, approaches rarely succeed over the long haul.

The selling cycle for the talent development industry is relatively long, perhaps as much as a year, although in my experience it averages around six months. In many cases summers are slow buying times because of vacations and Friday hours, while the end of Q4 is typically a busy time with budgets due for the upcoming year and current budgets needing to be spent before year end. Knowing these parameters will facilitate your planning.

Continuously engaging with the right prospects and customers through outbound sales and marketing efforts is one of the most important objectives of any sales cycle. Distributing thought leadership pieces and newsletters and delivering webinars are two ways to stay in touch, but there are other methods as well. Conducting customer conferences is a common technique, as is facilitating design meetings to ask your customers for input on new product development. Managing open houses and community services are two other ways to stay relevant and engage with prospects and customers. Perhaps the best way to stay in front of your buyer is to cultivate internal champions within client organizations who become your ears, eyes, and mouth in promoting your offer. Sure, this can take a good deal of time and hand-holding, and you might select the wrong person. But if you find the right person at the right time to assist with the selling process internally, you are likely to make much more headway.

Internet Prospecting

Later this chapter will explore the intricacies of Internet marketing, but for now let's introduce the idea of identifying prospects using the Internet. In today's marketing environment, offering "free" content can connect you with those interested in what you're selling. The thought is that if you don't provide the content to potential customers, they will discover it elsewhere amid the vast amount of free information available on the Internet or on social media. Why not utilize your experience to create a Facebook page or a blog, or tweet your marketing and sales messages and your whereabouts?

The barriers to entry into the industry are either diminishing or getting easier to overcome thanks to the greater reach offered by technology. It is not uncommon today to sign up for a webinar for which you are one of a thousand or more participants from throughout the world. Many firms in our industry use very targeted marketing tools to identify interested parties. Mailing lists are easier to assemble and distribute today than ever before, while reach is relatively inexpensive and streamlined.

Consider the self-help training programs advertised on the web. Tony Robbins-like motivational gurus are prolific on the Internet and they make millions of dollars. While not necessarily part of the talent development industry per se, Brendon Burchard and Eben Pagan, to name just two, reach hundreds of thousands of people through the Internet, selling online programs, in-person workshops, and premium live speeches. While their business-to-consumer marketing is very different from the business-to-business approach pervasive in the talent development industry, they offer support for devising a broad market strategy.

Accurate Forecasting

How do you identify quality prospects for your offer inexpensively and in a short amount of time? You have surely been on the other side of annoying robotic telemarketing campaigns. But reaching out to the workplace is a little different, particularly if your job performance depends on being able to capably deliver the products and services of the talent development industry. In this case, your potential clients are more likely to entertain a call from you to explore mutual interests.

Of all the sales challenges I have observed for talent development suppliers, the ability to accurately forecast sales is the most persistent. It often feels like sticking your finger in the air to get a feel for which way the wind is blowing. At a minimum, you need to keep an updated log of your pipeline: what you have sold but not yet booked (your backlog) and what you expect to sell (your frontlog). Without an accurate forecasting system, you will struggle to budget properly based on projects alone. I have heard many sales leaders assume their businesses can overcome their inability to accurately forecast sales by simply selling themselves out of a deep hole. This is not a meaningful strategy and rarely works.

To facilitate accurate forecasting, you will need an account planning system targeting prospective and current customers with specific strategies to win their business. The account plan should include a dashboard of success metrics for each account, the targeted outcomes, the expected milestones, any accountabilities, and ongoing progress to date. In other words, once you have landed that new account, how will you expand your business with the customer? You need to develop a specific strategy for types of customers, depending on their size, location, industry, and needs.

Pricing Strategies

Moving any product or service means pricing it so customers perceive value. This is true of anything we purchase. We are always calculating whether that purchase is worth it. With that in mind, there are three pricing strategies to consider: high, par, and low. The key is to assess what the market will bear, at the par level, and decide where your offer fits: What is the elasticity of your pricing? How far can it be stretched? How do your target markets dictate your pricing? Some buyers believe you get what you pay for and buy accordingly. Others search for the cheapest deal. While some buyers simply compare prices to ensure they are getting a fair deal consistent with the market, many are willing to pay a higher price if they think they are getting a better quality product.

Everyone wants a good deal. Take the iPhone, or any Apple product for that matter. Apple takes a high price strategy because it believes the designs and features of its products are significantly better than those of its competitors. The market dictates that people will pay more for something they think offers a unique value. The flip side is that you can also price yourself out of the market, especially with goods and services that are relative commodities. Why pay more for a program that looks like another unless you are receiving some value-added service that makes it worthwhile?

On the other end of the spectrum is the low-cost provider. These suppliers intend to reach more people and make up the price difference in volume. As such, they can afford to lower their price but only if they can reach more buyers through heavy mass marketing. They hope to attract more people and then, as appropriate, offer higher-end programs and services or simply continue to offer low-end pricing. For these suppliers the direct selling approach is probably too expensive to execute. The challenge with low-end pricing is that some buyers who believe that you get what you pay for might not entertain buying a low-cost product or service.

Some people think it is more difficult to increase your prices than decrease them. I'm not of that opinion. Once you set a price and reduce it, customers will see this and want to negotiate. (This excludes expected discounts on volume sales.) Smaller periodic price increases may actually be easier to enact, especially if you have earned the loyalty of customers who believe your offer creates value for them and their organizations. For the most part, these incremental increases can be justified by increased costs of doing business over time.

Deciding how to price falls under three broad categories in the talent development business: off-the-shelf products, day rates, and custom projects. They should all be priced based on your gross margin goal.

Product prices are typically fixed by quantity, with additional charges for custom treatments. The expectation is that larger quantity purchases will cost less—the bulk buying mentality. You can deliver this discount because larger print runs mean lower rinting costs for you per workbook or manual. Likewise, printers charge by quantity produced because of the scale achieved, and pass these relatively lower costs on to you, which you can then pass on to the customer. However, this assumes you are holding inventory. In today's just-in-time world, you may be able to print materials on demand, thus minimizing any inventory concerns.

In my experience, prices for in-class instruction and online learning are usually based on the cost of a facilitated day of instruction and the amount of seat time. Industry standards vary considerably based on the level of audience, the uniqueness of the content and instruction, and the experience of the facilitator. Prices for one day of classroom instruction can range from $99 for a public seminar for hundreds of people to $500 per participant for a fully developed classroom-based course. Assuming the optimal classroom size of 18 to 24 participants, this one day could run as high as $12,000. As the class gets longer the per-day per-participant price usually gets lower, so that a two-day course may cost only $750 per person and a three-day course only $1,200 per participant. The per-participant discount is calculated based on the number of days of instruction. Included in these prices are the facilitator's fees and the cost of materials for participant workbooks.

Conversely, day-rate pricing always depends on the expertise of the person charging the rate, the audience, and the uniqueness of the content. It is not uncommon that a senior-level audience engaged in a strategic planning exercise might end up with a $10,000+ per-day consultant; whereas, a good facilitator instructing a class on basic management to first-line supervisors might only charge $800 to $1,000 per day.

When determining day rates, one barometer is the value to the customer. To the extent possible, calculate the return on investment for your client given your offer in terms of revenue increases, cost savings, improved productivity, and net profits. This is where the evaluation of your programming and consulting solutions will pay off when you can directly link customer outcomes to your offer.

In general, a new consultant with fewer than 10 years of experience in the talent development field can charge anywhere from $1,500 to $2,000 per day. A more experienced 15- to 25-year veteran, $2,500 to $5,000. Highly educated, experienced senior-level consultants, $6,000 to $10,000. And the well-known superstar authors, $25,000. Some organizations are even willing to pay up to $75,000 for a two-hour presentation with the rare guru. Your rate will depend on how talented you are, your credentials, and what others have paid you in the past.

Finally, you can price by project. Usually on a fixed-price basis, this pricing model is attractive to customers who have budgeted for a certain amount and know exactly what they can afford. The downside is that if you price incorrectly and need longer to complete the project, you will undoubtedly lose money. One could argue that if the project is large enough, just having the cash flow to keep the lights on is worth losing a little, but you have to be careful. For example, you may underbid a project because you want to add another logo of a well-known and respected organization to your customer list. What you end up with is a new customer that has cost you money. As noted in chapter 8, not all customers or engagements are worth it.

Often, even product sales require additional implementation or consulting assistance. If you are going to price per project, you must develop an iron-clad contract, which should spell out the expected deliverables and allow for a process to initiate change orders when the customer wants more than was contracted. Even though this out-of-scope occasion may be difficult to accommodate, you have no recourse if you haven't spent time with the customer itemizing what they can expect to pay for at the end of the project. To avoid underbidding, you can tell the client you have put an X percent override on the project that will only be used in the case of a scope change, but will not be charged otherwise. This gives you and the customer some leeway throughout the project and may help you avoid nickel-and-diming your client on every little scope change item.

Sales Management

To keep the business development engine purring, you need superb sales managers who are not just in charge of growing sales, but more important developing their salespeople. If sales managers see their role as carrying a bag and are so worried about their own quotas, they won't have or take the time to hire, train, and nurture their sales team. In fact, they won't even be involved enough to fire those who aren't making the grade, which does not benefit them or the company. This is the danger of promoting the best salesperson to the sales manager position. You could end up with a person who isn't the best at managing others and a sales team down their top seller.

Successful sales management requires a standard and consistent selling process based on the best practices for your firm. Some sales professionals call this a playbook, illustrating the process, nuances, and details of effective selling for your business. A typical playbook should include sales goals, activities needed to reach those goals, tracking and monitoring tools, metrics and measurements, territory management, accountabilities, and pipeline management. Think of all the great sports team coaches who were consistently at the top of their game; for example, John Wooden, Vince Lombardi, Pia Sundhage, Márta Károlyi, Pat Summitt, or Scotty Bowman. They all have one thing in common: They have a system they bring to their sport and recruit or develop players who fit into it. Their players change from year to year, but what remains is the system they have perfected. Why shouldn't this be the same for sales managers? If the sales manager can create and follow a selling system and hire and nurture the salespeople to work the system, they too should be great coaches. At the end of the day, outstanding sales performance is all about preparation, practice, and training.

Sales Compensation

Compensation shouldn't be challenging if salespeople get paid based on their performance. This is pretty easy to compute. The difficulty lies in the distribution of these earnings—when and how much. Here are some general guidelines: First, there is the quota of how much the salesperson is expected to sell in a year. The more experienced the sales person, the higher the quota; more senior salespeople know the ropes, have established more clients, and usually have larger networks than more junior people. Quotas usually come with a bonus for reaching them. A good sales rep in talent development is expected to meet at least a $1 million quota, and it goes up from there.

Then there is the base salary. Sales representatives and sales executives, in the industry can make a base of anywhere from $85,000 to $150,000, although the top range may only go to those who sell a vast array of talent development services rather than just products. The base salary is usually guaranteed, but is also often used as a draw against which commissions are taken until the base is covered, at which time commissions are simply paid on sales. In addition to commissions, businesses offer bonuses for reps who reach certain sales milestones, and even "spot" bonuses for special deals. These bonuses might range from $5,000 to $10,000.

Sales managers can earn a base salary of $85,000 to $125,000, plus a decent commission override of what their salespeople generate and then even a bonus on top of that for exceeding quotas. Some businesses also have more junior employees called account managers, who generate leads that are fed to the more senior sales executives. These lead hunters might receive a base salary of anywhere from $65,000 to $85,000. They may close some themselves or simply hand the leads over to someone involved in direct sales force.

Finally, what also varies is the percentage of commission paid and when it is paid. Often, commissions increase as certain milestones are reached. Commission rates can range from 5 to 10 percent. Some in the industry believe the commission should be paid when the sale is made. Others believe it is more appropriate to pay when the invoice is sent. Still others believe salespeople shouldn't get paid until the client pays. An argument can be made for each, and yet a lot can happen between the sale and the client's actual payment. Waiting until payment is made will assure the sale was real and protect the business from inappropriately or prematurely paying out sales commissions. Many firms will pay in full 30 days after the sale is made; others will construct some percentage combination payment process for their salespeople, say 50 percent at time of sale and the balance upon client payment. And some commissions are paid out monthly, others quarterly. Regardless of the payout system used, you should align expectations between the salespeople and your organization from the beginning.

Location! Location! Location!: Sales Distribution Approaches

The age-old saying in retail operations is that distribution is all about location, location, location. What about for businesses in the talent development industry? In some ways having local access to clients makes selling to them more convenient. But as you grow, physical location becomes less important, and you'll need to focus on your digital network. The more visible you are the greater the potential that your distribution generates revenue.

Sometimes poorly developed programs or assessments do well with the right distribution, while expertly developed ones struggle to catch on. I've repeatedly seen bigger players with excellent sales systems, but not necessarily the most up-to-date products and services, outsell smaller players who don't have the resources for mass distribution but have more effective products and services. Perhaps the game changer and industry playing field leveler is in the network's ability to sell to more people at lower cost. Let's look at the "feet on the ground" distribution models and evaluate their pros and cons.

You have various sales channels at your disposal. The primary roles of sales distribution models include direct sales force, consultants, on-staff telemarketers, contracted telemarketers, licensed resellers, and authorized brokers. Table

6-1 compares the approaches on expense, margin, profitability, company control, ramp-up time, and offer knowledge.

Table 6-1. Sales Distribution Approaches

Variables Distribution	Direct Sales Force	On-staff Consultants	On-staff Tele-mar-keters	Contracted Tele-marketers	Licensed Resellers	Autho-rized Brokers
Expense	High	High	Medium	Medium	Low	Low
Margin	Low	Low	Medium	High	High	High
Profitability	Low	Low	High	High	Medium	Medium
Company Control	High	Medium	High	Medium	Medium	Low
Ramp-up Time	Long	Short	Medium	Long	Medium	Long
Offer Knowledge	Medium/High	High	Medium/High	Low/Medium	Medium	Medium

While this table should not be interpreted too literally because several variables could easily alter how expensive an approach is or how much control you have, it may serve as a guideline when evaluating how your business goes to market. The complexity of your offer, the experience of your sales force, the reputation of your business, and your past experience with the client can all influence the sale. Take the direct sales force, for example. From Table 6-1 one might conclude that it is the least effective approach due to expenses, both in the form of compensation and travel. It's typically much higher than most of the other sellers and thus yields less profitability. But this extra cost might be worth the more consistent brand image and messaging that a firm would be able to more effectively manage. In addition, this may be the best approach for complex sales because the seller has an opportunity to learn directly from colleagues on a daily basis. This point is important when introducing new offerings, which are more difficult in an indirect sales structure in which you do not employ the sales force.

For complex sales, the so-called eat what you kill method might work very well. Here expert consultants seek out the client, close the sale, and then deliver the offer. They can get closer to the clients' needs and navigate clients for additional sales much more readily than a pure salesperson. Of course, finding these types of people is often difficult, given the skill set required to do both. I have had significant trouble hiring very successful salespeople, who are accustomed to selling relatively generic products, and getting them to effectively adapt to selling consulting or customized services. Of course, the major downside to this approach is that the salesperson can't be selling, at least opening new accounts, if he is always delivering. You need an appropriate support and reward system for it to work.

Ultimately, selecting the right sales distribution model for any firm will depend on a number of variables not the least of which is its financial condition and cash flow. The most tempting and perhaps least financially risky approach is to turn over sales to third-party partners who cost less to manage, but who also may be the most difficult to control. Many companies include a number of these approaches simultaneously, although the potential for territory and customer overlap is high unless very clear guidelines are established. For example, many firms assign their own direct sales force to major accounts while providing smaller clients to licensed resellers.

Depending on the size, scope, and offer of your business, senior management may be involved in the sales process. The smaller you are the greater the need for senior leaders to interact with the client base to ensure complete understanding of their interests and needs. And although they don't have a sales quota number, they should make it a habit to periodically engage with customers. This includes everyone from senior technical, financial, marketing, and operations people to the CEO.

Much of the sales structure of an organization will depend on its business life cycle and go-to-market strategy. In addition to repeat business acquired by on-the-ground salespeople, lead generation is becoming more critical. You'll need people who can serve as both hunters (those better at uncovering new leads and prospects) and farmers (those better at expanding business deals with current customers), who are thus capable of selling deeper and wider into both new and existing accounts. Lead generation through telemarketing has become a necessity because it is a much lower-cost solution than having a group of on-the-ground salespeople hunting for those same leads. But lead generation is not as simple as calling numbers from paid lists. There is some science to the process that involves digital marketing expertise.

A Rose by Any Other Name Is Still a Rose: Marketing and Branding

When you come down to it, marketing has been around as long as humans have traded among themselves. It started with people telling stories of benefits and features that they needed to trade with one another. It involves finding someone who needs something you have or can make, convincing this person how your product can satisfy a need, and putting a value on what you are marketing to them.

Don Miller of StoryBrand suggests stories are the most compelling way to stimulate the brain. Most of us spend a good deal of time daydreaming until we get locked in by a story. Think of movies you have seen that have captured your attention. The best ones all have a common approach to engagement. They are like a music score that has come together from separate notes, which only make sense once combined. Likewise, a story is a sense-making device that offers clarity the brain longs for.

Company brands need a story peiple will remember. Those with a clear, focused message tend to outperform better products with an unclear message. Certain elements take place in memorable stories: There is always a hero who has some type of problem. The hero meets a guide who helps the hero address the problem by giving her a plan. This plan calls for the hero to perform some action resulting in a consequence, namely success or failure. For the talent development world this translates to a customer (the hero) who has a particular challenge; for example, getting her leaders to provide more effective feedback. The hero searches for someone—you as the guide—to help address this problem. You offer a plan to effectively manage the problem with a coaching program that calls them to action by engaging your business. The consequence is hopefully more effective internal leader coaches. Sounds simple, and it is (Miller 2016).

So what are the basics of marketing and branding your business? Foremost, marketing needs to be integrated with the selling process. Today, the two functions are blending in a significant way. They should be talking to each other every day, which has not always been the case with many sales and marketing functions. You might even house marketing and sales together. Ideally, your marketing activities should prime the potential market with interest, creating demand for what your business offers. Sales should satisfy that demand as quickly and effectively as possible and then send feedback to marketing about that demand so that marketing can make appropriate revisions to start the process over again.

From a pure marketing strategy perspective, the age-old basics of the 4Ps of a marketing mix are still relevant. For the talent development industry, this means:

- **Product:** Your offer, whether a product, program, or service that meets a specific customer need or demand.
- **Price:** What you charge for your offer, depending on its perceived value to the customer.
- **Promotion:** What marketing communication strategies and techniques you are using, including advertising, sales promotions, special offers, and public relations.
- **Place:** How you will deliver the offer to the customer through the most suitable channel for distribution.

Technology allows for more targeted approaches, thus minimizing the effectiveness of shotgun marketing practices. To this end, one business on whose board

I sit uses a "market mosaic" to describe how it reaches out to attract clients. When defining the potential landscape for business, it considers:

- market size
- market segmentation
- funding sources
- influencers
- accreditation climate (if appropriate)
- competition
- legislative climate
- company brand awareness
- access to resources (local and outsourced).

Each of these items represent a tile in the full mosaic. When you put them together, you get a full picture of what the market is and where you need to focus your attention. The business uses a three-pronged approach to optimizing its marketing opportunities: conduct a market assessment, create a strategy to address the market, and develop a playbook that spells out how you go about converting prospects to customers. This three-step plan provides an overarching approach to putting your marketing to work. The beauty of this approach is that you can apply it region by region, country by country, or by any other geographic or market segment relevant to your business.

One critical part of this mosaic is branding. Before making a purchase, buyers usually have an initial impression of the company offering the product. This initial impression is the result of branding. Think about companies such as Apple, Microsoft, IBM, Disney, and Coca-Cola. You likely have an impression of what these companies represent. You can even attribute different characteristics to them. They each stand for something, and through their marketing and selling methods they attempt to build positive brand awareness in the marketplace. Most important, regardless of what they stand for, you trust they will deliver what they say they will. You know that you will get what you pay for. They achieve this trust by persistently communicating a brand identity that reflects the consistent delivery of their promises.

Branding is equally important to your talent development business. How you are perceived in the marketplace determines the likelihood potential and current customers will consider your solutions to solve their problems. But how can you achieve a positive brand awareness? First, think from the customer's perspective. What are you known for? When they think of your business what are their expectations for what they will receive? When they are looking for a resource to address a particular challenge, who is top of mind? Second, turn the questions back to you. Can you deliver on your brand promise? Do you have the resources to meet their expectations? What is your current relationship with them? This is the give and take of branding.

My favorite example of an unmet brand promise is from United Airlines. For years United used the slogan "Fly the friendly skies of United." At the time, I had flown on a number of United's flights and they were anything but friendly. This included not only flight attendants but reservationists and gate personnel. The easiest way to lose customers is to over-promise and under-deliver. This was surely the case with United. Its employees' behavior was not aligned with its stated promise. Unfortunately, even after the merger with Continental, a generally well-perceived airline, United's brand did not improve much (Bennett 2016). On the other hand, Southwest Airlines makes no bones about its bare-bones brand, and in return you not only receive incredible service but pay less for it. Some of the mottos it has used over the years include "You're now free to move about the country," "The low fare airline," and "Grab your bag, it's on!" One recent slogan is "If it matters to you, it matters to us." There is little doubt Southwest has delivered on these slogans, or it wouldn't be consistently considered the top airline on *Fortune*'s annual most admired companies list.

Everything you do—how your employees behave, what your website looks like, how your collateral is packaged—contributes to communicating a brand message to your prospects and customers that you have a unique position in the marketplace. Because the talent development supplier market is very crowded, competitive, and fragmented, clearly articulating your value proposition through your branding and communicating how you are able and committed to deliver on your brand promise will help you stand out amid your competitors. Building this trust might even be a more valuable asset than a company being able to establish its uniqueness. Honesty, trustworthiness, and authenticity continue to be the top brand criteria today, even more so than the quality of products and services (Cohn & Wolfe 2014; Mindshare 2016).

In sum, how you are perceived in the marketplace is one of the most important items you can establish for your business, regardless of its size. Who you are and what you are in the eyes of both your prospects and clients will determine their expectations for your performance.

Marketing 2020: Getting and Staying Online

In the earlier days of marketing, stories were typically delivered to small groups. However, as communications technologies evolved, mass marketing soon emerged. It became possible to reach more people at once, whether through a sign outside of a trading post listing available wares and their prices, a distributed leaflet, a mail piece, or a print ad. While the essence of marketing has remained the same over the years, what has changed is the delivery vehicle with which you can distribute your message.

So, where does that leave you? When building a modern marketing strategy, you will be confronted with new tactics and approaches; for example, digital marketing, e-marketing, marketing automation, persona development, social advertising, search engine optimization, organic videos, and mobile.

This section aims to put you on the path toward effective marketing in the digital age. The first step is to recognize how rapidly online trends are changing and how new trends will influence your marketing strategy. In Table 6-2, take a look at the changes predicted in top trends just from 2014 to 2016.

Table 6-2. Top 7 Online Trends

2014	2016
1. Content marketing will be bigger than ever.	1. Video ads will start dominating.
2. Social media marketing will require more diversity.	2. App indexing will lead to an explosion of apps.
3. Image-centric content will rule.	3. Mobile will completely dominate desktop.
4. Less will be more.	4. Digital assistants will lead to a new kind of optimization.
5. Mobile friendly content will be necessary.	5. Virtual reality will emerge.
6. Ad retargeting will grow in effectiveness.	6. Wearable technology and the Internet of things will pave new ground.
7. SEO and social signals will become even more intertwined.	7. Advertising will become more expensive.

Source: DeMers (2013, 2015).

While similarities exist, it is notable how different the two lists are. The trends themselves are less important than what the continuous change represents for how you will leverage online tools and technologies for marketing. How will you best leverage online trends to build and grow your business? Let's jump into the basics that must be well understood before deciding on and implementing different marketing tactics. This starts with demand creation.

Demand Creation

Marketing serves to create demand for your product or service by driving awareness and interest through various points in the selling cycle. The Internet landscape has introduced new tools, techniques, and platforms by which you can create demand. It has also changed how potential and current customers interact with and consume your marketing. In fact, more than a third of people now prefer information gathering through Internet searches and social media communities over talking with their peers, colleagues, or industry analysts (Tom 2016).

There are two types of categories under which demand creation fits: inbound (responding to customers) and outbound (reaching out to customers) marketing. Inbound inquiries rose from 55 percent of all responses to marketing techniques in 2009 to 71 percent in 2015, while direct mail, email, and event inquiries (outbound) fell over that same period. The per-inquiry cost of responding to inbound marketing approaches is $25, compared with outbound marketing approaches at $41.50 (Tom 2016).

Given the relative cost of both approaches, it is no wonder companies are placing more emphasis on inbound marketing. But demand creation involves more than just inbound marketing. It also includes organized campaigns, lead qualification funnels, and scoring of marketing qualified leads, sales accepted leads, and sales qualified leads. The goal of this process is to deliver the right message to the right person at the right time, all aimed at facilitating a prospect's awareness and deliberation, and ultimately a favorable decision. Content serves as the foundation of an inbound strategy. A very powerful tool to create demand, content used in marketing needs to be focused on the buyer. First, you need to identify a buyer persona of whom you are targeting. Second, you need to align the buyer's purchasing journey of education, solution, and vendor selection with your offer. And third, you need to align your marketing campaign with the placement of your content. Inbound marketing comes to an end when the buyer responds. Today, inbound marketing has become more effective through e-marketing.

Internet marketing and demand creation is moving to a mobile focus. As Christophe Morin (2016) of SalesBrain reports, there is a mobile tsunami taking place the world over. In 2015, 75 percent of the U.S. population had a smartphone, which is expected to rise to 95 percent by 2018. Furthermore, people spend an average of about three hours a day on their smartphones. Mobile is revolutionizing content, so your marketing message needs to be not only readily available but also quick, simple, sensory, and emotion and story driven.

What Is E-Marketing?

E-marketing, or digital marketing, is simply the use of the Internet and digital media capabilities to help sell your products and services. These digital technologies should be used to support your traditional marketing efforts, regardless of the size and type of your talent development business. A strong e-marketing strategy will help your business communicate the right messages for your products and services to your targeted audience. What is different from traditional marketing approaches is the greater scope and options to make it happen. You can integrate all these options to feed off one another, thus simplifying the process significantly through electronic customer relationship management and other business management functions.

Promoting your brand, influencing buyer preference, and increasing sales are all objectives of e-marketing. But first you need a clear definition of how your e-marketing campaign will drive sales and how you will monitor its progress. Would you like to use your Internet presence to sell to your clients, serve your customers, educate the world, save money, promote giving, or build your brand? Depending on which one or more of these are your goals, your e-marketing actions will be very different. For example, if your goal is to market your website to drive business, you can leverage pay-for-click models where your website is promoted through a search engine and you pay a nominal fee each time someone clicks to your page. This can be accomplished through search engine optimization. You can also create a viral-free campaign through sites such as Facebook, LinkedIn, or Twitter. Or you can use affiliate reselling approaches wherein you pay other sites to promote yours.

You will want to set realistic, relevant, and specific targets and establish a system of metrics that allows you to monitor and measure progress at any point in time. For example, you might want to use e-marketing objectives to increase online sales by 10 percent the next year, or reduce the annual cost of direct marketing by 20 percent through email marketing, or improve customer retention by 15 percent a year for the next three years.

Benefits of E-Marketing

While building an online presence, e-marketing can provide you with unprecedented access to mass markets at an affordable price and allow you to create a personalized marketing approach. Its value is in its flexibility and cost-effectiveness for any size firm. Think of the hard copy print savings for your company if you offer your brochure online and can edit it with a click of a few buttons rather than running off to a printing machine. In addition, your e-marketing campaign can take place around the clock every day of the year.

E-marketing also allows you to pinpoint specific customer demographics and market just to that segment. Furthermore, you can conduct one-to-one marketing by responding to online requests. Personalizing marketing approaches is not a particularly new idea, but the power of the Internet to facilitate it is extraordinary.

Analytics programs enable you to monitor progress and track results on the effectiveness of your e-marketing approaches. You can get greater insight into your interested prospects through the demographic information you receive from your visitors. However, before you get started with e-marketing, it is very important you have some skills and know-how to run an e-campaign effectively. If not, you run the risk of wasting your valuable resources with a poor campaign.

Strategies for E-Marketing

While many businesses use e-marketing to sell products, almost half reportedly do not have an e-marketing strategy, according to research across a sample of industries (Chaffey 2017). Knowing how to use e-marketing is essential to your growth. You need to have a sense of your online market share and value proposition to understand your online customers' insights. So what do you need to consider when creating or refining your digital marketing strategy?

There are three categories of e-marketing delivery: the web (e-commerce and SEO), email (advertising and promotional mailings) and social media (viral and social networking). The strategies for each are different. For instance, social media is a form of online communications focused on obtaining community-based input, collaboration, and content sharing. The primary intent of a social media strategy is to reach and connect with your customers, where sharing is facilitated through sites such as Facebook, Twitter, and YouTube. In contrast, you should use your website to specifically sell and promote your business and its offer.

The cornerstone of an e-marketing strategy is content marketing, which includes video marketing, blogs, training videos, demos, podcasts, and gaming. Through content marketing, you can create and distribute valuable and relevant information targeted to attract and retain a specific audience, hopefully resulting in a purchasing decision. Unlike direct selling efforts, which typically involve promoting your products and services, relevant information is instead offered that might inform your potential buyers in ways they appreciate, thus leading to more business and loyalty from them.

Your e-marketing plan will not seem all that different from your traditional offline marketing plan. You can start with five basic steps:

1. Conduct a strategic analysis to assess your target audience's needs.
2. Define strategic objectives aligned with your organization's vision.
3. Formulate those strategies through positioning, differentiating, and prioritizing.
4. Implement through careful execution of all steps.
5. Measure your results (Otalcan 2016).

Looking forward, what are some of the current and likely trends in digital marketing?

- **Segmentation:** More focus is placed on targeting specific markets.
- **Influencer Marketing:** Key nodes are determined within related communities that are influencers and can be reached through paid advertising and customer relationship management software.
- **Online Behavioral Advertising:** Data are collected about user activity to market to the user's specific interests and preferences.
- **Collaborative Environments:** The business, technology service provider, and external agencies work together to optimize efforts and share resources.
- **Remarketing:** Targeted information focused on a particular interest category or defined audience (Chaffey 2016).

Hopefully, this primer will help you jump-start your e-marketing approach, whether you develop it internally or outsource it. Either option has pros and cons depending on your needs and resources. As you look to build your business and clientele, you should explore contracting a company that specializes in lead generation, social media facilitation, branding, and e-marketing. Once you are off and running, you can bring it in-house with dedicated staff or continue with some combination of resources to meet your needs.

Just Enough or Just-in-Time?: Delivering the Goods

The growth strategies of focus and differentiation are often difficult to achieve as a competitive edge in the talent development industry. What might be more attainable is a growth strategy predicated on how well you curate and deliver your content. However, the skill sets for delivering consulting services and for delivering packaged products are vastly different. Truly great consultants possess deep expertise, have strong presentation capabilities, and are attentive and good listeners. On the other hand, creating a program requires considerably stronger project management capability, instructional expertise, and facilitation skills.

Competitive advantage through delivery stems from Michael Treacy and Fred Wiersema's customer intimacy discipline in their 1995 book, *The Discipline of Market Leaders*. It's true that sometimes excellent products and services do not infiltrate the marketplace as should be expected, while others of considerably lesser value outsell what appear to be more effective products. A lot more of this success comes from how well the deliverables are provided to the customer. Chapter 8 will explore the dynamics of customer service and the value it offers a firm independent of the quality, uniqueness, and marketability of its offer. Suffice it to say, any consistently successful firm, no matter its size or age, is unlikely to be successful if it does not devote attention to the customer service element of delivering an offer.

Conclusion

Once you've developed your offer, you may feel exhausted, hoping that it will simply sell itself. However, as this chapter illustrates, your business will not go far if you do not invest in marketing and selling your offer. You need a high-powered sales and marketing machine that communicates your brand promise and unique value proposition. While on-the-ground sales distribution continues to dominate the selling landscape in the talent development industry, the use of less expensive and further reaching technology-enabled tools has altered the way selling takes place today. At the very least, marketing and sales activities must be inextricably intertwined to get the most out of each. It is clearly a case where one plus one equals three.

Reflection Questions

BUILDING A WELL-OILED MACHINE: YOUR BUSINESS DEVELOPMENT ENGINE

- What does your business development engine look like?
- Where can you add power to it?
- Where is grease needed to get it running more smoothly?
- What pricing strategies have you put in place and how are they meeting the needs of your marketplace?

LOCATION! LOCATION! LOCATION!: DISTRIBUTION APPROACHES

- What sales distribution methods have worked or not worked for you?
- How would you change your approach based on this analysis?

A ROSE BY ANY OTHER NAME IS STILL A ROSE: MARKETING AND BRANDING

- What does your market mosaic look like and how is it facilitating the growth of your business?
- How have you established a brand in the marketplace?
- How is your brand distinguishing you from your competition?

- How are you using your marketing plan as a strategy for growing your business?
- What's your story brand?

MARKETING 2020: GETTING AND STAYING ONLINE

- What is your e-marketing strategy?
- What are you currently doing with e-marketing that you could improve upon?
- What measurements do you already plan to have in place to assess your return on investment in your e-marketing efforts?

JUST ENOUGH OR JUST-IN-TIME?: DELIVERING THE GOODS

- What are some examples in which delivery of services trumped all else for a talent development firm you know?
- Where was customer service so strong that it overshadowed some obvious weaknesses in the rest of the business?
- What examples do you know if in which poor delivery of services could not overcome the strengths of an industry leader?

7

OPERATING PROFITABLY AND SUSTAINABLY

*Investing in management means building
communications systems, business processes, feedback,
and routines that let you scale the business and team
as efficiently as possible.*
—Fred Wilson

Differentiating your offer and making it available to potential clients will all be for naught if you cannot operate your business profitably and your systems and processes to produce and sell it cannot be replicated and scaled. Even if you're a one-person consulting practice, you still need to cover your costs to keep the lights on. Of course, if you want to become a larger business, generating profit, whether by selling more or cutting costs, is a major consideration. Doing both simultaneously delivers the biggest bang for your buck.

This chapter focuses on how to operate a business profitably over the long haul. You'll learn about managing finances, building a strong leadership team, taking calculated risks, growing your business through scale, creating a back-office infrastructure that can maintain and grow your business, serving and retaining your most valuable customers, and perhaps most important, managing the talent in your own business.

Keeping Your Head Above Water: Maintaining Financial Health

Tracking and measuring your performance on a weekly and monthly basis is critical to business success. Often, the metrics used to do this are called key performance indicators (KPIs), which tell you how you are doing at any point in time. You will want to develop your own dashboard to help track and manage KPIs. One such dashboard, called the Balanced Scorecard, was introduced by Kaplan and Norton (1992), and is set up to measure four overall business components: financial, customers, process, and people. Organizations decide the most relevant KPIs for their business under each of these headings.

Your KPIs should focus on the barometers that measure your success. That said, most organizations use variations of the same indicators, which are typically related to sales, operations, customers, production, and finance. In fact, the others will tend to drive financial performance.

Given the various business models and opportunities for gaining competitive advantage in the talent development industry described in this book, is there a replicable formula that leads to sustainable growth? One barometer of insight is what potential purchasers of talent development firms look for when considering an acquisition, merger, or add-on. The most important criterion for purchasers is the business's current financial success. The following information offers the basics of what you need to know about the finances of your business. For those interested in delving into the details, I recommend *Fundamentals of Corporate Finance* and *Foundations of Financial Management*.

Key Financial Metrics

Revenue drives the bottom line, which is the true measure of a business's ability to consistently generate money. Generating money through your offer while controlling costs dictates margin strength. Strong or high margins can often translate into scalability, thus taking advantage of replication as well as the opportunity to grow relatively unencumbered. For example, a technology platform that can deliver both assessment and training can be expanded to an infinite number of users by increasing memory and storage capacity at significantly less expense for each additional user.

But increased revenue does not automatically translate to improved bottom-line results, unless you manage to incur no new expenses as revenue increases. In fact, increased revenue can result in a decrease in net income, at least temporarily. Assume for a moment that to achieve those revenue increases you must make more costly investments that reduce the bottom line. Growing businesses typically operate in financial cycles. They grow, plateau, grow some more, plateau again, and so on. Making judicious investments will result in incremental revenue that will indeed drop to the bottom line until more investments are made for even greater growth.

A Financial Metrics Primer

Three key financial statements are used to assess a company's performance and financial position, which need to be managed and addressed at least on a monthly basis: profit and loss, balance sheet, and cash flow.

A **profit and loss statement**, or income statement, summarizes revenue (value of products and services a company sells) and expenses (cost of goods sold, fixed costs, variable costs) generated by the company over the entire reporting period. It is a statement of earnings, statement of operations, or statement of income. The basic equation on which an income statement is based is Revenues – Expenses = Net Income.

EBITDA (earnings before interest, taxes, depreciation, and amortization) is a measure of a company's operating performance. Essentially, it's a way to evaluate a company's performance without having to factor in financing decisions, accounting decisions, or tax environments. Profit, or net income, is the amount remaining after all costs, depreciation, interest, taxes, and other expenses have been deducted from total sales. Gross margin is a company's profit before operating expenses, interest payments, and taxes.

A **balance sheet** is a statement of how much money is in an account. It consists of two categories: assets and liabilities. An asset can be current or fixed and is an economic resource that can be owned and is expected to provide future economic benefits. A current asset is cash or any asset that can be reasonably converted to cash within a year—for example, cash and cash equivalents, accounts receivable, inventory, prepaid expenses. and property and equipment. Long-term assets, or fixed assets, are expected to be consumed or converted to cash after one year's time, and are listed on the balance sheet beneath current assets. Property (such as office space or buildings) and equipment are common long-term assets. A liability is a claim on a company's assets, such as payroll, bonuses, legal settlements, payments to vendors, contracts, and certain types of leases. Current liabilities are due in less than one year. Accrued liabilities are records of revenue and expenses in the periods in which they are incurred. Liabilities due in more than a year are considered long-term liabilities, .

A **cash flow statement** measures the cash generated or used by a company in a given period and identifies how much is readily on hand. Cash flow is simply the cash expected to be generated by an investment, asset, or business.

Despite margin strength, the guiding force for assessing company worth is sustained EBITDA growth. While margin strength and EBITDA growth tend to be correlated, it is possible that a business with strong and consistent margins might show depressed EBITDA because of lack of sales, marketing, or administrative cost controls.

Talent development companies are typically offered and bought based on a multiple of EBITDA (that is X times a company's EBITDA) not revenue, although a multiple of revenue is often used as an industry barometer. That said, on occasion a relatively unprofitable business will be acquired for one or two assets that when taken alone bring considerable long-term value to the acquiring business.

For example, I know of a firm bought for its unique selection technology, which was then converted into training product assets, not for its bottom-line performance. These assets brought value to the acquirer that was far greater than the value of the firm's management or even good will. So, when some of the senior leaders left relatively soon after the acquisition, there wasn't much concern because the acquiring firm had already derived far greater value from the purchase of the product assets and expected to obtain more down the road.

Another example is a company that has potential for success but needs new leadership or a different business model to achieve it. Such a company can often be acquired relatively cheaply. The company's assets might be represented by original intellectual property or assessment tools with confidential algorithms. Finally, businesses burdened by extensive debt, wherein the "debt service" obligation significantly affects the bottom line, may find an evaluation based more on top-line revenue, indicating its potential cash generating capability, than purely on EBITDA. It is also important to acknowledge that while these same debt-burdened companies may have cash-flow problems, their EBITDA may not be significantly affected because interest expense is taken out of the equation and principal debt service is not included in the income statement but rather on the balance sheet.

EBITDA reveals the gross margins the business is able to obtain: what is left after cost of sales are deducted from top-line revenues. Higher margins will almost always deliver high bottom-line EBITDA because there is more money left to spend on people, capital, and other expenses before netting out earnings and subsequently net profit.

But while EBITDA describes a firm's current state of financial stability, it doesn't tell the whole story. Looking at the balance sheet will reveal the actual long-term health of a company, as it describes the accumulated liabilities, usually in the form of short- and long-term debt and payables against its assets. Where the liabilities are significantly greater than the company's assets, additional scrutiny is necessary. The interest payments on considerable debt, or debt service, can be difficult to manage and overcome. Thus, it is possible a firm's P&L profit and loss statement can look healthy while its underlying financial burden is far too exposed to warrant it being acquired by another company. There is little question, however, that potential buyers and sellers will expect both the P&L and balance sheet to look healthy. Organizations with debt-laden balance sheets may end up either left with the seller to address or result in discounted valuations.

Budgeting

Proper annual budgeting is critical to running a sustainably effective operation. Budgeting involves not only forecasting the income statement but also transferring that forecasted income statement into a comprehensive cash flow, which then drives the balance sheet. Despite having a fabulous offer that customers want and are willing to pay for, many businesses simply budget themselves out of existence. This shouldn't be possible when revenue is strong and expenses are reasonably under control.

But setting a budget that can't be supported is the main reason businesses lose money and ultimately fail. Oftentimes, this may stem from a successful year when everything seemed to be working. A feeling of bravado and invincibility sets in. To take advantage of the previous year's growth, an even more audacious goal is set, which the owner or sales leadership believes it can achieve. They may be overconfident or it may simply be a poorly informed business decision. In either case, no one wants to push back, so groupthink prevails.

To achieve the revenue goal, the business will need additional resources: more people, expanded marketing, and new product development. With a budget based on top-line revenue it is easy to justify this spending on the additional resources needed. But, if that revenue level is not met, and the spending still takes place, the company will start operating at a loss. Sales leadership believes it can crawl out of the hole if it just has more time to do so. Operations is on the verge of installing new systems that were budgeted for and pulling back now would be a waste of time and money. And what will happen to the employee friendly culture if people have to be laid off? Unfortunately, this is a common scenario that's only solved by draconian but necessary actions.

Often, the impact will go beyond the current year and may last several years, because the business will have to borrow its way out of trouble, increasing its long-term debt and accompanying debt service to pay it off, and tapping its line of credit. This could have been avoided by taking a more measured and realistic view of the business and the environment in which it is operating. Conservative budgeting is one way to grow in an insightful and informative manner.

While budgeting will typically reflect your annual goals, it is wise to review these financial metrics on a 9 + 3, or 6 + 6 revolving timeline. That is, you will want to keep track of not just how you are doing as it relates to your annual budget and goals, but also on a plus or minus three- to six-month cycle from any point in time. This will offer you both a backward and frontward assessment of your business.

Cash Management

Chapter 5 discussed what your business offers in the context of whether content is king. Looking at the bigger picture, cash is the real king. Without cash to pay for the expenses of the business, including debt service, you will find it difficult to invest in growth. By knowing how much cash is on hand, you know how much is available to run your business. It also indicates the line of credit you may need to cover short-term cash flow. Finally, it provides resources when you need long-term financing to invest in business assets or when you face any shortfalls in running your business on a monthly basis. Many businesses fail because they are undercapitalized, meaning they don't generate enough cash to not only keep the doors open but to invest in their future as well.

There are a number of guidelines to help you determine how much cash your business should have on hand—for example, three to six months' worth of expenses. However, each business is different. It's more critical to know how to effectively manage your cash. Failing to either generate enough or not managing it properly will mean you will have to borrow money to fuel the business. While there are times when it may seem relatively cheap to borrow cash, you never know when its cost will increase beyond your means. And, of course, the type of borrowing will dictate the terms you can get. If you borrow from a bank on either a revolving short-term credit loan or a long-term note, the rates are going to be much lower than if you use your personal or business credit card to obtain cash.

Establishing a strong partnership with a bank is critically important to keeping your business running smoothly. Just keep in mind that debt service—those fees the bank charges you for access to their money—can mount to a point in which they may be hard to pay off. The inability to consistently reduce your debt can ruin your balance sheet. If you're not able to show a bank you can service that debt reliably, the result will be more-stringent terms or simply termination of the relationship. Banks loan money on the confidence that your business will not only be able to service that loan, but also that it will be around for a long time.

Building Leadership Muscle: Strong Management Matters

Strong leadership and management with deep bench strength influences industry success. Despite the importance of creating value for your customers and its impact on customer retention, value alone is not enough. If the business does not possess the leadership that can deliver this value, it is highly unlikely that it will be leveraged for growth. Has the company's leadership demonstrated operational expertise? Does it have the experience and capability to help the company grow? Does it truly understand the business and industry it is in? These questions and more must be answered affirmatively if the business is going to achieve long-term success.

Strong leaders and their teams consistently turn around failing organizations just by giving focused direction, setting clear expectations, instilling strong confidence, providing empathetic support, and rewarding excellent performance. Jim Collins and Morten Hansen (2011) concluded from their research that long-term sustainable growth firms possess management teams that demonstrate a sufficient amount of what they call 10X Leadership. This construct is defined by the four capabilities of Fanatic Discipline, Empirical Creativity, Productive Paranoia, and Level 5 Ambition. Long-term sustainably successful businesses have leaders who possess much more of these qualities than do their less successful industry counterparts.

In contrast, weak leaders can doom businesses. While they may be successful in starting the business, they may come up short as the company sets out to grow through readily repeatable processes. Take for example, operations. The very details required to install and evaluate disciplined processes that help scale a business are often anathema to the right-brain visionaries who founded the business; instead, at some point, the business needs more professional leadership—except in unusual cases (such as Bill Gates or Steve Jobs, and even they hired operations people)—to take it to the next level and beyond.

In his 1996 book, *Only the Paranoid Survive*, former Intel CEO Andy Grove states that all great entrepreneurs live in paranoia. While comfortable in their skin and with the decisions they make, these entrepreneurs typically doubt themselves, which doesn't allow them to become overconfident. This keeps them balanced. However, they are also unable to let go by delegating responsibility to others, believing no one can do it better than they can. They are reluctant to bring on new people who have more experience than they do and who may interfere with how the business has always operated. However, sometimes you just have to let go to grow.

I once sat on a board whose CEO needed to be replaced because of his less-than-stellar performance. He simply could not take the company to the next level because of his inability to lead. After a long search, the board found a professional manager to replace him who had never worked in the industry, but who had a lot of experience leading organizational growth in much larger companies. It took him less than a year to make the necessary changes in the business, fill out his management team, and start what turned out to be an incredible five-year growth curve. At that point, the company was sold for more than three times top revenues and nine times EBITDA.

As you look forward to building and growing your business, how will you transition from the innovative entrepreneur to the professional leader? The professional leader needs to be a very talented person who not only has the operational skills and experience to grow the company, but also is sensitive to and appreciative of the past, which has served as the foundation for the company's existence. Certainly, a balance of creativity, innovation, and discipline is the best combination.

When forming and evaluating your top management team, you shouldn't become too top heavy. You don't want too many functional leaders who stay tethered to their desk and don't produce revenue. Smaller businesses must employ people who affect the top line, including the senior management team. It is a fine balance. Having a strong management team ensures you build adequate management bench strength—not only to run the business, but also for succession planning—whether you relinquish some of the day-to-day operations or sell the business. The issue is that you can't build bench strength without testing people to find out if they are up to the task, which means creating management opportunities for them to demonstrate their mettle.

John Kotter (2016) has long argued that management and leadership require different skill sets. Management involves discipline, planning, controlling, processes, and efficiency, while leadership involves future thinking, communicating, aligning, motivating, and mobilizing. In short, managers do things right and leaders do the right things. However, Kotter is the first to say that while many companies may start out with great leadership, the sustainably successful ones embody great management as well. As some organizations grow their products, services, and reach, they tend to overplay the management structure role, which results in a hierarchy that pushes out entrepreneurship and stifles profitable growth. The question is, can an organization be reliable, efficient, and predictable while also agile, flexible, and adaptable? Kotter would say yes, but only if it can recreate the original organization in some or many forms.

The good news for the talent development industry is that as the pace quickens in an ever-changing world, so does the need for new learning. It stands to reason that no one is more well-positioned to both lead and manage a business successfully than those who cut their teeth in the talent development industry. Only time will tell if we can live up to this challenge.

As a leader, do you seek talent differently and hire in unusual ways? Do you look for intelligent, creative, and flexible people, and are you willing to adapt the job or organization to fit their talents? Do you set high expectations and encourage significant growth? Do you take it upon yourself to serve as a mentor or coach?

Take Risks, Not Chances: Managing and Measuring Risk

Every organization faces some degree of risk as it grows and matures, and it is difficult to succeed without taking risks. The majority of risks fall into the broad categories of strategy, finances, operations, compliance, and reputation. As with any company, whether a small startup or huge multinational conglomerate, operating profitably and sustainably depends almost exclusively on making decisions that advance the business while minimizing the likelihood of making bad decisions. While you can't fully dismiss that some chance might be involved in any decision, it's prudent to ensure that decisions follow protocols designed to minimize serious risk.

Taking well-calculated risks involves determining the consequences of a particular action by conducting significant analysis and preparation. Some years ago a sports psychologist studied risktakers, including sky divers, race car drivers, and aerobatic pilots, and concluded they were not only extremely cautious but conducted a serious amount of intelligence when preparing for their ventures to combat their lack of confidence or commitment and fear (Kriegel and Patler 1985). In other words, they got a much better handle on "if this happens, then that will happen" before engaging in their risky ventures.

Contrast this with making decisions and leaving outcomes to chance. You can only calculate the probability when the possible outcomes are relatively finite. For example, the chance a coin will be heads when you flip it is 50-50. Taking a chance that all will work out to your advantage—that your coin will land on heads—has ruined countless companies over the years.

How do you effectively manage risk? The challenge is taking risks that are likely to pay off or playing it safe all the time, thus minimizing a big payoff. Take online learning from the talent development supplier perspective: 25 years ago, many people in the industry saw that online learning could play a big role in the future, yet some suppliers are still slow to acknowledge its influence and as such are seeing their products and services suffer. Times change rapidly, and unforeseen disruptions can devastate a business if they are not addressed.

There are two basic decision-making options when contemplating future risks: proactively anticipate the future or wait for the future and then react and adapt. Either option can work; your approach depends on your level of risk tolerance. Adopting a little of both covers the bases. Here are 11 guidelines for managing risk to cover these bases:

1. Create a long-term strategy that anticipates the eventualities of change. Use this plan as a guidepost to evaluate big decisions.

2. Ensure senior management is committed to ongoing risk assessment.

3. Embrace diversity of thought, not only among senior management but all employees. This will ensure that many opinions and ideas will be considered.

4. Encourage, reinforce, and reward a culture of effective risk management throughout the enterprise, and provide appropriate training in the value and application of risk management.

5. Develop a strong relationship and interact frequently with your bank to ensure your loan covenants are within stipulations. It's important to ensure that your bank and other lenders continue to provide needed capital for your growth.

6. Comply with all government laws affecting the business. Those related to safety, the environment, immigration, customs, health and human services, and taxes require constant vigilance.

7. Manage your customer base by ensuring your business is focused on more than just a few customers. Ideally, no one customer should have more than 10 percent of your business so that you're not overly dependent on them.

8. Protect your proprietary intellectual capital and the way you differentiate your offer. Ensure all legal actions are taken to copyright and trademark what you own so others don't illegally use it. Monitor as best you can.

9. Manage your distribution network, whether in-house or contracted out, such that your business, not your salespeople, owns the customer relationship. Admittedly, this is not always possible if you're using external sales resources, but managing the appropriate use of your products and services is your job.

10. Manage your inventory so you don't run out of capabilities to serve your customers. In today's digital world we don't think much about running out of program materials because reproduction is a click away. But how

readily available are these resources and more important do you have employees who are capable of delivering them?

11. While no one can control the occurrence of a natural catastrophe, you should ensure that if one occurs you have proper insurance. How will you guard against fires, flooding, power outages, hurricanes, and earthquakes from hurting or destroying your business?

Of course, managing against risk does not mean you have to avoid taking risks. As Facebook founder and CEO Mark Zuckerberg said: "In a world that changes really quickly, the only strategy that is guaranteed to fail is not taking risks (Beahm 2013)."

Getting More for Less: The Scalability Factor

One of the biggest challenges for businesses is achieving scalability. In theory, scaling a business means eliminating costs and time to produce and distribute products and services, resulting in greater margins and more profitability. The underlying proposition of scaling is relatively simple: Create replicable processes that take less time and labor to produce results. This is as true in the talent development supplier industry as it is in any other.

But if scalability is this simple, why aren't all firms hugely profitable? The answer is that implementation is not as easy as it sounds, especially if it involves re-imagining the underlying processes organizations use to operate and go to market. Just as it is easier and less expensive to sell to an existing client rather than a new prospect, it is easier and less expensive to not remake the business model—even if it can result in improved success.

There are at least three general functions in the talent development supplier industry in which scalability is feasible:
- development of the offer
- distribution of products and services
- operation of the business.

Offer Development

Once you develop the offer, either a product or consulting service, how can you scale it? How can you create a readily replicable product or service that doesn't need to be retooled every time you sell it?

For the product category, this means developing a training workshop, assessment instrument, software application, and so on. Or you can consider a learning management system (LMS) platform, which supports the ready use of plug-and-play learning modules that have been created in software compliant code. The LMS stays the same while the products can differ in content and even design.

Some people in the industry believe that the more customized a program is the less profitable the deliverable will be. Client organizations frequently have to decide whether to "make or buy"; that is, to create custom programs or purchase off-the-shelf programs. Even suppliers who create custom-developed programs can achieve scale by replication and effectively executing every time a program is created, regardless of the type of labor needed to create these programs.

Mass customization is one way to scale the development of off-the-shelf programs. A common scaling technique used by many businesses, mass customization means that the core offer accounts for 80 percent of the needs of the target market, while the remaining 20 percent allows for tailoring or customizing the offering to the specific needs of buyers. It provides quicker time to market, digitized formats, on-demand production and delivery, minimal finished goods inventory, and product or service modularization.

One of my favorite examples of mass customization is the Hertz Corporation. If you have ever rented a car from them, you may have thought that the car assigned to you was specifically customized for you. Why? Because when you approach the electronic reservation board, it has your name and parking space number in lights. All you have to do is go to that spot, where the keys are in the ignition and the trunk is up. Even the exiting process has been scaled to save you time. The truth is that you basically get the same car as the next person whose name was also in lights. Hertz is able to scale the car rental process because it can easily replicate the experience across thousands of renters with minimal adjustments needed.

In the talent development supplier industry, mass customization examples run from training program materials that simply add a client's branding (cosmetic); those that include custom role plays and case studies (collaborative); and online learning programs for which learners control their individual learning paths (adaptive). Alternatively, mass customization of workshops may not involve tailoring the prepackaged materials, but rather creating a facilitative experience that meets the unique needs of the client and its end-users (transparent). The same can be said for online learning programs created with off-the-shelf authoring tools, reducing time and costs during the product development cycle. Often, a minimal number of screens can be tailored to make the end product look like it was developed specifically for each customer (Cohen and Pine 2007). For example, Lexipol, a SaaS-based education and training company, provides police, fire, and correctional institutions with a training platform it easily and frequently updates when there are changes in specific state and federal policies and regulations, while 80 percent of the content typically remains the same across jurisdictions.

Consulting services also can benefit from a mass customization business model. For example, there are many strategic planning processes and organizational change models that use simple templates, which are customizable when completed with each client's unique information and insight. In other words, the process or model is continuously replicated to fit any set of customer data.

Product or Service Distribution

Distributing products and services at scale can get you to market faster and more effectively than your competitors. Some products and services require a time-consuming, face-to-face sales model, particularly when in-field salespeople must locate the right buyer, define the appropriate need, and then match that need to the prevailing offer. As a result of this labor-intensive and expensive sales model, many firms have a more scalable way to create (or farm out) the lead-generation capability. In this scenario, lead hunters provide already qualified leads at significantly less cost than feet-on-the-street farmers who sell, follow up, and attempt to develop long-term relationships with clients.

Other ways to scale sales and marketing efforts include the creation of pricing and proposal templates, deploying direct email and webinar opportunities to reach out to prospective clients, and setting up reseller arrangements with domestic and international partners. These partners can range from inserting your offer (or components of it) into widely distributed catalogs to licensing arrangements with international distributors.

Consider the earlier example of John Wiley & Sons' Inscape Publishing, which distributes the DiSC inventory, has scaled its distribution. Inscape does not have a direct sales force. Instead, it offers its assessment inventory to nearly 2,000 worldwide authorized partners, or value-added resellers, that market and sell their offering. The firm provides consistent support to these distributors, including some global marketing activities, but the business itself does not directly sell the inventory to end-user organizations.

Business Operations

Scalability opportunities for business operations include the use of technology and the integration of internal services. For many businesses, the most logical scalability option is structuring more effective and straightforward internal processes, whether they employ technology platforms, human resources applications, or back-office finance and accounting utilities. Some popular examples include time sheets for recording labor efforts expended on projects, human resource information systems, sales reporting tools, and CRM platforms. What is most important is to determine the key processes that drive the business and scale them appropriately.

Technological scaling opportunities are abundant and will continue to reduce back-office costs as those technologies become more robust. One front of the house process that has benefitted from technology, though, is that of project management. The value of having a project management mentality and tool set to create a product, both generic and custom, is too great to calculate. Some complex development processes can be reduced to a series of steps, timelines, and milestones, all programmed into a software tool, such as MS Project, which serve to organize the project information and manage it to completion. Professionally managed projects will also produce significant financial returns. Any steps that can be eliminated from project management procedures should result in greater margins and speed to market. This results in a repeatable project management process with accompanying tools, enabling fast and lean production, rather than having to reinvent the wheel every time a new project surfaces. Such a well-thought-out process is applicable to small internal operational projects, as well as the development of any product or service offerings mentioned previously.

Examples of additional operational scaling opportunities through the use of technology include Salesforce.com, HubSpot, Marketo, or Pardot for sales and marketing; Great Plains and Quick Books for accounting; Microsoft Dynamics and PeopleSoft for integration; and Insperity and Zenefits for payroll and benefits. A host of others use documentation, cost containment, and technological streamlining to manage their entire business.

Cleaning Up the Backyard: Where Are Your Processes and Systems?

While it is easy to focus on your client-facing systems, do not neglect your internal ones. For example, are they working properly for you and your staff? Failing to review your internal processes and systems and letting them become unmanageable is akin to placing all your unused junk in your backyard, creating an eyesore for your neighbors. Eventually, you will have to clean it up. Likewise, cleaning up your back-office systems will improve the look of your business to your most important neighbors: your employees and customers. If your employees see a careless and sloppy operation from above, they are likely to model that same carelessness in how they interact both internally and externally.

There are two overriding goals for installing systems and processes in your business. The first is to create efficient internal management functions that give you the right data at the right time to make quality decisions. The second, while inclusive of the first, is to make it easy for your customers to deal with you. Customers might love your product or services, but fall out of love with you as a supplier if you are difficult to deal with. Take any cable company, for example. You might love the high-speed connections your supplier provides, but find navigating its customer service a nightmare. This can easily be the case for any talent development supplier. Operating profitably over the long haul means ensuring your systems and processes are not only in place but working well for your business both internally and externally. A well-run organization can be a clear differentiator in the marketplace, while a sloppy and error-prone one will not last very long.

However, simply installing systems can be taxing and counterproductive. You do not want to pigeonhole people who work best out of the box. Having a modicum of structure with certain systems and processes ensures that you're not over-engineering the business. For example, you should have an employee handbook that clearly documents expectations for employee behavior. This is not only helpful to employees so that they understand expectations, but it will also help you justify personnel decisions that can be supported by the HR systems in place, including those involving performance management and compensation. In addition, you need a sound project management process in place to ensure meeting timeline and cost objectives. Finally, you need a system for periodic customer feedback. Reaching out to customers in a more formal, systematic, and professional manner will provide you with important information that can facilitate satisfaction, loyalty, and retention. Leaving it to chance is shortsighted.

Fortunately, you can incorporate all of these processes and systems with easy-to-implement software tools. Enterprise resource planning (ERP) or CRM systems, such as Salesforce, include add-on modules that cover the broad spectrum of back-office systems. But having these tools in place is only the first step in organizing your business so that you have the right data to determine how it is performing. There is always room for improvement, which is where process improvement methodologies come in to play.

Business process improvement helps organizations continually improve their internal processes in a systematic manner and includes both process redesign and business process reengineering. Its primary goal is to reduce cost and cycle time, and where necessary introduce process changes to improve product or service quality that best match the needs of your customers. Methodologies that improve processes include Six Sigma, Lean Management, Kaizen, and Hoshin Planning.

The process for cleaning up your backyard includes three basic steps: (Consider how each relates to the discussion about mission, vision, and values in chapter 3.)

1. Define your strategic goals and purpose. Who are you, what do you do, and why do you do it?
2. Determine your customers and stakeholders. Whom do you serve?
3. Align your business processes to achieve the goals of your business. How can you improve them?

Suffice it to say, improving the quality of your processes and maintaining acceptable levels of performance quality are critical factors in the overall long-term success of your business.

Hire, Fire, Rehire, Retire: Talent Management in Changing Times

The major expense item for most companies, regardless of size, is compensation and benefits, often more than 50 percent of all operating costs. Given the importance of acquiring, developing, and retaining qualified employees, which is not unlike finding qualified customers, effectively managing your talent can make or break your overall success. After all, who should know more about this topic than you? Let's take a moment to remind ourselves of what we tell our clients: People are a business' most important asset.

I clearly recall my first company that specialized in creating custom business simulations for selecting managers and salespeople. We sold these simulations, as well as how to effectively evaluate job candidates using them, to our clients, all of whom praised them as the most valid and reliable selection tools available. We even had research to back up our claims. But did we use these simulations to select our own staff? Shamefully no, at least not until the day a client asked us how, not if, we used these when selecting our own personnel. We had already made a number of hiring mistakes so we decided to utilize our own simulations and from that point on we made better selection decisions. The talent development challenges your clients face might often mirror those you face, so it is in your best interest to practice what you preach. And why not? If your offer is good enough for your customers, it should be good enough for you.

There is another advantage to effectively managing your talent beyond simply fully growing your business to consistently meet the needs of your customers. Investors consider the quality of your internal talent, especially your more senior leaders. Yes, financials are important, but your people are responsible for continually making your financials look good. This is as true for your customers as it is for you. Investors look long and hard at the talent levels of organizations to assess the growth potential of a business.

Aligning Job Competencies

That you need employees to make a business run is no different from needing fuel to make a car run. However, just as it is critical to know the most effective octane rating for your particular car, you need to know the characteristics of the talent most effective for your business and culture. So how do you ensure you have the talent best qualified to deliver the results you need? The key is understanding what you want the person to be able to do. Too often we assume their experience and expertise will be enough to get them through the day; therefore we don't always share our performance expectations with them.

One way to fix this is to create a business value chain that aligns your expected business outcomes with the capabilities the business needs to achieve those outcomes. From these capabilities you can determine what competencies are needed to demonstrate those capabilities. Table 7-1 gives an example of what this might look like.

Table 7-1. Business Value Chain

Competency	Organizational Capability	Business Outcome
Strategic Thinking	Strategy Integration and Alignment	Strategy-driven Culture
Service Excellence	Relationship Management	X Percent Customer Retention
Creativity	Innovation	X Percent Increase in New vs. Current Program Sales
Collaboration	Team Alignment	Employee Engagement
People Development	Talent Management	Top three in Industry Talent Attraction and Retention
Project Management	Process Improvement	X Percent Reduction in Rework
Business Acumen	Financial Analysis	X Percent Increase in EBITDA

For example, assume one of your business outcomes is 90 percent customer retention. The overall organization capability you would need to possess to achieve this would be relationship management, and the accompanying competency, service excellence. Service excellence can then be broken down into the knowledge, skills, and attitudes that comprise it. This simple and straightforward approach can help you get a handle on your own talent needs by focusing on exactly what you are trying to achieve as a business.

Preparing for the Future

As the workplace and workers continue to evolve, you need to pay attention to major changes and prepare for the future. Here are four of these changes already beginning to shape the future of the industry:

1. **Demographics and talent shortage:** Do you have the right people in the right place with the right skills at the right time and right price?

2. **Individual rules:** Do you know how to get the greatest productivity from an increasingly complex and diverse workforce?

3. **Rising sophistication:** Are you using sophisticated management approaches to manage your people assets—as you are with your other assets?

4. **Technology revolution:** Are you ready for the affect of revolutionary technologies on the ways your people and business operate?

To address employee challenges, consider classifying your people into categories, which allows you to optimize their contribution to your business. Basically, there are two dimensions to this: roll impact and skill competency. Roll impact measures the risk of a skill shortage or deficiency that may undermine your business success if not managed properly. Skill complexity can be thought of as the cost of owning that talent. Figure 7-1 below illustrates this as a 2 x 2 matrix.

Figure 7-1. Talent Role Capabilities

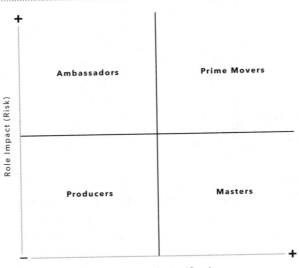

These employee roles can be described in the following way:

- *Prime movers* are most critical to creating and delivering your organization's distinguishing value proposition to customers and long-term economic value for your organization.
- *Ambassadors* deliver your organization's brand promise directly to customers and may have innate behavioral attributes that are available in the market but are often hard to find or identify.
- *Masters* are accomplished practitioners who have knowledge, skills, and disciplines that meet professional or marketplace standards.
- *Producers* have behaviors and skills that are generally available in the market or can be developed very quickly.

The costs of "bad" talent can be at best draining in the short term and devastating in the long term. This classification may help you identify, hire, and retain the right type of people for your business. Few will demonstrate all these capabilities at once. Some will obviously be stronger in certain areas than others. You will need to assess your talent needs and the gaps in helping your business create value for your customers. When it comes to talent, the path to long-term success is to always hire those who are better than you are.

Is What You Give What You Get?

The major challenge with those entering the workforce is trying to compete with new companies that provide all kinds of benefits to their employees. To attract the best and the brightest, certain benefits have become standard in the workplace. Granted your business is probably not competing with larger companies, but there still may be an expectation for benefits you haven't thought were necessary or even desired. Some talent development firms are very sensitive to what is taking place on a national level with their own clients, and are trying to match benefits: paid personal time off, sabbaticals after a certain number of years of employment, free lunches, and remote office days each week are common and becoming more and more expected.

While many of these benefits are becoming the norm, companies should not ignore other aspects of the employer-employee relationship. Companies that excel at retaining their workers view their employees in three distinct categories—people, professionals, and society members—and adjust their benefits accordingly. For example, the people category focuses on some of the options noted above, such as sabbaticals, time off, and flexible schedules. The focus on the employee as a professional includes training and development and tuition reimbursement benefits. And the focus on them as society members includes benefits such as participating in community service projects and creating nonprofit endowments.

That said, employees stay with companies largely because of the autonomy they receive, the team effort and collaborative culture they experience, and the smart people with whom they work (Bond 2016). And let's not forget that one of the top items correlating with job engagement and low turnover from Gallup's 12-item questionnaire is "I have a best friend at work," which some say is a proxy for trust. Employees still look for those internal needs of achievement, affiliation, and autonomy.

The more tangible benefits may require more thought as a relatively small business because of their financial implications for items such as profit sharing, stock options, bonuses, medical benefits, and 50 to 100 percent matching 401(k) contributions. They have a direct bottom-line implication for your business. The question becomes, do you get more productivity from employees in return for these benefits? No one knows for sure but we do know a happy employee is likely to be more productive than an unhappy one, and unhappiness can often be attributed to what they are not receiving that their peers are at other businesses. It is a fine line to draw. Clearly you have to make sure you don't break the bank with benefits; on the other hand, to attract and retain good employees you may have to stretch the compensation and benefits budget more than you had hoped, which might include collaborative workspaces, flexible hours, and sabbaticals.

After adequate healthcare and savings benefits, I always favored profit-sharing as a way to best engage employees for their own and the company's benefit. Such a plan ensures everyone benefits from operating efficiently and shares in the profitability of the company. To execute this approach, you could set a target profitability above which profit sharing takes place. This way, the company is ensured of retaining a certain amount of its profits before distribution. For example, say your business target for the year is 10 percent net profit. Assuming you reach this level, any amount above it would be shared with employees on the basis of a percentage of their salary. It could be all the extra profit or some predetermined percentage of it. There are many pros and cons that won't be explored here other than to say profit sharing should be carefully considered. While compensation isn't as important to employee satisfaction, it is when compared to people doing the same job. It is about fairness.

Whether it is fair compensation, interesting work, opportunity for development, or a best friend at work, attracting and retaining the best employees for your business is critical to its success. And figuring out the comp and benefits formula is a major part of that success. The costs of turnover are significant when considering lost time and productivity of a job that's not filled, the time it takes to train a new employee, the ramp up time to get full productivity, and the impact on the culture of the business.

There are ways to avoid many of the comp and benefits challenges. While perhaps not ideal, you can maintain a relatively small full-time staff supported largely by 1099 independent contractors; this reduces costs and allows for more staffing flexibility. This is best when you can't keep everyone on staff pulling their utilization weight. That is, they aren't paying for themselves, so the idea of a variable employment roster makes a lot of sense. Oftentimes the best candidates for these roles, such as contract facilitators, are former employees who prefer a more flexible schedule or those who have "retired" but would like part-time work.

However, there is one huge caveat. Know the tax and employment law regarding independent contractors. Recent cases have classified what companies thought were contractors as actually employees subject to payroll deductions and other tax-related items. One talent development supplier, which thought it had followed all the published legal workforce guidelines, had to pay nearly $500,000 in back taxes to the IRS. And this amount didn't include the costs of legal counsel to fight the claim.

From Cradle to Grave

One of the most frequent complaints employees have about smaller businesses is they expect newly hired employees to find their way on their own. Granted, while this "test" will tell you a lot about the initiative and resourcefulness of these people, it may also considerably slow down their ramp up time. This is why it is helpful to have a formal orientation and onboarding process. Getting new people up to speed as quickly as possible will help their performance and sense of belonging, particularly as they start to pull their weight and visibly contribute to the business. Perhaps you assign a "buddy" employee who will be responsible for guiding the new employee along the way, complemented with a standard documented process. If you are large enough to have a designated human resources office, it can take on this responsibility as well. This shouldn't be done haphazardly, but rather with a specific plan with timelines, milestones, and expected outcomes.

Once a person is fully onboarded, it is then important to periodically test the waters by orchestrating check-ins. This will go a long way toward heading off any discontent or ongoing issues. The process doesn't have to be complex. In fact, the shorter and more to the point the better. One way to execute this is to ask people to circle one of three options that illustrates how they are feeling about their employment situation—glad, sad, or mad—and provide space for comments in Figure 7-2. Sort of like the net promoter score (NPS) for customers.

Figure 7-2. How Do You Feel About Your Employment Situation?

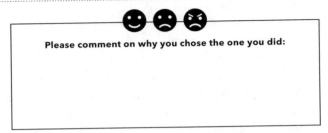

Does Culture Eat Strategy for Breakfast?: The C Factor

Above all, operating profitably and sustainably requires a strong culture promoting a respectful and productive environment. But culture can differ from one organization to another. More specifically, culture means a lot of things to different people and the multigenerational wants and needs are likely to differ significantly.

There are a lot of data that show common elements for the best places to work. In his preface to the "2016 Best Companies to Work For" edition of *Fortune*, editor Alan Murray (2016a), writes that what defines a great workplace is not just free food, generous benefits, and nap pods, but rather one common element, culture.

But what exactly makes a great culture and thus a best place to work? According to the Great Place to Work organization, there are three basic ingredients:

1. **Trust**, as measured by that between employees and management
2. **Pride**, as visible through the amount people take in their work, teams, organization, or brand
3. **Camaraderie**, as noted by a supportive, warm, and friendly relationship between employees.

What is most important about culture is it is no longer a nice-to-have, soft, and unmeasurable factor in a business's success. It is now a critical cog in an organization's performance. For example, the 100 Best Companies to Work For had significantly less turnover than their respective industry averages across all industries; sometimes as much a 50 percent less. Annualized stock market returns between 1997 and 2014 for these Best Companies were nearly twice that of the general market. And here's what is even more interesting: Small and medium great place to work companies (less than 500 employees) perform better than larger ones (more than 500) on the trust index, and voluntary turnover is nearly a third the U.S. average. Culture is important across the board of any size company, even the small ones (Bond 2016).

What is the strategy for attracting the talent you want for a best place to work company? There are six simple elements:

1. Provide robust opportunities for growth and development.
2. Highlight the impact employees can make by working at your company.
3. Ensure pay is fair and benefits are enticing.
4. Employ creative recruiting tactics.
5. Make a phenomenal first impression.
6. Make the company's unique culture a selling point (Bond 2016).

Despite an over-focus on generational differences, young people require the same elements from the work culture as older generations: an opportunity to grow and succeed, to have work-life balance, to have a sense of purpose in what they are doing, for there to be transparency with senior management on its plans, to collaborate across all borders, and to embrace diversity in the workplace.

Conclusion

All of what has thus far been presented in this book are simply the basics for building and growing any talent development operation, whether from an external consultancy's role or that of an internal corporate practitioner. At the end of the day, the proof is indeed in the pudding. And the pudding of success, as in any business, is best described in financial and operating performance. If you can't make a profit in your business, you won't be able to sustain it for very long. You do well by doing good work, which is purchased again and again by customers, which allows you to be profitable, thus sustaining your business to continue to do well by doing good work.

Achieving this end state doesn't simply come on a lark or hope. It involves hard work and expertise in areas for which you may not have been trained or are even interested in learning. Recall, this is by and large an entrepreneurial industry that requires not only an unbridled passion for what you do, but also an attention to operational details involving financial management, customer service, risk management, processes and systems, quality control, and leadership and talent management. To say one of these is more important than the others is not understanding the enormity and complexity of the business. All are equally critical to your success, and any significant misstep for any one of them can lead to failure. This is why it is so important to find and develop people who already have the mindset, skill set, and toolset needed to help you manage your business efficiently and effectively, thus closing the gaps in your own capabilities and interests.

Reflection Questions

KEEPING YOUR HEAD ABOVE WATER: MAINTAINING FINANCIAL HEALTH

- How would you evaluate your relationship with your bank?
- What can you do to ensure it continues as a strong partnership?
- What are signs in your P&L and balance sheet statements that require you to reconsider how you are managing your business financially?
- How have you gone about proactively managing your cash flow?

BUILDING LEADERSHIP MUSCLE: STRONG MANAGEMENT MATTERS

- Where is your firm in its growth cycle? Has it stagnated?
- Is the founder still calling all the shots? Has your CEO passed his prime?
- Is it time to consider bringing in professional leadership to take your firm to the next level?
- How would you rate yourself and your leadership team on being superbosses?

TAKE RISKS, NOT CHANCES: MANAGING AND MEASURING RISK

- How are you managing risk in your business?
- What are some impending decisions you need to make that are relatively risky?
- What risks have you taken that have or have not panned out?
- What are the reasons for these different outcomes?
- Which of the above needs immediate attention?

GETTING MORE FOR LESS: THE SCALABILITY FACTOR

- What scaling examples do you already use in your business?
- What can your organization do more effectively to scale its three key business areas: offer development, distribution, and operations?
- How have you quantified the improved results your business has achieved through scalability?

CLEANING UP THE BACKYARD: WHERE ARE YOUR PROCESSES AND SYSTEMS?

- What processes and systems in your business need the most attention?
- What are you doing to improve these?
- How are you ensuring your customers find it easy to do business with you?

HIRE, FIRE, REHIRE, RETIRE, RIGHT: TALENT MANAGEMENT IN CHANGING TIMES

- What are you doing to plan your talent needs according to the demands of your business?
- What competencies do your employees need and how aligned are they with the expected outcomes for your business?
- How are your compensation and benefits set up to maximize employee productivity?
- What are you doing to ensure an efficient onboarding and checking system for your employees?

DOES CULTURE EAT STRATEGY FOR BREAKFAST?: THE C FACTOR

- What are you doing to create a culture representative of a best company to work for?
- What are your limits to providing benefits to employees?
- How are you facilitating a happy and productive workplace?

SERVING YOUR CUSTOMERS AND YOUR NEEDS

*Know what your customers want most and what your
company does best. Focus on where those two meet.*
—Kevin Stirtz

The pulse of any business is best kept beating by serving your customers effectively. Whether this is done profitably or not is another story. In general, customer service is about three basic components:

1. **Purpose:** Embracing and meeting the needs of your customers
    is why you are in business.
2. **Delivery:** Improve the processes delivering your products and
    services to the customer, allowing them to achieve their stated
    business results.
3. **Retention:** Ensure the loyalty of your customers by exceeding
    their expectations.

Master these three components, and you will be in business for a long time. Fail on any one, however, and you might find yourself with no one left to serve. The object of this chapter is not to rehash all that's been written about what makes great customer service: winning customer loyalty, dealing with difficult customers, and managing their expectations. The business case for good customer service is by now relatively elementary, so let's delve deeper into how to find, choose, and serve your customers more effectively.

Server or Servant?: Customer Service Today

You have likely heard the sales mantra that it takes five to 10 times the cost to sell to a new customer than to resell to an existing one. Whether this is true or not isn't as important as the fact that it makes sense. But retaining your current customers is never easy. This addresses how you go about finding and keeping the right customers—those who can deliver long-term profitability to you at a reasonable cost. Most businesses consider their best customers to be those for whom they can create significant value. This is difficult to argue with because if you offer them value, especially for their own customers, they are likely to come back to you for products and services. What's most important is choosing the *right* customers for your business.

Choosing Your Customers

Are you choosing your customers, or are they choosing you? You may think you are choosing them when in fact they are deciding whether they want you to serve them. What if you could focus on choosing the best customers for you? Life would be much easier and less stressful, but that's easier said than done. However, there is a formula proposed by Robert Simons (2014) in a *Harvard Business Review* article describing four key steps to choosing the right customer:

1. **Identify Your primary customers:** Know whom you are targeting and why. Your primary customer needs to reflect your company's perspective (mission and culture) so you can optimize the energy and creativity of your people serving the customer. You should also match your capabilities with the needs of your customers. Your core competency should translate to the customers you seek who will most benefit from that competency. Finally, you should determine the profit potential your customers can bring to you; don't chase those that will cost you more to serve than you can make from serving them.

2. **Understand what your primary customers value:** After identifying your best customers, determine what they most value about your offer. Are they price conscious? Do they require technical help? Do they expect expertise?

3. **Allocate resources to win:** Next, focus on making them lifelong customers by ensuring they get what they need when they need it.

4. **Make the control processes interactive:** Stay on top of your customers' needs. Create a frequent dialogue with them that informs you of any changes in what they want and expect from you.

If you and your customers have formed a strong partnership in which you depend on one another, helping to fulfill your respective missions and objectives, you should have customers who stay with you until their needs or your ability to satisfy them are met.

Listening to Your Customers

More than 308 organizational learning buyers were surveyed on the items that make a high-quality learning partner, as well as what makes a learning product great (Anderson 2014, 48-50). Results showed the top five items were quality of product, results produced by the product, product value, easy to work with, and thought leadership or innovation. Of the items that made a product great, the most important considerations were can be configured, meets end-user expectations, is appropriate for employees, and fits organizational context. The areas in which learning partners were least meeting the buyers' needs were in learning analytics and learning technologies.

These results provide a clear path to constructing your offer and relationships so they meet the wants and desires of your customers. Unfortunately, this is not a simple task, especially if you have to reconfigure your current business model to meet these needs.

Building Long-Term Customer Relationships

Obtaining a client can launch your business, but retaining that client and others will help you drive sales and keep you in business. Client retention requires frequent in-person interaction, especially in the talent development supplier industry where your value proposition is tied to the impact people have on organizational success. Despite technology making communication easier, you're still more likely to build lasting relationships through person-to-person connections. And having great relationships can go a long way in masking any of your weaknesses and any mistakes you may make.

Client relationships start with you being able to address your clients' needs. The longer you can satisfy those needs, the longer your relationship will thrive. But if it is this simple, why aren't all our relationships lasting? The essence of positive relationships is in the strength of the connection, which requires significant attention to be obtained, nourished, and sustained over time. So while the solution sounds simple, many businesses fail in the execution.

To build better relationships you must understand mutual interests and needs, link them to expected business results, develop a meaningful execution plan, and execute the plan flawlessly. To execute effectively, three relationships must work in harmony:
- between the seller as a whole and the customer
- between the various distribution channels and the seller's employees
- between the customer and the seller's employees.

Within each of these relationships is the people-to-people connection that will make or break those chains (Cohen 2004, 41-46).

You will probably spend a significant amount of your budget figuring out ways to reach, attract, and improve your relationships with your customers, whether it's marketing and customer strategy development, event planning and management, channel development, integrated communications strategies, employee incentives, or analytics and measurement. However, at the core of these tactics is building better relationships. Here are some techniques to ensure these relationships endure.

First, and foremost, you need to align your employees' behavior with how you want to be portrayed in the marketplace; in essence, your brand promise (see chapter 6). It is what you stand for, how you want to be perceived, and what customers should expect from you (Scafario 2011). Ensuring customer-facing employees understand this and how they can project themselves to customers is paramount to building better relationships. Deliver on your value proposition, which is different from your brand promise. Your value proposition outlines what customers will get in exchange for their time, money, and effort—the benefit derived by customers minus the cost or risk required to receive that benefit. Ramp up the level of real engagement your employees have with your business. The more involved and engaged your employees are with what your business represents and where it is going, the more likely they will present themselves to customers in a way closely representing the brand promise and value proposition of the business. This is how relationships between a company and a customer are built and reinforced one interaction at a time.

Keeping Your Customers

Customer loyalty comes down to three general rules:

1. Some customers are more predictable and loyal no matter what company they are doing business with.
2. Some customers are more profitable than others (for example, spend more money, pay their bills on time, require less service).
3. Some customers find a company's products and services more valuable than those of their competitors (Reichheld 1996).

So what makes some customers more profitable? Simply stated, every product or service comes with a base profit, so the longer you have a customer the greater the likelihood they will make more purchases over time. These customers become more profitable because they know you better, they don't waste time requesting services you don't provide, and they understand where to get the information they need. This results in lower operating costs. They are more likely to recommend others to your business, and are not totally averse to paying higher prices than new customers because they are likely to get promotions, discounts, and special prices from you in return. This defines a true win-win partnership. First-year acquisition costs are the same for any customer, but after that, they virtually disappear.

It is easy to calculate the lifetime value of a customer, or how much a customer is likely to spend with an organization during its lifetime, provided the customer remains satisfied and loyal. With that, you can determine the potential long-term value of your best customers. This will help you appreciate the importance of serving your customers. Appendix B offers a simple exercise that illustrates this.

Calculating the lifetime value not only includes what the customer pays for your services over a lifetime, but what it additionally offers you from referrals. It can be a very large number. Now, compare this with the highest paying customer you had for just one year. How does what they paid you compare with the lifetime value of your most loyal customer?

While this seems like an obvious point, many businesses don't take stock of just how much a great customer is worth. They focus on the short-term value of their customers and how to maximize that number. Some estimates are that 65 percent of the average company's business comes from its present and satisfied customers. But , remember, just because they are satisfied does not mean they are loyal. So it's important to not only keep them satisfied, but convince them to become loyal.

Figure 8-1 combines the evaluation of the experience you create for your customers (positive or negative) with the level of your customer's expectations (positive, neutral, negative). In *Zones of Retention*, Heskett, et al. (1997) contend that just keeping customers satisfied is not enough to keep them loyal. Loyal customers, those in the zone of affection, do not only have positive experiences. They also have positive to neutral expectations of that experience—whether you consistently meet or exceed their expectations with a positive customer experience.

Those who have negative expectations for customer service as well as a negative experience move closer and closer to the zone of defection. Those in the middle appear to be content in that their expectations are being met. Yet, their customer experience is relatively neutral, thus they are more prone to change suppliers, particularly if their needs, such as affordability, are better met elsewhere. Knowing where your customers are on the zones of retention continuum is critical to retaining those who are already loyal and appealing to those who aren't yet in that camp.

Figure 8-1. Zones of Retention

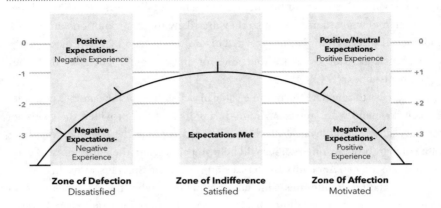

What Is the Loyalty Effect?

Frederick Reichheld's net Ppomotor score (NPS)—"the one number you need to grow"—provides insight into how well you are doing on the customer-loyalty barometer (Reichheld 2003). It asks customers one question on a scale of 0-10: "How likely are you to recommend (insert company name) to a friend or colleague?" Over time, a customer's response is most highly correlated with actual purchasing patterns and ultimately the growth of your business.

The NPS is calculated by taking the percentage of respondents who give a rating of 9 or 10 (promoters) minus the percentage who give a rating of 0 to 6 (detractors). Neutrals are 7s and 8s and are not part of the calculation. The score can vary considerably from minuses—having far more detractors than promoters—all the way to a theoretical 100 percent, which equates to no detractors at all. The reality, however, is that every business has detractors so NPSs of even 50 percent are considered relatively decent and those in the 70+ percent range are extremely rare and hard to obtain. Such companies as USAA, Harley-Davidson, Costco, Amazon, eBay, and Vanguard have been reported to have NPS values greater than 70 percent. However, the average firm plugs along at an NPS value of 5 to 10 percent. Reichheld's research over a 10-year period revealed companies with the highest ratio of promoters to detractors in their sector typically enjoyed strong profits and healthy growth (2006).

Yet another measure of loyalty is provided by the Walker Loyalty Index shown in Figure 8-2.

Figure 8-2. Walker Loyalty Matrix

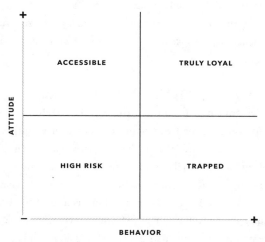

Source: Walker (2016).

This approach to assessing customer loyalty presents the opportunity to segment loyalty by creating a scatter diagram in which each customer lies on the graph at the intersection of their responses to "Do you like us?" (attitude) and "Do you need us?" (behavior). Then it becomes useful to develop specific action plans for each quadrant. Figure 8-3 below provides sample hypothetical results from a customer satisfaction survey.

Figure 8-3. Sample Walker Loyalty Matrix Scattergram

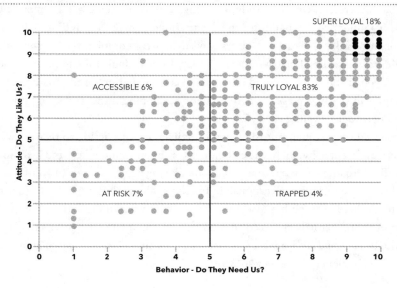

Regardless of how you assess the loyalty and longtime value of your customers, it's important to conduct customer service satisfaction surveys. By using continuous feedback mechanisms, preferably formal but also attainable through personal communications, you will get a sense of your customers' interest in continuing to be served by you.

Service Recovery Strategies

Say your customers continue to land in the Zone of Defection and are risks to leave you. How do you recover from poor service? Is it even possible? Not only is it possible, but it also pays off. Customers whose problems and complaints are handled quickly and satisfactorily tend to think more highly of those organizations than they did before they engaged in their requests (Krishna, Dangayach, and Sharma 2014, 263-277). Ironically, while there is a limit to customer patience, research continually shows that quality customer service leads to greater customer loyalty with more profit for your business (Hart, Heskett, and Sasser 1990).

In practice, it would seem relatively easy to employ methods for service recovery: apologize, ask for forgiveness, fix or remedy the problem, perhaps compensate in some way, and then follow up. So why do some companies continue to provide poor service? There are likely two major reasons: First, they don't have a systematically applied approach for addressing these complaints. Second, they look externally rather than internally to fix their problems. They don't spend the time and resources necessary to correct the processes and structures inside the company that are likely the reason for poor service.

Just imagine how much easier it would be to overcome poor service if you had such a system. One way to look at this issue is to create a 2 x 2 matrix that provides guidance for handling these situations, which you and your business consistently follow. Figure 8-4 offers ways to address complaints. Each complaint would be classified along two dimensions: who is at fault for the poor service—that is, you or the customer; and how critical is the situation for the customer? The examples in the figure are for actual talent development incidents, and how you might consider handling each case.

Based on the quadrant the situation falls into, your action to recover would be very different. Obviously, the criticalness of the situation is key, and it shouldn't be difficult to identify what that could look like to your customer. In addition, you need to figure out who is responsible for the problem, but always consider that you might be. Research has also shown that those who thought their complaints were not satisfactorily resolved told 28 people about their negative experience. On the other hand, those who felt satisfied only told 10 to 16 people about their positive experience (Freeman 2013).

Figure 8-4. Strategies for Service Recovery

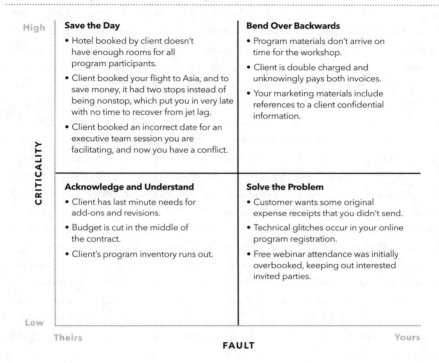

Getting Less for More: Customer Acquisition Costs

As you build your business, you will need to consider the cost to acquire customers who buy your product or service. Acquisition costs may include the research, marketing, and advertising expenses. To calculate them, add the cost of marketing and sales (including salaries and overhead) and divide by the number of customers you acquire during a specific timeframe.

Of course, you need to consider the customer acquisition cost (CAC) along with other data, especially the value of the customer to the company and the resulting return on investment of that acquisition. Your CACs should not exceed the lifetime value of your customer; otherwise, you will lose money in the long term. For example, if you spend $25,000 to acquire 10 customers, your CAC is $2,500 per customer. The question becomes, is this a worthwhile amount to spend? The answer depends on your business model, your offer, and how much you are charging for it. You need to calculate how much return business you will obtain from each client.

The more personal touch required to convert a customer, the less overall return on acquisition. Consider this when deciding whether you should implement a direct sales force or a web-generated lead conversion. The longer it takes for a salesperson to acquire a customer, the greater the CAC and the less your potential profit margin. Top-notch salespeople who can ramp up very quickly are at a premium.

Besides reducing the costs of acquiring your customers, how can you improve your CAC? Foremost, executing well in your targeted market will improve your CAC because the more targeted your sales and marketing, the less time and money it will take to land those customers. With these existing customers, you can upsell or cross-sell products and services to them. For example, a customer might value implementation services for the programs it already uses, such as follow-up trainer training, participant certification programs, or even administration of back-office operations, such as course registration, internal marketing, and program evaluation. By vertically integrating the services your clients need to internally deliver your offering, you can take some tasks off their plates and get paid to do so. The costs of acquiring this new business for a current customer would be minimal because you know them well and you are positioned to add value to their business.

There are two other ways you can optimize your CAC. First, you can test different website configurations or calls to action, thus deepening your understanding of what is taking place. Second, you can automate your sales and marketing process. Taking costs out of the sales process by streamlining it will go a long way toward improving your bottom line (Kiss Metrics 2016).

But the CAC can also be misleading. For instance, if you have just opened up a new territory or put a new person into an existing territory, you can expect your acquisition costs to be higher than they are in a mature territory with seasoned salespeople. Also, if you have made significant upgrades to your website, or even created a new one, which you rely on to drive traffic, it may take a while to get the type of traction needed to drive business and fine-tune it to improve your SEO. Keep in mind that your own business dynamics and operations can cloud the CAC calculation.

Why, When, and How to Fire Your Customers: Assessing Customer Worth

Having said all of the above about acquiring and retaining loyal customers, some customers are not worth keeping—those with whom it is hard to have a profitable relationship. Even the experts advocating service excellence, such as Fred Reichheld (1996) and James L. Heskett, W. Earl Sasser, and Leonard A. Schlesinger (1997), admit that there are bad customers. However, the lifetime value of these customers might not match the costs to service them. They might not be loyal, sometimes coming to you to buy your products and other times buying from a competitor, or their CAC may far outweigh their return on investment.

Bad customers can be financially and emotionally taxing, so much so you actually lose money as you spend a disproportionate amount of time serving their difficult-to-satisfy needs. So while your talent development business offers a service to customers, you should not feel beholden to the matra customer is always right.

You want customers who not only desire and appreciate help, but who are also willing to participate in the collaborative relationship required of a true partnership—one that almost always ensures a successful outcome. Such relationships are the basis for long-term loyal customer interactions. In fact, happy customers spend 140 percent more than unhappy ones and tell an average of nine people about their experience (Markidan 2014). They are also easier to resell to than having to approach new prospects. But even if you focus on shaping relationships at the outset, ensuring expectations are clear not only about the deliverables and their associated costs, not all your customers will be perfect. So how do you "fire" a bad customer?

Signs That a Client Should Be Fired

We have all worked with customers who are delightful people and mean no intentional harm, but we still wanted to fire them. In some cases, they made it very difficult to complete the work on time in a high-quality manner because they were not responsive. For example, you might not have been able to get a hold of them without sending multiple emails and voicemails.

Then there are those clients who do not review various versions of the deliverables, even though they agreed to as part of their contract. I had such an experience with a customer. When the customer looked at the last review of a program that was ready to go live the following week, she communicated that it wasn't what she wanted despite approving the design weeks before. I ended up being her scapegoat and was forced to settle for half of the contracted project fees. If you are in a similar position, it can be tough to swallow. You may be upset, but it's important to remain ethical and professional in dealing with an unfortunate situation.

To avoid this happening again, you need to recognize when to let go of bad customers. Every minute you spend trying to address a bad customer's issues is a minute you lose satisfying the good ones (Markidan 2014). I developed five major categories with a colleague to assess when it's time to move on: integrity, professional, personal, interpersonal, and organizational (Cohen and Reinhart 2000).

- **Integrity:** Misrepresentation of the company's need for your services; kickback suggestions to return something to them, typically money under the table for their willingness to do business with you (which actually happened to me); going back on one's word, such as subsequently disagreeing with a signed agreement.

- **Professional:** Bad mouthing colleagues and other departments; changing dates and commitments at the last minute; changing expectations in the middle of a project; not agreeing to pay you for work you have done; blaming you for a failure you didn't have anything to do with that would save face for the client.
- **Personal:** Unrealistic demands that interfere with completing the agreed-to work; repeated changes in scope because of personal reasons that might cause suspicions about the real reasons for the changes.
- **Interpersonal:** Disrespectful behavior and rudeness; talking behind one's back; excusing oneself in the middle of a requested and scheduled presentation without apology.
- **Organizational:** Culture and political dysfunction; blocking access to key stakeholders.

Bad customers can require constant contact, be abusive to your staff, receive complaints from their own staff, frequently swap vendors and tell everyone about it, question even agreed-upon invoices, continually change work scope, are frequently unavailable, and constantly try gaming the system (van Opzeeland 2015). If a customer demonstrates any (or all) of these characteristics, it's probably time to end your partnership.

Effectively Leaving Your Customers

Is there a way to predict that someone will be a bad customer before you work with one? Probably not, unless you were warned by colleagues who already experienced one. You may be able to pick up on signs during the prospecting, contracting, and selling process. For example, they are more difficult to deal with up front, they rarely compliment your work, they always complain about some aspect, they are quick to throw you under the bus, or they are constantly posturing and covering their butts. You may hear their own employees tell stories about their bad behavior and privately agree with your verbalized observations in passing.

Even though you know that the customer is not always right, you might still find it difficult to let them go. However, there are many ways to leave your customers:

- **Say goodbye:** Be simple but straightforward while being polite, positive, and appreciative. Finish what you are currently working on for them. You still don't want to leave them in a lurch. Maintain your professional approach at all times.

- **Tell it like it is:** Express your dissatisfaction with the working conditions and make it clear that you aren't providing them with your best output. Be honest regarding why the relationship isn't working, as long as you say goodbye in a professional manner. Who knows, the dialogue may open your customers' eyes.
- **Quit but stay:** Grin and bear it by completing all that you owe them and never work for them again.
- **Leave without pay:** It's difficult to do but also quite admirable. It allows all to save face as you settle up.
- **Negotiate a settlement:** A little better than not being paid but worth trying. Perhaps this might include reframing the situation so that the customer sees it as an advantage.
- **Do whatever you're told:** It's hard to swallow, but it's another grin and bear it approach. It's the old "just do it" mantra, but never darken their doors again.
- **Bide your time:** Get comfortable with where you are in the workflow and explore how you may have contributed to the problem. Learn from it.

Of course, you can combine any of these options, which will depend on how long you have served the client, how many other projects you have with that client and your other clients, and how many other parts of their organization you or your colleagues are working with.

But don't confuse a challenging customer with a bad one. By actually solving that customer's problem, you could improve your offer for many others. While bad customers are rude and abrasive, make unreasonable demands, and threaten to complain about you to everyone they can, they are not necessarily bad people. These situations may not warrant any service recovery strategy, just one for service ending.

Conclusion

At the end of the day, you should keep several things in mind when serving customers. Most important, without them you have no business. On the other hand, difficult to satisfy customers can lead to unprofitable business in both the short and long term. If you spend all your time, money, and effort trying to satisfy them, you are taking valuable resources away from good customers who are willing to partner with you, provide a pleasant mutually beneficial experience, and ultimately recommend you to others.

Reflection Questions

SERVER OR SERVANT?: CUSTOMER SERVICE TODAY

- How have you gone about choosing your customers?
- Why do your buyers want you to continue to serve them?
- How aligned are your brand promise and value proposition with your business' s demonstrated behavior with your customers?
- Why are your customers loyal to you?
- How are you measuring the loyalty of your customers?
- What strategies can you use to ensure that your customer service is top-notch?

GETTING LESS FOR MORE: CUSTOMER ACQUISITION COSTS

- What are your customer acquisition costs?
- How do they compare for current for new customers?
- What can you do to improve your CAC?

WHY, WHEN, AND HOW TO FIRE YOUR CUSTOMERS: ASSESSING CUSTOMER WORTH

- What signs signal a bad customer?
- What have you done with your bad customers?
- How are they different from good customers? How have you dealt with them?
- What have you done to fire them?

PART 3

MOVING FORWARD

OVERCOMING BARRIERS TO GROWTH AND SUCCESS

Problems do not go away. They must be worked
through or else they remain, forever a barrier to the
growth and development of the spirit.
—M. Scott Peck

This book is meant to offer you some best practices for building a successful business. So I would be remiss if I didn't explore the barriers that can impede success and the ways you can overcome them. Knowing about these potential barriers ahead of time will help you overcome them. This chapter offers lessons in building a successful business in the talent development area. We'll start with the most important lesson of all. Keep your eyes open and your head out of the sand.

Putting Your Head in the Sand: A Recipe for Failure

Previous chapters discussed the five ingredients necessary to achieve success: financial health, value creation, your special sauce, strong management, and a business development engine. But what is likely to happen if you do not include these ingredients in your strategic and execution plans? Well, the absence of any one of the five is likely to make it more difficult to succeed. But what else could get in the way of success?

A few barriers come to mind. The first is relying on just one product or service. Certainly, many firms are known for, and in fact built on, one training product, software program, assessment inventory, or unique business service. But few have shown sustained growth without expanding their offer, even if that means creating off-shoots or extensions of their foundational program. Once clients have bought and used that offer, they will look for the next product or service from that company, especially if they have had a positive experience with the first one. Because we also know the cost of obtaining business from a current customer is significantly lower than finding a new one, it behooves a supplier to continue to upsell and cross-sell with new products and services.

A second barrier is when a firm's guru or visionary loses his leadership performance capability or interest. The very traits and capabilities that made the founder so successful often get in the way of growing the business. Recall my example of Larry Wilson in chapter 1. If the founder can't step away when it becomes evident his management competence has peaked, the company will likely flounder.

The third barrier, very much related to the founders' problem, is the tendency to look for the next best thing. Never satisfied with simply improving what they have already created, they much prefer to create what hasn't yet been discovered. It is inherent in their entrepreneurial nature to pursue the next big thing. This lack of focus not only causes chaos among their employees but ends up taking attention from the original product or service that got the company off the ground. As a result, the business becomes stale, doesn't keep up with new customer needs, and becomes open for competitive sniping.

Finally, as organizations grow they become more dependent on the quality of talent they bring in, develop, and retain. Meanwhile, the founders have either moved on to something better in their minds or are no longer with the firm. The irony is that by not paying attention to the talent management demands of their own talent development business, the firm is likely to fail.

That said, every failure provides an opportunity for future success. Mistakes can serve as the foundation for success if they're taken seriously and learned from. The argument for the idea of "failing first, learning next, improving thereafter" has some currency. Failing fast and often could provide the stepping stones to success. George Vukotich (2016, 27-29), the senior vice president of programming at 1871, a business and innovation incubator, argues that "failing fast is good for business," stating it often can be the quickest and least expensive way to learn—and in many cases create the shortest path to success, particularly for start-up and small organizations looking to grow.

Vukotich cites a study by CB Insights reporting the top 20 reasons start-ups fail, offering multiple reasons why failing faster is a good thing. Among the top reason were no market need (42 percent of failures), ran out of cash (29 percent), not the right team (23 percent), got outcompeted (19 percent), pricing (18 percent), cost issues (17 percent), poor product (17 percent), and need or lack of business model (17 percent). Any of these reasons could easily stunt growth, not just contribute to failure.

So what are some of the mistakes typically made in creating a successful talent development firm? Perhaps too many to list, but here's a start, sorted by category. Most of these have been represented, in one way or the other, in previous chapters, so you might want to check off those that resonate with you.

People

- Hiring successful product salespeople to sell pure consulting services and vice-versa.
- Hiring the wrong sales leaders (or no one at all).
- Selecting an unqualified or inexperienced business partner.
- Relying too much on others to make the business work for you.
- Conducting careless background checks regardless of who recommended the potential hire.
- Poorly communicating to your staff what's in it for them.
- Allowing poor performers to stay on longer than they should.
- Hiring the wrong finance director.

Marketing and Offer

- Having an unclear vision of where you want to go and when you want to get there.
- Branding unclearly and ambiguously.
- Being unable to live up to your value proposition.
- Using a poorly thought-out project management system to deliver your offer.
- Trying to become all things to all clients and not focusing on your strengths.
- Not understanding successful product development is best attained through the collaboration of a variety of people, knowledge, and experience.
- Making claims of effectiveness of your offer you can't support.
- Failing to develop a marketing plan that incorporates updated online tools.

Operations

- Failing to create a strategic plan or not adhering to one you have created.
- Not turning over your finances to a qualified person or firm.
- Merging your business or selling it for the wrong reason (for example, to pay off your debt, to get out of dealing with administrative demands, or to free you up to write a book).
- Being too inflexible to adapt to market changes.

- Handing off responsibility for overall operations to someone without staying closely in touch with the business.
- Merging pure consulting services with a pure product offer.
- Not employing appropriate legal counsel.
- Not protecting your intellectual property.
- Failing to understand the intricacies of expanding internationally before doing so.
- Assuming you can't be ripped off because you have copyrighted all your materials.
- Misunderstanding the legal parameters of different sales channels, such as licensees, distributors, and partners.

Industry

- Applying other industry principles of success to how you run your business (for example, assuming the publishing business is the same as the talent development business because both produce books and manuals).
- Not applying universal principles that work from other industries.
- Failing to understand the competitive landscape of the industry.
- Not understanding the most likely industry trends and altering your offer to take them into account.

Personal

- Not listening to your employees about problem staff members.
- Checking out of the business before it is operating smoothly and profitably.
- Taking excessive time off.
- Showing off your financial success in the face of others' struggles, especially if the business is teetering.
- Taking most of the credit for your success without giving proper recognition and credit to others.
- Turning the business over to your yet-to-be qualified family members or putting them in positions that readily expose their inadequacies.

As you review this list, some items may appear obvious, others not so much. The only caveat is that not all mistakes happen all the time. There are plenty of exceptions to every rule.

And here is the good news. We all can learn from our mistakes as long as we know when we made them, why we did so, and how we can avoid them in the future. Julian Birkinshaw and Martine Haas (2016) call it "return on failure," suggesting you can increase your acceptance of failure by simply recognizing the benefits of failed projects, the customer insights gained, the people involved, and the make-up of your organization. They suggest assessing the assets and liabilities of failed initiatives, sharing lessons learned, and understanding if there are any patterns of yours and your organization's failures.

Dodging Hurdles:
Enabling Success by Avoiding Barriers

Over the years, I have watched the industry survive the ups and downs of the global economy. Simultaneously, I have seen the corporate world realize the strategic value that the human capital asset can create. Through these and others' observations, several best practices have come into focus that may help you think through what needs to be put in place to ensure the long-term success of a talent development firm (Rosen 2016).

Continuous Innovation

It's difficult to sustain long-term growth in the talent development industry—or any industry, for that matter—without continuous innovation and reinvention to reflect evolving and maturing customer demands. For instance, the introduction of technology-enabled talent development solutions alone has significantly changed and will continue to alter the competitive landscape. Unfortunately, the talent development industry has a long way to go before it can comfortably predict its future business success.

Growth Planning

There is little substitute for strategic growth planning, particularly in an evolving industry. The challenge is how to stabilize your plan in such conditions. Suffice it to say, five-year horizons are too far off to think that today's plan will still be relevant. Instead, growth planning should focus on the short term, somewhere within the two- to three-year window. More important, every plan needs to be reviewed frequently for relevance and revised to meet ever-changing customer needs. As the saying goes, if you don't take the time to plan for the future, the future will plan for you.

Of course, most plans fail not because of how they're constructed, but because of how they're executed. Firms should not position growth planning as an exercise to appease leaders, partners, and customers who want to know where the business is headed. Rather, growth planning should lay out an executable plan to achieve a specific vision. If leaders fail to share the plan with the entire organization or simply translate it into execution and accountability goals, it isn't worth the paper on which it was written.

Solid Bench of Committed Practitioners

It certainly shouldn't shock anyone in this industry how important it is to recruit, select, develop, and retain the right people. This is particularly critical for your business, which likely relies heavily on expertise and experience to serve its customers. After all, this is what we profess to our own clients. Unfortunately, the talent development industry doesn't always follow its own advice. Indeed, contrary to logical expectations, many talent development firms are not the best at managing their own human capital.

Regardless of how well your mission, vision, values, and strategic plan are spelled out, you can only hope your employees are equally committed to carrying them out the way you thought they should be. Surely, you can influence and to some degree even control how they operate, but having a group of committed co-workers who buy into your vision will go a long way toward enabling the success of the business, even if other key elements are missing or incomplete. Committed, passionate employees help you get things in order if they are out of sync.

Visionary Leadership

Without strong and insightful leadership, few companies in any space will survive very long—at least not without great cost and pain. Two distinct sets of competencies are needed for leaders to be effective, especially in relatively small entrepreneurial environments. First, leaders must possess a long-term vision for the business—the ability to see the forest for the trees. Second, leaders must be operationally effective and understand the various business levers they will need to pull—the ability to achieve the vision. Unfortunately, these capabilities are hard to find in a single leader. In fact, they seem to be at opposite ends of the continuum. At minimum, leaders' deficiencies need to be buttressed by those around them.

Too often, though, many talent development firm founders refuse to relinquish their duties to others with much better qualifications and experience, particularly with financial and back-office operations, as well as customer-facing areas such as business development and marketing. Strong leaders will surround themselves with people who are much better equipped to address the challenges of each business function. It's more than just delegation and empowerment; it's getting out of the way.

Pipeline of Motivated Prospects

Without customers, you will have no business. So getting and keeping them happy is critical to your success, which takes time, skill, and leadership through a smooth-running business development engine. There are many prospects to draw from and no one company in the talent development industry owns them all.

Indeed, even the best and largest suppliers have a relatively small percentage of the total potential customer base. If your focus is on the Fortune 500, for example, having a 10 percent share would be very desirable. There is an abundance of potential customers who could use talent development products and services. The key is how to reach, identify, and bring in prospects who will ultimately provide a long-term sustainable base. That is, how can you motivate your prospects to become paying clients?

Certainly, your offer and the way it is messaged are key to attaining a pipeline of motivated prospects. However, some organizations are just not interested in what you have to offer, and no matter your efforts you will be unable to motivate them to buy. Still, other organizations might not really know what they need to improve their talent development performance. Any compelling message that can initially reach and attract them could ultimately lead to a prospect motivated enough to remain a client.

Dependable Sales Engine

Your business development engine plays a key role in obtaining clients. As you may recall, if any components of the business change so must the sales engine. However, this isn't always feasible, at least not in the short term. New offers may be created, while old ones are shelved. New people may come on board, while experienced employees retire. The most important element of a sales engine is how dependable it is under changing circumstances. It is like a house. If the structural bones are in place, it will stand the test of time regardless of what renovations are made. The house will be dependable because the foundation is strong and reliable. This is no different for the sales engine in your business.

Success Disasters

Let's assume you feel pretty good about having most, if not all, of the success enablers noted above in place in your business. Congratulations. But the reality is that despite your success, you may still have to worry about one more thing: the potential disaster that your success could bring. Most notably, you may be growing so rapidly that you and your senior leadership can't keep up. This may mean you can't hire fast enough, develop the people you have to take on greater roles and responsibilities, or sustain the capital to purchase better and larger back-office systems.

If you can't keep up with your client's demand you will end up failing to deliver on your promise. Many small companies are not savvy enough to recognize this, but if they can plan for it, they can implement the changes necessary for growth. You may argue this is a nice problem to have and you are willing to do what it takes to make it work, but you may not be the right person to take the business to the next level. Will you be prepared to let go to grow?

Managing Your Circles: Making a Difference

To overcome barriers to growth, you have to decide where to devote your time and energy. If you are spending a disproportionate amount of time putting out fires, this is time you aren't devoting to growing your business. On the other hand, if you let a flame grow into a forest fire, it can be devastating for the growth of your business. You have to toe the line between managing everyday barriers and attending to the details of long-range growth.

One way to take on these barriers is to figure out how to manage what's in front of you. A great model for assessing this comes from Stephen Covey's *7 Habits of Highly Effective People* (2004). Covey states that highly effective people know how to compartmentalize what they can actually influence versus what they should be concerned about but not necessarily possess the circumstances to truly manage. He called these the circles of influence and concern.

The circle of concern includes what you truly care about in terms of personal issues such as health, career, and relationships to more global challenges, such as climate change, war, and the economy. The circle of influence encompasses what you have the power to influence and it is typically smaller than the circle of concern. Covey recommends widening your circle of influence thus reducing the size of your circle of concern. In essence, this gives you more control over your life and the decisions you make. He says the problems most people face fall into one of three area direct control (problems involving one's own behavior), indirect control (problems involving other people's behavior), and no control (problems we can do nothing about such as our past or the realities of the present).

What has always been surprising, however, is that Covey never talked about a "circle of control" even though he acknowledges that these three areas of problems involve control. Indeed, there are really three circles, with the inner-most being the circle of control. Clearly the more you can enlarge this circle the smaller those of concern and influence will be. Granted, none of us have total control, but we have options that can make a huge difference in overcoming barriers to our success. So the model should look something like Figure 9-1.

Figure 9-1. Three Circles of Self-Management

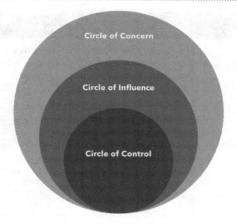

At the end of the day, you have to make decisions that will help your business succeed. You must then figure out which issues and challenges are game stoppers. Which of those appear disastrous but are really only blips on the screen soon to pass? Figuring out the most important elements of your business model and what can impede its success is your number one priority. What you can control, influence, or be concerned about will influence the degree to which you should and can be involved in how your business is run.

Taking into account the size of your business, your role in it, and some gray areas between circles, Table 9-1 provides some examples that might spur your thinking and help you focus, or refocus, the amount of time you are spending overcoming barriers to growth.

When you face a problem or challenge that impedes growth, you need to figure out how you would classify it. If it's in the circle of control, what can you do to manage it? Once you know, act quickly and decisively to do so. If it's in the circle of influence, what's the likelihood your influence will have any affect on the results? That is, rather than obsess about something you would like to fix but aren't likely to given the circumstances, your time would be better spent on changes that can be made. When something outside your influence becomes the center of your attention, more critical issues aren't typically addressed. If it is difficult to resolve, then cut your losses early and move on. Similarly, the argument applies to your circle of concern. Again, it's not worth your time to obsess about something that will have little to no influence on the growth and success of your business. Choose carefully, prioritize, and act on what will make a difference.

Table 9-1. Managing Your Barriers to Growth

Circle of Control	Circle of Influence	Circle of Concern
Mission, vision, values	How work gets done	How your competitors are doing
Performance expectations and standards	Performance and productivity	Industry dynamics and trends
Financial goals	Knowing what others need	Copyright and IP laws
Capital expenses	Value creation	Claims of effectiveness of competing programs
Knowing what you want	Business focus	How the industry goes to market
Industry knowledge	Execution	The future of the industry
Hiring and firing decisions	Morals and ethics	Industry disruption
Marketing messaging	Culture	Competitive landscape
Personal communications	Back-office processes and systems	Emergence of technology solutions
Risk management	Service quality	Bad customers
Exit strategies	Strategic planning	External environment
Advisory board selection	Advisory board members	Advisory board behavior
Senior team selection and development	Senior team performance and development	Senior team behavior

Advisory Boards: Why and Why Not?

Perhaps the best way to overcome, if not entirely avoid, barriers to growth is to engage and embrace the experience, expertise, and wisdom of those who can help you navigate the many challenges your business will face. By seeking external help from experienced business leaders, you can gain access to key connections. Your advisory board can hold your senior team accountable for decisions, advocate for game-changing ideas, and obtain commitment for taking productive action.

I have been extremely fortunate to have served on 15 formal or informal advisory boards of firms in the training and education/talent development industry. These have included small $1-10 million skill training companies, larger $15-50 million compliance education businesses, a $100 million private secondary school system, and even a more than $125 million college.

So what is the role of an advisory board and when is one needed? How might you go about forming and evaluating one? To be clear, the difference between boards of public versus private companies is relatively simple. The former not only includes true fiduciary responsibilities but also legal accountability, whereas the latter only requests advice and does not require any legal obligation. Where the advisory-only capacity for a privately held company might cross over into a stronger fiduciary role is when members are also investors and own stock in the business or when the company has been formed under certain legal parameters such as an ESOP (Employee Stock Option Plan).

Let's address the private businesses in the industry contemplating either forming their own board or rethinking their current one. There are really only four overarching steps to creating an advisory board:

1. determining the need
2. identifying the advisers
3. managing the board
4. evaluating the board's performance.

Advisory Boards in the Talent Development Industry

You've likely read about the involvement and importance of boards for public companies. But what about in the talent development supplier industry? Consider some small survey data on how talent development suppliers have used these boards. One study surveyed 25 companies whose average size was $21.6 million and had been in business for an average of 26 years. Seventy-one percent had some form of board. The average board had five members, three of whom were external to the business and one of whom was from outside the talent development industry. Typically, no term limits were given and there was typically a board chair who was either internal or external to the business. The average meeting occurred every three and half months for a five-hour session. The average fee paid for each full meeting was $3,150, plus travel expenses. The most discussed topics tended to be about strategic issues and operational challenges. In the end, most respondents believed their boards provided significant value and help and that the time and money spent was well worth it (Cohen and Whiteley 2015).

Determining the Need

Why do you need a board? Is it worth the additional time, commitment, and money you currently are not using? The simple answer is to provide you with outside strategic guidance. But a board is also theoretically designed to hold the CEO accountable by periodically monitoring the performance of the business. A board should not be involved in the day-to-day operations of the business although it should fully understand how the business works. A truly value-added board will keep its firm from making costly mistakes so it can actually help grow the business.

"Done right, a formal Board can accelerate success and reassure all stakeholders," says David Shaw (2013), founder and CEO of Knightsbridge Human Capital Solutions. He says the benefits of a formally constituted board, beyond holding the CEO accountable, include providing comfort to financial institution lenders, protecting shareholder interests of all investors beyond majority stakeholders, and offering an independent and diverse external voice. Boards can also help ensure the right balance between how much you are working "on the business" versus "in the business," help you map the direction of your business, and help you move from an entrepreneurial to a professionally managed firm.

Identifying the Advisers

How do you select a board? Foremost, you want advisers who have "been there, done that," people who either have an expertise in an area relatively deficient in the business or have extensive industry experience or success growing a business in a similar or adjacent industry.

Gaps in expertise that would benefit from an outside board member include customer relations management, social media and Internet marketing, international expansion, sales and channel distribution, legal and compliance issues, product development, and operations. Filling a board with outside expertise that closes some of these gaps is a strategically sound investment, both in terms of the money and time it will save you.

Should board members be current or prospective clients? While certainly a case could be made for this, I would advocate that it's not a good idea for at least two reasons. The first is the buyer-seller relationship you either have or will have will be compromised. In fact, your client may not even be able to purchase from you because of the conflict of interest. Second, this type of board member may not be open and honest with you for fear of undermining that relationship. That said, it is beneficial to have a former buyer of either your own offer or other companies in the industry. Such a person can provide critical insight into the buying process of programs and services from a customer's perspective.

Your board members should also embrace and share the values and management style of your business so they are not behaving or speaking inconsistently with your persona. This doesn't mean they have to look and talk like you. In fact, it's better to have board members who have different but complementary styles and are comfortable challenging one another during difficult times. Above all, they should come with very good reputations. Well thought of and respected board members can serve as a credibility builder for both internal and external interests.

Managing a Board

What are your board members' responsibilities? Their greatest value is in helping you think and act at a strategic level based on past experience and knowledge. In addition, they should be called on as advisers in your succession planning process, as a fresh pair of eyes to review the integrity of your financials, and even as an external monitor of the culture of your company. The challenge for you and your board members is to know when to take charge, when to partner, and when to stay out of the way (Charan, Casey, and Useem 2014). This will vary depending on the structure and ownership of your business. A venture capital equity owned firm will undoubtedly be more involved in the business than those serving more in a mentoring capacity or those meeting infrequently to conduct a "smell" test of how the business is performing.

How often, how long, or even how your board meetings are conducted will depend on your specific needs. Some boards meet monthly or quarterly; others twice a year. Most find in-person meetings the most productive but many smaller firms who can't consistently afford the travel and fees associated with a board meeting conduct them virtually. Some complement in-person meetings with periodic conference calls. Ultimately, the responsibility for ensuring overall board effectiveness rests with you, the owner or CEO of the business, or in some cases a designated board chair.

Board Committees

Creating important committees is another facet of board management. Almost all firms establish compensation and CEO performance evaluation committees. Others create a financial affairs sub-committee as well. And some combine them. In addition, ad hoc committees are often established to assist with special projects and challenges. For example, in the event of merger or acquisition opportunities, there may be a subset of the board that oversees the work involved in making decisions.

Be sure to formalize whatever arrangement you have established. Get a signed nondisclosure agreement (NDA) and a noncompete agreement fully describing your expectations for board members, as well as the fees and expenses you will pay them and their length of tenure on the board. Board continuity serves companies well, but as the business evolves and grows, it's a good idea to rotate in board members to bring in new experiences. Board members who stay on too long can get too complacent and may not want to rock the boat. The issue of term limits has reasonable pros and cons. In either case, however, a mechanism should be put in place to periodically evaluate board member performance. Finally, well-managed boards have a formal agenda; updated financial and sales and marketing results, which are provided before each meeting, and an executive session conducted by the board at the end of the meeting to give feedback to the CEO.

Evaluating the Board's Performance

How do you evaluate a board? Whether it is new or long-standing, the board should be periodically assessed to determine whether you are getting what you expected from each member, individually as well as collectively. According to a survey conducted by the National Association of Corporate Directors, more than 90 percent of boards conduct full evaluations and almost 83 percent conduct committee evaluations. But less than half of boards said they evaluate individual directors (Gwin and Vavrek 2011, 68-69). While these results generally describe larger companies with public boards, we can extrapolate that evaluations are essential to good governance practices. The type and extent of these evaluations depends in large part on the type of board; for example, to keep the company in compliance with government or industry requirements; to oversee and monitor their company's strategic objectives; or to engage in internal talent development, succession planning, and overall capability development. The background of the directors needed to meet these three type of boards will be different and should be evaluated as such.

It's critical to determine which of the following nine potential areas for board evaluation are most important to your business given the time of the evaluation, and understanding that business needs will undoubtedly change over time.

- **Acceleration:** challenging the business to think out-of-the-box by facilitating rapid yet thoughtful decision making and innovative growth
- **Access:** providing connections to relevant people and organizations that can provide information conducive to the effective operation and growth of the business
- **Accountability:** holding the CEO and senior team to do what they say they will do by periodically checking on, probing, and challenging progress status
- **Achievement:** challenging the business to not only reach, but exceed, its measureable goals and objectives in a predictably frequent manner
- **Action:** encouraging and supporting positive movement toward growth objectives aligned with the business's mission, purpose, and values

- **Advantage:** ensuring the business is continually competitive in its marketplace through intelligent decision making and forethought
- **Advice:** offering strategic insight and perspective on operational, business development, talent management, and overall growth challenges
- **Alignment:** monitoring the consistency of the organization's vision, mission, and values with its daily operating activities and decisions
- **Assessment:** periodically evaluating the organization's individual talent, culture, and performance

Whether you are contemplating creating a board or seeking to evaluate its performance, Appendix C offers a form based on thse nine factors (Cohen and Whiteley, 2014). If the former, it can be used to help you assess what you want to get from a board before selecting it. If the latter, then you can not only assess what is important to you but also how your board is performing against those criteria.

Interestingly, a survey conducted by McKinsey in 2013 on board responsibilities illustrated some startling results. Only 34 percent of 772 directors surveyed agreed the boards on which they served fully understood their companies' strategies. Furthermore, only 22 percent said their boards were fully aware of how their companies created value, and just 16 percent claimed their boards had a strong understanding of the dynamics of the companies' industry (Barton and Wiseman 2015). This would seem to be a basic requirement of any board member for any business; otherwise, how can a director offer counsel without frequently invoking, "this is the way we did it in my industry (or at my company)." Furthermore, when asked what their boards could do better to help the company, CEOs consistently responded with just five items:

1. Focus on the risks most crucial to the company's future.
2. Do your homework.
3. Bring broad relevant knowledge to the table.
4. Do more to constructively challenge strategy.
5. Make succession less disruptive to the business (Sonnenfeld, Kusin, and Walton 2013).

While these CEOs were from major public corporations, these lessons can also be applied at a smaller talent development firm.

That said, the key to what makes a great board great is less structural and procedural than it is social. As Jeffrey Sonnenfeld (2002) has stated from his years of experience studying board effectiveness, "The most involved, diligent, value-adding boards may or may not follow every recommendation in the good-governance handbook. What distinguishes exemplary boards is that they are robust, effective social systems." What he meant by this is they are characterized by:

- a virtuous cycle of respect, trust, and candor
- a culture of open dissent
- a fluid portfolio of roles
- individual accountability
- performance evaluation.

As you consider establishing a board or evaluating the performance of your existing one, use the research and observations here to optimize its value to you and your business.

Conclusion

Success is often fleeting, so the real question is not as much how you achieve it but rather how you sustain it. Anyone who has been in or run a business recognizes that failure can come at any time due to unforeseen and unimaginable economic, environmental, technological, and personal changes. Plan as we may, the future does have a plan of its own. If this weren't the case, there wouldn't be an insurance industry.

What insurance can you put in place to navigate the chaotic waters? Certainly, accepting their eventuality is a good first step because it will keep you on the lookout for signs that things may be changing. Going full bore without looking both behind and to your sides is a recipe for failure. Asking for and accepting assistance from those who have experience can help you avoid calamitous mistakes. It's also important to be proactive in first identifying the signs and then addressing them with realistic and measured solutions. You might not avoid all of them, but at least you will be prepared and not surprised if they emerge.

Reflection Questions

Putting Your Head in the Sand: A Recipe for Failure

- There are numerous ingredients for failure among talent development firms, many of which aren't unique to the industry. What others have you observed and even experienced?
- Which ones worry you the most regarding your own business and what are you doing about managing away from them?
- What mistakes have you made and what have you learned from them?

DODGING HURDLES: ENABLING SUCCESS FACTORS BY AVOIDING BARRIERS

- Of the critical success factors noted, which ones are you most comfortable with in your own business, and why?
- What can you do to improve in those areas you aren't so strong?
- What have you observed about the overall pattern of critical success factors in other outside suppliers with whom you have dealt?
- Are there any signs of your business running into a "success disaster?"

MANAGING YOUR CIRCLES: MAKING A DIFFERENCE

- What are some of the barriers to growth you have faced?
- What have you done to overcome them?
- What are the relative sizes of your circles of control, influence, and concern?
- How have you altered their size to fit the needs of your business?

ADVISORY BOARDS: WHY AND WHY NOT?

- What are your business needs that would make you consider creating an advisory board?
- Which of the board performance criteria are most important to your business now and why?
- What do you expect to get from your board?
- If you currently have a board, how would you evaluate its performance on the nine contribution areas, as well as Sonnenfeld's five factors for creating a great board?

10

ESTABLISHING YOUR GROWTH PLAN AND EXITING

It is always wise to look ahead, but
difficult to look further than you can see.
—Winston Churchill

Perhaps the most difficult aspect of building and running any business is anticipating the future. Certainly, you can assume that some events are likely to happen; although you may not know when. For example, the economy will ebb and flow; when and by how much is more difficult to predict. Knowing that you cannot necessarily foresee the future means that you should at least prepare for it, whether by being extra conservative or by devoting all your time, effort, and money to only one product system or market.

Disruption strikes every industry. At some point, the talent development industry will likely face its own "black swan," or unpredictable event (Taleb 2007). One might argue whatever it is and whenever it takes place will affect everyone the same way, unless you can somehow get out in front of it (Read or watch *The Big Short* for an example of how a very few were able to predict a future that others weren't able to see, and how they profited handsomely.) This chapter addresses ways to grow, regardless of what may happen in the future, possible disruptions on the horizon, and how to think about and plan for your own exit strategy.

Pathways to Growth: Let Me Count the Ways

Paving your pathway to growth is much more difficult than simply following a straight line. Growth is a multi-evel proposition for improving both the top and bottom lines and there are many strategies for each. It also depends on where you are and where you want to go. For example, as you move from a startup to even a couple of million dollars in revenue, you will have to grow by converting what might be a small practice into a full-fledged business (chapter 2). When you get to $5 million in revenue you will need to start thinking about putting a formal infrastructure in place. As you double in size, you will need to hire and involve managers who understand what needs to be done to sustain growth at that level. From there, these factors multiply several times. Relatively few consulting businesses ever reach $20 million. These revenue milestones will require a different pathway to growth or at least a different emphasis on how to grow.

This book is not just about the talent development supplier industry, in general. It is more specifically about building and growing a business in this space. Once entrepreneurs get off the ground, they often wonder how they can not only sustain their businesses but also make them successful. Growth is high on the list of interests of most suppliers. In fact, the Instructional Systems Association (ISA), a trade group of about 80 learning and development suppliers, conducted a survey to identify what its members most wanted to discuss at its 2016 annual conference. A survey asked 71 companies to rate 13 topics, which had been suggested to ISA in recent years, on which were first, second, and third most important. The four leading topics, regardless of company size, were "overall company growth," "marketing tools to accelerate growth," "structure and growth for sales and marketing," and "company growth through partnerships and acquisitions" (ISA 2016).

With growth in mind, business leaders must build the appropriate infrastructure, strategy, competitive offer, and business model that will sustainably deliver the results they seek. They must create quality content and products, find and onboard sales talent, add new markets and penetrate existing ones, and balance between analog and digital marketing tools.

Keep in mind that the opposite of growth is failure. In fact, this is the very premise of George Ainsworth-Land's seminal book, *Grow or Die* (1973), which we explore in more detail later. Ainsworth-Land was the first to posit transformation theory in which he described the structure of change in all natural systems, including organizations. If systems don't grow they atrophy at best and die at worst.

This section will identify ways to grow and explore comparative analysis. But you cannot tackle the ultimate challenge of business growth without a little structure. While the following categories are pitted against each other, because the tactics are different for each, this is not to say you can't do both. At the risk of oversimplifying these categories, let's start with the highest level: organic versus inorganic.

Organic Versus Inorganic

Organic growth involves building on an existing structure and system, whereas inorganic growth generally entails the purchase of companies that are bolted-on to the original structure. The rationale for focusing on inorganic growth is that it can relatively quickly increase top- and bottom-line numbers, as well as EBITDA, assuming a healthy add-on. The traditional rationale for these add-ons is to either fill existing holes in the current offer or spread out the offer into new markets. The downside involves possibly disrupting both the acquiring and acquired businesses with the integration of different cultures, processes, and systems that are difficult to manage. To mitigate this downside, many acquiring companies allow the acquired ones to stand alone until they can be integrated. However, companies can grow fast organically, although without a significant capital infusion the growth might not occur as quickly. Then again, organic growth can be less painful and perhaps build on a stronger foundation.

Customer Expansion Versus Penetration

No business can succeed without a steady stream of customers. When it comes to growth, adding new customers and penetrating current ones offer two paths forward. Because it costs more to earn a new customer than it does to get an existing one to purchase more, customer penetration may seem like the most direct and immediately effective approach to growth. However, relying solely on mining existing customers can be dangerous. You cannot expect them to repeatedly come back, and at some point, you will fully tap the potential business you can win from them. Expanding your customer base not only opens new doors but naturally broadens the potential for subsequently penetrating those new customers. Without paying attention to expanding your customer base, your growth will start to slow as current customers become former ones.

Restricted Versus Broadened Distribution

Where you distribute products and services offers other paths to growth. One option is to focus locally by state or region. Becoming a well-known business in a certain geographic area can spur growth, but depending on the region's size and make-up, this could be very limiting. A natural approach in most industries calls for broadening your geographic footprint, ultimately internationally, rather than only serving a local market. Domestic expansion typically involves creating a presence with either feet on the ground or local offices, all of which adds to managing expenses and people. However, it does not present the same challenges as moving internationally. Many businesses in the talent development supplier industry have stumbled over exchange rates, local production capabilities, language barriers, and ownership or licensing considerations when expanding internationally. Several talent development businesses have expanded internationally by providing licensed distribution in other countries, only to subsequently buy them back to gain more control over delivery quality and financial accounting.

You can also add channels that serve additional markets and industries. For example, you might start out servicing the corporate marketplace and discover that with a little tweaking your offer could serve the primary education market as well. Consider Grace Hill, which caters to the multifamily housing industry—apartment complexes, military housing, and college dorms—all linked by the need to comply with fair housing legislation. To go beyond just teaching compliance, Grace Hill expanded its offer to other areas, such as leasing, maintenance, office management, and even leadership. Or consider Mintra Group, based in Norway. It focuses on compliance and safety in the oil and gas industry, particularly serving ocean rigs. Mintra Group realized that both the maritime and shipping and construction industries face similar issues as the oil and gas industry and thus offered the possibility of transferring its current programs and services to these industries with relatively little adaptation.

Another growth option is to license tools and programs to smaller and local consulting practices already working with clients in industries you would have trouble reaching. This allows you to simply rely on your partners to do the selling, while you focus on product development. Depending on the structure of the licensing deal, this can be a very profitable way to grow, boosting both top- and bottom-line financial performance. If the deal permits the licensee to produce or publish the materials, you can see extremely large profit margins. In fact, the revenue may all drop to the bottom line, particularly if the product development costs have already been sunk or amortized.

Existing Versus New Products

How you approach offering your programs and services is another pathway to growth. You can offer new products that have improved and expanded on current ones (incremental changes), repurposed for new markets and delivery methods (substantial changes), or even brand-new ones (transformational changes). For smaller, undercapitalized businesses, the first two present more realistic opportunities to grow. After all, the cost of creating a brand-new product is often very expensive. Any means of offsetting these costs, including incremental product extensions, would improve margins. As mentioned in chapter 1, the talent development supplier businesses that have been around for a long time still generate most of their revenue (70 percent) from their original programs. At some point, they decided that creating brand-new programs and products was either too difficult or expensive, although many have.

By building off incremental or substantial changes to your products, you can bundle elements of different programs and products into new offers. By piecing together these elements to meet specific client needs, you can expand the pipeline. Or if applicable to your offer, you can add optional consulting implementation services to ensure seamless integration after the product sale. An example of a talent development business that has expanded its offer into other segments of its original risk mitigation training business is NAVEX Global. NAVEX provides corporations with online information and training on a multitude of compliance-related issues. The company started with just two topics in employment law and eventually branched out to all types of compliance-related issues, including bribery and corruption, regulatory, corporate fraud, harassment and discrimination, diversity and inclusion, and employee retaliation.

In addition to bundling your products or services, you can also explore offering subscription services. This recurring and relatively predictable revenue business model can improve margins the longer clients subscribe. Or you can develop certifications that other consultants and internal practitioners would need to deliver your products and services to clients, perhaps with recertification requirements after a certain amount of time. This ongoing revenue model, if positioned properly, can lead to sustained growth.

Price Increases Versus Cost Cuts

You can also exploit two distinct financial solutions to boost your margins and create growth. First is periodically increasing prices. Slow but steady small price increases can stem the tide of some industry downturns and accelerate growth during good times. Of course, you must make sure these price increases are not offset by operational cost increases brought on by your growth. That said, price increases can help overcome some expected operational cost increases.

Second is appropriately cutting costs that do not negatively affect the future of the business. Two of the largest P&L items are the cost of sales and employee compensation. You can explore indirect distribution, rather than having your own sales force. In addition, you can convert some other fixed employee labor costs to variable contractor fees. Similarly, office space considerations that reduce the amount of fixed space particularly for mobile employees can provide quick returns on increased profits and growth.

Accelerated Growth

Every industry has organizations that seem to grow faster than their competitors, including talent development. A recent study conducted of a dozen fast-growing talent development suppliers revealed the strategies for their accelerated growth (100 percent or more over five years; Wilkinson 2016). The companies ranged in size from just less than $10 million in revenue to more than $150 million. They included the John Maxwell Company, Development Dimensions International, Crisis Prevention Institute, Root Learning, Paradigm Learning, ExperiencePoint, Ariel Group, Brooks Group, Acumen Learning, Management Concepts, LHH Knightsbridge, and Wiley.

Five basic growth strategies emerged:

- **Sales team and partner growth:** expanding the sales team, partner network, or other distribution channels
- **Marketing investment:** increasing investments in more sophisticated marketing strategies to attract qualified leads
- **Thought leadership:** positioning the business, or an individual within it, as a leading authority on a subject through publications, conferences, and blogs
- **Operational excellence:** building a sustainable and repeatable business model that could be replicated across multiple geographies, customer types, or product ideas
- **Product line expansion:** adding new products and services that capture additional business from existing customers while expanding into adjacent customer types.

To sustain growth, whether at a normal or accelerated pace, you must put the necessary systems and people in place to effectively manage it. Otherwise, the proverbial "success-disaster" is likely to emerge and eventually pull your business under.

Growth Constraints

What are some factors that could severely restrain growth? If you aren't able to quickly convey the benefits of your offer to those you want to do business with, you will struggle to differentiate yourself from your competitors. If your business development engine reflects no systematic sales process, account management methodology, or significant salesperson skill set, it will be very difficult for you to sell and close deals. If you don't have a focused and targeted sales and marketing campaign, you aren't likely to pinpoint opportunities to go after. If your back-office systems are inadequate to manage your business, resulting in frequent breakdowns, you will be unable to increase your scope of business. If your culture is toxic resulting in frequent turnover, it will be hard to develop the cohesion needed to sustain significant growth. If your leadership is not forward thinking, you will not be prepared to take on the many challenges of the new day. And finally, if you have no governance plan for how to manage your business through the future, you will most likely not be able to meet the demands of sustainable growth.

Grow or Die: Is Reinvention Required or Realistic?

In George Ainsworth-Land's *Grow or Die*, he posed the theory of transformation, now a cornerstone of strategic planning and organizational transformation in companies throughout the world. The underpinning belief proposed is that growth is the most basic and universal of all drives, whether biological, psychological, chemical, physical, or cultural. Furthermore, it has been a long-standing intrinsic drive of our ancestors. Ainsworth-Land suggests applying his theory to the growth of organizations, which, like nature, grow through a process of de- and reconstruction in a pattern of formation, self-imitation, success, and then renewal. If renewal doesn't take place the organism simply dies.

According to Ainsworth-Land, change occurs as a series of interlocking Sigmoid curves (S-curves), each with two or three points in which the rules of survival change if the entity is to continue growing (Figure 10-1). There are three phases: formative (phase 1), normative (phase 2), and integrative (phase 3). Phase 1 is characterized by experimentation during which the organization attempts to find a connection with its environment. Think how you might attempt to determine if your offer resonates in the marketplace. Some organizations can die at this point before finding this connection.

Assuming you make it through phase 1, the rules of survival then change, requiring you to replicate, or create normative patterns responsible for what you have done to be successful. If you navigate phase 2, you will continue on a path of continued growth limited only by the resources you have available to support it. But eventually these resources for success are consumed or become irrelevant as market conditions change. To progress, keep pace, and jump over any resource barriers, something has to give. This is where innovation or reinvention and integration enter the picture (phase 3), and where significant change must take place to avoid decline. (Ainsworth-Land calls this a bifurcation, or division of something into two branches or parts.) In Figure 10-1, at the top of the S-curve you either move forward through a plateau of stagnant performance or reinvent your business and start phase 1 again, beginning a new S-curve.

Figure 10-1. George Ainsworth-Land's Growth Curve

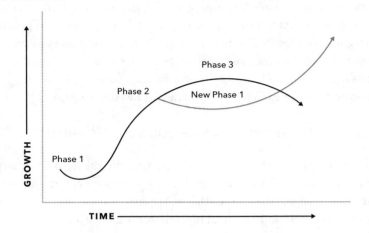

Think of phase 1 as the entrepreneurial phase, from which your business becomes successful and grows. At some point, however, you must diversify, or at a minimum innovate, through an incremental, substantial, or transformative change to maintain your relevance in the marketplace. Of course, you first need to be aware of where you are on the growth curve.

More recent support of Ainsworth-Land's theory is illustrated by research conducted about the average lifespan of U.S. public companies, defined by how long it takes to delist them. In 1970 the average lifespan of a company was 55 years. Just 40 years later in 2010 lifespan had decreased to 31.6 years. The main reason offered for this change was a company's failure to adapt to increasing complexity. Just like biological species, companies are complex adaptive systems that must continually evolve, often in somewhat unpredictable ways (Reeves, Levin, and Ueda 2014, 47-55). With all the disruption taking place today, and likely in the future, it should not be surprising to see that the average company lifespan continues to drop as companies fail to adapt to change.

The conclusion you might draw from Ainsworth-Land's theory is that growth is required for long-term success. While growth appears to be most desirable given the alternative, there is always the chance that highly accelerated and successful growth can come with drawbacks. That is, you can become successful in such a short amount of time that you haven't adequately prepared your business to handle this growth and thus fall into that black hole of the success-disaster paradigm. The irony of success potentially breeding failure makes building and sustaining a business a long and hard process. You might think it would be a problem you'd like to address, but it could be one that you don't have the wherewithal, bandwidth, or tools to manage. The lesson is that growth needs to be managed and planned just as you might lay out your strategy for the upcoming year. Not doing so will likely result in failure.

But most organizations are designed to operate, not innovate. So what does reinvention look like? How do you know when to reinvent? "Knowing when to undertake deliberate strategic transformation—when to change a company's core products or business model—may be the hardest decision a leader faces," according to Mark Bertolini, David Duncan, and Andrew Waldeck (2015, 92-101). The authors offer five interrelated "fault lines" that may indicate that the foundation of your business is unstable and it's time to consider reinventing yourself: Do you serve the right customers? Do you use the right performance metrics to measure success? Are you positioned properly with the right competitive advantages? Do you deploy the right business model for the future? Do your employees and partners possess the right talents? If you spot these fault lines in your business model, it might be time to reinvent. After all, some level of continuous reinvention is not only necessary but realistic depending on how your business is doing.

Growth can be painful, the thought alone may bring tears to your eyes and queasiness to your stomach, whether you are a one-person consulting practice or a several hundred-person business. Growth requires taking some risks, being uncomfortable, and charting new territory. The journey can be fraught with surprise and unexpected events, but it also can be celebrated by these very same events. The good news is that by keeping your eyes wide open and consciously making choices with which you are most comfortable, you will be able to successfully manage and even overcome any difficulties.

Industry Disruption: Predicting the Black Swan

Disruption is at the forefront of everyone's thoughts in the business world today; whether it's Uber or Lyft disrupting the car service industry while not owning any cars; Airbnb for booking lodging without owning any properties; Netflix for watching movies and TV shows; Facebook for distributing content; or Coursera for offering post-secondary education.

The rate of disruption, how long it takes for an industry to change, has fallen from more than 10 years in the 1960s to less than three years today (Sanders 2016). While most people view technology as the main reason for disruption these days, it is actually the use and application of technology that is disruptive. It's less about the next disruption that will affect our day-to-day lives, but rather when it will occur and how will we adapt to it.

Consider some past disruptive technologies and how they affected established markets (Table 10-1).

Table 10-1. Sample Disruptive Technologies

Industry	Disruptive Technology	Disrupted Market
Academia	Wikipedia	Encyclopedias
Communications	Telephone	Telegraph
Communications	Cell Phone	Land Lines
Retail	Online	Bricks and Mortar
Computer	Smartphones	PCs and PDAs
Medical	Ultrasound	Radiology (X-Rays)
Medical	Arthroscopic and Endoscropic	Open Surgery
Transportation	Steamboats	Sailing Ships
Transportation	Automobiles	Railroads
Printing	Digital Printing	Offset Printing
Publishing	Word Processing	Typewriters

A recent McKinsey Global Institute report identified 12 technologies that could "drive massive economic transformations and disruptions in the coming years" (Maynila, et al. 2013). Of the list, five are not too far removed from the world of talent development:

- the mobile Internet
- automation of knowledge work
- the Internet of things
- cloud technology
- advanced robotics.

Some of these technologies are already becoming established in the talent development industry. Surely advanced robotics will influence not only the way work gets done but who does it. The call for training on just how to operate and monitor robots will be necessary, as will reskilling those replaced by them. Mobile technology, largely through the automation of knowledge work, is becoming more and more advanced such that streaming video and other work tool applications will influence what workers have at their immediate disposal to learn and apply to their everyday tasks.

Just take a look at the traditional management consulting industry. Clayton Christensen, Dina Wang, and Derek van Bever posit that it is on the cusp of disruption if not already in the midst of it (2013, 107-113). The few very large companies, the one-stop solution shops, of McKinsey, Bain, Boston Consulting Group, and Accenture are all facing severe competition from "facilitated network" firms that rely on modularizing their offers, democratizing knowledge, specializing, and developing strong partnerships. These newer and typically smaller firms are structured around enabling the exchange of products and services, whereas the older solution shop firms are structured primarily to diagnose and solve problems whose scope is undefined. Even long-standing bastions of success in the consulting world can quickly be subject to vast alterations based on somewhat sudden and unpredictable customer, economic, and environmental changes.

You can react to disruption in two ways, according to Tim Sanders (2016), former YAHOO! chief solutions officer. You can either walk in the valley of despair or the land of innovation. Disruption will happen, but how are you going to react? Just as there are stages of accepting death as posited by Elisabeth Kübler-Ross (1969), Sanders offers similar phases to denying the change brought on by disruption: shock, rejection, resistance, explanation, approval, and identification. Reacting properly to disruption also means focusing on what is really disruptive, painful, and permanent, and addressing your response in collaboration with your colleagues. Rapid problem solving is the only sustainable competitive advantage in today's ever-changing business environment, if you do it faster than your competitors.

How, then, can you prepare for the next disruption, the next black swan? Three principal characteristics describe such an event: it is unpredictable; it carries a massive impact; and after it has taken place there is a strong tendency to rationalize its occurrence as less random and more predictable than first thought. This third characteristic is the most interesting aspect of disruption. We seem to understand why the event happened only after the fact, which would suggest we could have put together enough evidence to predict it had we thought about it a little more. However, we tend to deal better with that which we know because it is difficult to address that which we do not. So we focus on the facts of the past and present rather than generalize to the future. What this exposes us to is a certain vulnerability to oversimplify the facts we do have and thus restrict ourselves from imagining the impossible events with negative consequences.

What disruptions might hit the talent development industry and how best can you react to them? Working from the three major drivers of the industry—content, instruction, and delivery—there is little question disruption is likely to emerge around delivery technologies. It is more unlikely to come from new content, theories or processes, or new learning theories or instructional techniques, although more work is being done on neuroscience's affect on learning.

We can already see how learning is being transformed with shorter durations, say 20 to 30 minutes, whether in the physical or virtual classroom. This could disrupt those who are uncomfortable with longer drawn-out learning modules of several hours at a time, regardless of how many breaks are provided. Certainly the learning experience is evolving as well, with vendors providing everything from more sophisticated simulations to virtual and augmented reality learning experiences, to gamification of content. There are some new software categories emerging driven by content in the areas of feedback, engagement and culture management, and transfer of learning (Bersin by Deloitte 2015). Content is also being consolidated by vendors such as Skillsoft, Grovo, Floqq, Vodeclic, Lynda.com, Udemy, and getdegreed. While these companies are not disrupting the content of the courses, they do change the way learners access the courses.

Technology disruptions have affected online employee tools and organization-wide learning platforms, and will continue to do so with the use of more powerful mobile apps. Anywhere, anytime, anything learning has become the status quo. In the overall talent management space there appears to be an even greater likelihood of disruptive technology. Employee tools, mobile apps, ERP platforms, talent bidding, talent on demand, human collaboration with machines, online video, smart data, and predictive analytics are just a few of these (Neal and Sonsino 2015, 30-35).

The question ultimately is whether content, instruction, or delivery innovations will affect the future and success of your business model if not explored and incorporated into your offer. According to Clayton Christensen, Michael Raynor, and Rory McDonald (2015), you might be wise not to overreact to disruption by dismantling a still-profitable business; instead, strengthen your relationships with your core customers while simultaneously creating a new business focused on the growth opportunities arising from the disruption.

Exit Strategies: Why, When, Who, What, and How?

Assuming your business performs well and either embraces or successfully dodges emerging disruptions, it may be time for you to think about cashing out—to reap the rewards, at least financially, for your hard work, long hours, and multiple sacrifices. The good news for owners is the market for acquiring and buying out talent development businesses continues to be strong. The question for business owners, though, is far more complicated than simply deciding whether or not to sell. For instance, although you may be motivated by the money you'll receive, you may still want to contribute to the growth of the business—and the industry. With this in mind, owners must clearly understand that they will need to let go of the personal and professional control they currently hold. This last point is the most difficult adjustment factor. It changes everything. After all, no one wants to see their legacy tarnished.

Despite plenty of activity, 75 to 80 percent of mergers and acquisitions fail. To ensure a smooth transition, you need to consider the intentions of the acquiring company. Acquiring companies are prone to want to "take" from acquired businesses rather than "give" to them. They see targeted companies as a means to strengthen their own businesses or fill certain gaps, whether through client lists and relationships, products, and even brand reputation. However, they overlook the short- and long-term integration challenges. Acquiring companies that give back to their acquisitions to buttress those businesses tend to be more successful, whether by providing needed capital, offering better managerial oversight, transferring a resident skill or knowledge, or sharing resources (Martin 2016).

This is no different in the talent development supplier industry. Too many companies have failed to leverage being merged or acquired. Certainly, part of this involves the founder and senior leadership team leaving after their earn-out time has passed. But usually it comes down to culture integration of human capital. To make sure the transition is smooth, try following this road map for success (Carroll 2014, 20-23):

1. Conduct significant due diligence and planning prior to the merger or acquisition.
2. At the outset objectively, consistently, and fairly map the most capable talent to appropriate roles.
3. Consolidate the sales force through a fact-based assignment of account responsibilities to preserve customer relationships, retain the best talent, and drive sales force effectiveness.
4. Consciously commit to a long-term relationship with the intent to make it work.
5. If at first you don't succeed, try again. Execute and refine as you go, sometimes taking necessary baby steps to build a model of success.

I have gone through the sale of a few firms in this industry—as the owner, as a partner, as a senior executive, and as a buyer. Some experiences were wonderful; others didn't work out as well. Here are some key questions you as a business owner, CEO, or senior executive will need to consider when contemplating the decision to sell your business.

Why Sell in the First Place?

What is motivating you to sell? For some owners, personal life changes such as health issues will provide enough reason. Other owners may find it is time to semi- or fully retire, because they seek a different pace of life or are just tired of doing the same thing every day. Still other owners may think they have taken the business as far as they can, and they need to turn it over to professional growth-oriented experts. These are all valid reasons.

As you think through this process make sure you have built up a very strong senior management team that can manage succession planning for the short term and then the long term. You will need to let go sooner rather than later, so ensuring you have the people in place to move the business forward will not only prepare you emotionally to move on, but will be evaluated very positively by buyers.

Whom Should You Seek as a Buyer?

You do not want to turn your business over to just any company. It is important to consider the type of buyer your firm is most suited to attract. There are two types to consider: strategic buyers and financial buyers. Strategic buyers see opportunities for growth through adding new capabilities to already existing aligned businesses. It might include a different set of content or delivery methodology, or even geographic reach, but by and large it is intent on adding the business to its existing portfolio. A strategic buyer might want to integrate the new business into its brand, or it might want the new business to remain relatively independent but still overall part of its brand. For the most part, strategic buyers aren't necessarily interested in reselling their businesses, at least not in the short term. An example is the Wiley acquisition of Inscape, Profiles International, and Cross-Knowledge to add to its training business, originally largely provided through Pfeiffer and Deltak.

Financial buyers are most likely to come from a private-equity background and expect a strong return on their investment over this time. They are more interested in building a portfolio of businesses at the lowest price, growing it, and selling it at the highest price within a relatively short window of perhaps three to five years. Often, they will achieve this by buying a "platform" firm, one that is already doing well, perhaps even an industry leader, and continuing to grow it organically but also by adding on additional businesses. In these cases, the added firms lose their branded identity and become part of the firm that acquired them. In other cases, a total rebranding of the acquired firm takes place. Another is when Employment Law Training acquired three other businesses, one of which was even larger than itself, and combined them into a new branded entity called NAVEX.

These two types of buyers are very different in their intentions and expectations, except for wanting to build sustainably profitable businesses. The most important thing to determine is how your wants and needs (as the current owner) match the buyer's future plans. For instance, if you want to continue working in the business, the buyer needs to be open to finding an executive position for you.

If you plan to stay on for a period as an executive, you should understand the difference between strategic and financial buyers in how they evaluate and retain senior leadership. Strategic buyers put more emphasis on the quality of the team, especially that of the CEO, because they take the long view and expect that CEO to protect the culture of its business, integrate capabilities with other businesses under the same umbrella, and take the business to a new level. Financial buyers are quicker to pull the cord on the CEO if they don't think that individual can grow the business rapidly. For example, in every case in which I have been a board member of a private equity owned firm, the CEO was replaced within about 18 months of purchase with someone who had a track record of growing much larger businesses.

Integration is typically more of a challenge for strategic buyers who want to bring the businesses together under the same umbrella. This involves a likely change in leadership and the challenge of merging cultures. Strategic buyers offer financial economies of scale by streamlining back-office operations into a central place, rather than having separate operations for each business it acquires. An example would be Korn-Ferry International, which has bought seven different companies in this space, and now branded as Korn-Ferry Hay Group, they benefit from single source human resources, legal, and, in large part, information technology services. On the other hand, most financial buyers, particularly those in private equity, have little interest in integrating office operations across many of its independent firms. While they may bundle firms into a portfolio, they want to remain flexible to allow for selling individual firms if needed. To reduce expenses of their companies, they might bundle their buying power to achieve certain discounted purchases for office supplies, healthcare, technology services, and so on.

Also be sure to consider the type of noncompete agreement that will be enforced to keep you from working in the industry, and for how long. Having a clear personal vision will help determine which type of buyer will fit best with your needs.

Snapshot of Industry Players

Although the names often change, it is sometimes difficult to know the players without a scorecard. Below is a partial list of some current players in the talent development industry and what companies they've bought (and in some cases sold) within the last several years.

Strategic Buyers

- Korn-Ferry, International (Personnel Decisions/Ninth House, Lore, Pivot, Leader Source, Global Novations, Lominger, Hay)
- John Wiley & Sons (Inscape, Pfeiffer, CrossKnowledge, Deltak, Profiles International)
- Lee Hecht Harrison/Adecco (Knightsbridge, Penna)
- IBM (Kenexa)
- GP Strategies (Sandy Corp., Blessing-White)
- Heidrick & Struggles (Co Company, Senn-Delaney, Decision Strategies, International)
- SAP (Success Factors)

Financial Buyers

- Renovus (Ariel, Linkage, Telemedia, Prime, Better Communications)
- Providence Equity Partners (TwentyEighty: Miller Heiman, Vital Smarts, ESI, Forum, Achieve Global, Huthwaite, Omega, Edmentum/Archipelago Learning/Plato, Ascend Learning)
- The Riverside Company (Crisis Prevention Institute, OnCourse Learning, Employment Law Training/NAVEX, Lexipol, Grace Hill, Mintra, Alchemy, Learning Seat, Bohemian Interactive)
- IIR (16 firms that conduct conferences and workshops in specific areas such as energy, agro-chemicals, legal compliance, financial, and healthcare)

When Is the Right Time to Sell?

While there may not be a perfect time to sell a business, there are logically good and bad times to sell. For example, it's a good time to sell when the market is active and buyers are interested. You will be more likely to get a better price for your business than during leaner times. Also, it's a good time when your business is financially strong—with both the current and projected top and bottom lines. A strong financial history will only add to this formula. There is no financial gain in selling your business at the lowest possible price. In addition, if you are saddled with long-term debt, but see a path out, you might want to wait until you can break even because this will undoubtedly serve to discount what you sell for.

Beyond sound financial criteria such as your business's sales and profit growth history, how can you become an attractive target in the talent development space? Businesses that focus on one, or just a few, targeted audiences are particularly attractive. This could be industry specific: healthcare, finance, oil and gas, or law enforcement, multifamily housing. Or job specific: salespeople, engineers, duty-to-care professionals, law enforcement. Of course, the less competition in any of these targets the more attractive the seller.

Firms with a recurring revenue gained through subscriptions, SaaS business models, and platform libraries are also attractive in their performance predictability. The steady cash flow, assuming high customer retention rates, makes these businesses much easier to control. Possessing a very clear and uncomplicated offer and owning a significant portion of market share are also appealing. Other factors include concentration of customers, scalability, brand reputation, and management team caliber.

All buyers, whether strategic or financial, will conduct significant due diligence prior to fully engaging a seller. Beyond the criteria discussed already, they also analyze the competitive landscape into which the potential acquisition fits. As a potential seller, it's important to recognize how your business compares to the competition. ALM Intelligence, formerly Kennedy Consulting Research & Advisory, conducts competitive analysis in the human capital space and uses a 2 x 2 framework to judge the breadth and depth of consulting capabilities within companies (Figure 10-2). In general, the most favored companies would be in the upper right—high in both breadth and depth—and the least favored in the lower left.

While this tool can identify relative positions in a particular competitive space, it can be misleading if you only draw this conclusion. For example, a firm in the upper left (high in depth, low in breadth) would likely be narrowly focused in one area or perhaps one offering. For an acquirer, this might actually be desirable, particularly if that capability doesn't already exist in its business. Similarly, a firm with a wide breadth of capabilities might serve the growth needs of an otherwise narrow offer from another business. Depending on the strategic intent of the match between buyer and seller, where they fall will help to determine the competitive advantage, or lack thereof, of potential acquisitions.

Figure 10-2. Breadth and Depth of Companies

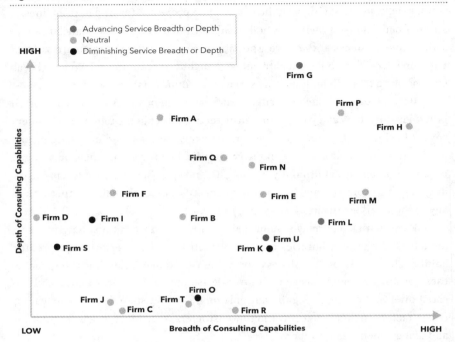

Source: DeVito (2016).

If you have decided that selling is a potential option, you might consider hiring a consultant or firm that is well versed in the industry to help you get ready to go to market. This partner would have extensive experience guiding companies to shore up any glaring weaknesses that may get in the way of a sale. It would conduct an assessment of the strengths and weaknesses of the business from the eyes of a potential buyer and then make recommendations for improving them to put your best foot forward. This effort could cost from $8,500 to $15,000 for one or two days of input (Aldersea 2016). The time and expense may be well worth it to ensure you get the best offer for your business.

How Do You Go About the Sale?

The process of letting others in the industry know you are thinking of selling your business while simultaneously maintaining confidentiality is complicated. To get started, make it known to both private investors and industry leaders (for whom you think are a good match) that you are potentially interested in selling your business. Of course, once you admit to this, potential buyers may assume some level of eagerness or desperation on your part, thus reducing your negotiating leverage. You can also retain a professional firm to broker your sale; their job is to seek potential interested parties and negotiate a deal for you. But perhaps the most professional way is to retain an investment banking firm whose role is to help value your business, understand your goals, seek appropriate interested parties, and then advise you on negotiating and closing the deal.

Selecting the right partner through this process is important as well and entails requesting proposals, meeting with candidates, generating specific criteria you are looking for, and making a final decision. You will need to be on the same page in terms of what you are looking for or how long you will continue to look for a buyer. The selling process can take a lot of your, your senior team's, and your board's time, if you have one.

The upside to retaining an investment banking firm is that it understands the business of putting deals together, maintaining extremely high confidentiality during the process. It can help you be more realistic, while casting a wide net of potential buyers, particularly in the private equity space. The downside is that these services can be expensive. For example, you might expect to pay a monthly retainer fee of $8,000-$12,000, plus out-of-pocket expenses, for a three- to six-month period. Once you have sold, they typically take 3-5 percent of the purchase price, minus the fees you have already paid.

If you're financially healthy, a leader in your particular niche with a sustainable and competitive value proposition, you might find private-equity investors approaching you on their own. For example, the private-equity firm, The Riverside Company, has a training and education vertical that seeks companies in the compliance business that are largely subscription revenue based, ideally in a SaaS environment. It looks for companies whose offer helps its clients stay up-to-date on required state or federal legislation, such as employment law, fair-housing, law enforcement procedures, or required certification standards for home inspectors and healthcare professionals.

What Can You Sell For?

Because most of the purchases in the talent development industry are by private firms, it is difficult to truly know the prices paid for acquired companies. And some public companies do not disclose smaller purchases within their total business, or in some ways they mask these purchases. Through the right sources, we can at least come to some very good educated guesses to offer guidelines on what you might be able to sell your company for.

Strategic buyers try to meet the asking price of the seller and negotiate around managing the risk associated with any issues integrating cultures and retaining leadership talent. With relatively scarce assets and plenty of cash, some strategic buyers will spend a premium, eventually obtaining enough scalability to fit acquisitions into a strategic road map. Because they intend to be in the business for the long haul, overpaying isn't that critical.

Financial buyers base their decisions and offer prices on three factors: growth rate, cyclicality, and margins. If your business has a 10 percent or higher compound annual growth rate, or recurring revenue, and a 20 percent or higher EBITDA margin, you might easily sell for 10 to 12 times your EBITDA. However, most training supplier companies trade at six to nine times EBITDA, and at 0.75 to 1.2 times revenue, because they tend to be cyclical without recurring revenue. Of course, there are exceptions. One late 2016 resale of a talent development supplier went for an amazing 16 times EBITDA and seven times revenue. These figures differ somewhat if the business is strictly considered a management or HR consulting firm: EBITDA multiples averaged a little higher—at 10.6 for management consultancies (range of 7.8 to 14.9) and at 8.5 for HR consulting firms (range of 6.7 to 12.6)—from 2006 to 2013.

One commonality across deals, however, is that the vast majority involve some type of earn-out. That is, hardly any buy-outs are totally upfront. Some 40-60 percent could be paid in upfront cash, with the remaining amount paid out over two to three years depending on performance. This allows the acquiring company to protect its investment.

Another relative commonality across types of buyers is the criteria considered when considering a purchase. Although both look strongly at the financial condition of the business, the financial buyer typically ranks these criteria in the following order: gross margin, EBITDA, EBITDA growth, revenue, and revenue growth. In addition, the quality of clients and the intellectual property owned by the business are key purchase criteria, with the latter being very important to a strategic buyer.

Table 10-2 offers examples of some relatively recent purchases and the rough estimated purchase numbers.

Table 10-2. Snapshot of Recent Purchases in the Industry

Year	Purchasee	Purchaser	Estimated Amount	Multiple
2016	Hay Group	Korn-Ferry	$452 million	2.25 x revenue
2016	Decision Strategies Int'l.	Heidrick & Struggles	$9.2 million	0.8-1.2 x revenue
2015	Knightsbridge	Lee Hecht Harrison/ Adecco	N/A	1.4 x revenue
2015	Cross Knowledge	John Wiley & Sons	$175 million	N/A
2015	Inscape Publishing	John Wiley & Sons	$85 million	3 x revenue
2015	Smart Pros, Ltd.	Kaplan	N/A	0.9 x revenue; 12.3 x EBITDA
2014	NAVEX	Vista Equity	$500 million	4+ x revenue; 10-13 x EBITDA
2014	OnCourse Learning	CIP Capital	$90 million	4+ x revenue
2013	Vital Smarts	Providence Equity Partners	$100+ million	2+ x revenue; 5 x EBITDA
2013	Informa*	Providence Equity Partners	$180 million	0.9 x revenue; 7.7 x EBITDA
2011	Crisis Prevention Institute	Brockway Moran & Partners	$111 million	3.4 x revenue; 9 x EBITDA

*Training firm assets including Miller Heiman, Omega, Huthwaite, Achieve Global, Forum, ESI International, now rebranded as TwentyEighty, under Providence.

What Are Your Next Steps?

When you are ready to sell, most deals will involve keeping you, and perhaps select senior managers, around for at least a negotiated transition period. You might slot in at some executive position or just as a board member. Depending on how the deal is constructed, it could be laden with earn-outs over a period of years, based on the continued performance of the business.

This does not mean that you are fully protected from being fired before the end of the contract. Just know once you give up majority ownership of your business, you are at the mercy of the buying entity. Although this sounds logical, many owners fail to understand the consequences of the sale. In my experience, there's been more discomfort with deals down the road. As such, early exits from the business, after the sale, happen more frequently.

So just like any business initiative, deciding to sell your business requires a well-thought-out plan. Don't go into it without having carefully deliberated all the possible parameters and dynamics involved—not the least of which is the impact your exit will have on you and your current staff. Be sure to engage some trusted advisers who have navigated these waters before, and who understand the pros and cons of exiting a business.

Conclusion

What's exciting about the talent development industry is that it is ever evolving, which can also be frustrating. Just when you think you have put all the right pieces in place, along comes an industry change you either didn't see coming or are ill-equipped to address. Nonetheless, an objective bystander would likely agree the industry is still evolving and to the extent its future is tied to technological innovation and workplace demographics, it will continue to evolve.

The good news is there are many pathways to coexist with these rapid and massive changes, as long as you are committed to growth. Without such a commitment your willingness to move away from the status quo will be stunted and the changes will overcome your ability to move forward. Whether you are interested in exiting your business, leaving it to your family, or just letting it dissolve, there are strategies you can embrace that will make any of these options viable; just be very clear on what you want, where you want to go, and how you want to get there.

Reflection Questions

PATHWAYS TO GROWTH: LET ME COUNT THE WAYS
- What are the best ways for you to grow your business?
- What influence will these approaches have on both your top and bottom lines?

GROW OR DIE: IS REINVENTION REQUIRED OR REALISTIC?
- What growth phase are you currently in?
- What is your pathway to growth beyond that?
- What growth options do you have?
- What can you do to bifurcate your business before a decline sets in?

INDUSTRY DISRUPTION: PREDICTING THE BLACK SWAN

- What are potentially the most disruptive innovations you are seeing that could affect the future of your business?
- What have you done to incorporate disruptive, or even just substantial, innovation in your business?
- How prepared are you to address the challenges a black swan will present to the growth of your business?

EXIT STRATEGIES: WHY, WHEN, WHO, WHAT, AND HOW?

- What considerations do you have for exiting your business?
- What reasons have you given for why you would want to do this?
- What does your plan look like?
- Why wouldn't you want to explore this option?
- How have you positioned yourself for exiting the business financially?
- What type of acquirer would fit your needs best, a strategic or financial buyer, and why?

11

LOOKING AHEAD
AND BEYOND

The weaker the data available upon which to base one's
conclusion, the greater the precision which should be
quoted in order to give the data authenticity.
—*Norman Ralph Augustine*

In this book, I have tried to combine my decades of experience with industry voices from trusted sources and research to be as precise as possible in laying out the best path for building and growing your talent development firm. That said, no one can accurately predict what tomorrow holds for the industry, especially in this VUCA (volatile, uncertain, complex, ambiguous) world. Instead, you can do your best to get ahead of the curve by being vigilant and sensitive to what's next. If you are committed to building and growing a sustainable business, you must look ahead with the same diligence as you learn from your past and operate in the present.

What's in Store?: 2017 and Beyond

Society is just entering the next and fourth industrial revolution, one of artificial intelligence, robotics, big data, and quantum computing (Murray 2016b). As World Economic Forum founder Klaus Schwab (2015) said, "The speed of current breakthroughs has no historical precedent. When compared to previous industrial revolutions, the Fourth is evolving at an exponential rather than a linear pace."

So what does this fourth industrial revolution hold for the talent development industry? The talent development industry has already experienced disruption over the last 15 to 20 years, as organizations spend less time on instructor-led, face-to-face experiences, down from 70 percent of all training in the early 2000s to 51 percent in 2015 (ATD 2015b). (This number dropped further for information and software companies, at less than 40 percent.) While not completely abandoning the benefits of live in-person instruction, organizations are blending learning solutions that pair instructor-led training with newer media platforms. And they are moving the physical classroom experience to a virtual synchronous instructor-led training environment, thus combining the benefits of live interaction with efficiency, cost, and scale.

With new technologies, such as those for collaborative, gaming, and mobile experiences, you'll have myriad new opportunities to design and deliver your offering. How you shape your business will in large part be determined by how you adapt to these technologies. Employees will increasingly want to guide their own learning. The proliferation of readily available learning resources will affect how most workers will learn in the future. The workforce is changing from a much older, perhaps less technologically sophisticated and comfortable individual to one who has for the most part grown up learning with technology-enabled platforms and will be less tolerant of traditional approaches.

What is difficult to predict is the timetable for all these changes to fully take place—and the exact interaction between the forces of worker demographics and technological change. You cannot leave Gen Xers and even Baby Boomers alone while Millennials and Gen Zers emerge as the new workforce. The older generations will also want the most efficient learning approach, whether technologically enabled or not, so as to not waste their time, even as they overcome a potential unwillingness to accept new learning modes. Accommodating this changing, more modern workforce means organizations will need to adapt to more modern learning. And so will your offer.

The current digital transformation will change the face of organizations—their structure, culture, and speed to innovate. Technology will not only enable companies to perform better; it will define what business these companies are in (Chambers 2016). As Josh Bersin (2016) notes, "wake up to the new world of learning." Here are just a few examples of how technology will play out in the talent development industry, and thus what you might want to consider in building and growing your firm.

Self-Service Learning

Growing from the need to make learning available to anyone, anytime, anywhere is the potential to buy learning opportunities and online catalogs of programming. Think Amazon for learning, or a self-serve portal for whatever learning you need whenever it is needed. A personal learning site that not only tracks progress toward established training outcomes but becomes a personal portfolio for career development and advancement. (See, for example, Career Engagement Group's

Fuel 50 platform.) Learners pay for each experience just as they might when buying any product online, from books to televisions. How might this potentially affect your business? For starters, it might reduce the need for your specialized services and certainly compete with your offer, as companies turn to this platform rather than look externally for in-person suppliers.

Microlearning

Bite-size and microlearning experiences of very frequent three- to five-minute bursts of information make it more easily understood and assimilated, thus avoiding information overload. Repeated retrieval of new information, distributed practice or rehearsals over time, and deeply encoding mental associations of new with exiting knowledge for better retention all show improved retention results. In today's information-intense and increased-demand-for-knowledge fast-paced world, microlearning approaches can help the learner focus on just what needs to be absorbed at the greatest moment of need. While instructor-led classroom experiences will not disappear, organizations are likely to see more workers access what they need to learn when they need to learn it from powerful platforms. And because of the capability of technology to bring learning to the worker, it will be more continuous; assessments and follow-up messages and activities will be available after training. In fact, systems are just starting to allow organizations to develop their own custom learning curriculum made up of a host of mini-lessons particularly relevant to their organization's culture and business strategy. These will be increasingly refined to meet both the organization's and its learners' needs.

Mobile

The workforce of tomorrow will continue to become more mobile. In 2015, 37 percent of U.S. workers reported that they have telecommuted before for their job, up from 9 percent in 1995 (Jones 2015). This movement to mobile workers comes as businesses begin to close down certain facilities and move their staff, especially from call centers to home offices. This will now require a different set of collaboration and decision-making skills, as well as discipline and independence, not to mention the need for virtual leadership skills, all of which you might help organizations and their employees develop.

Learning Management Systems (LMSs)

The LMS industry is $3 billion in size and growing at 20 percent per year (Bersin 2016). But the traditional LMS is best at managing training costs and reducing instruction time. As a result, most LMS users are displeased with their platform

(Hall 2016). Perhaps this is because the traditional LMS isn't designed to incorporate video very well. The majority of LMS providers distribute traditional learning materials, not high-quality streamed video-based learning. Video is everywhere in every device publication and communication medium: One billion people regularly watch video on YouTube; the number of hours rose 60 percent in 2015; and two billion people worldwide have video-enabled smartphones (Bersin 2016). The proliferation of new LMS platforms promise more comprehensive and effective learning in the workplace.

Gaming

As the gaming industry continues to flourish at home, gaming experiences will be transfered to the workplace. Companies are creating learning and knowledge platforms that do more than just provide content. They also enable follow-up tracking and data analytics to help both the learner and the organization assess progress and identify further learning needs, not only on an individual basis but for an entire organization.

Simulation

The use of true simulated environments through virtual and augmented reality or other means has arrived. Virtual reality is the next major computing and communications platform after mobile phones, according to Mark Zuckerberg (Del Prado 2015). Devices such as Facebook's Oculus Rift and Samsung's Gear VR are already available for virtual reality-enabled programs. Then there's Google's Glass, a forerunner for augmented reality tools. Virtual and augmented reality are likely to change immensely how we communicate with one another, how we "travel," and how we consume content. Certainly, it can affect how and where workers are trained.

Artificial Intelligence

The term deep learning has begun to surface wherein systems learn by themselves through repeated pattern recognition, similar to but much more complex than when your mobile keyboard automatically suggests words as you type. Artificial intelligence holds promise in enhancing the learning experience, primarily through assessment and prescription for development. By 2018, three million workers will be supervised by a nonhuman boss; 45 percent of the fastest growing companies will have fewer employees than smart machines (Gartner 2015). Improving this technology will advance the learning capacity of individuals and their corporations several fold to achieve the three end goals of faster, cheaper, and better.

Robotics

Based on the influx of robotic solutions, some aspect of learning in the future will reside in teaching people how to teach or interact with robotic devices. What opportunity might this present your business to assist organizations in retraining the employees that remain? Surely, organizations will be tasked with upskilling their staff to remain competitive in the human capital landscape. But if robots do leave companies with fewer workers to develop and train, you will need to adjust your products and services.

***

The future of the talent development industry—and thus talent development firms—looks brighter than ever with new technologies for addressing emerging workforce and learner demands. The future of the industry will be wrapped in advanced technology; faster, more precise, and shorter learning experiences; and social, personal, on-demand learning platforms. Learning itself is being reinvented, largely driven by the ubiquity of devices capable of extreme mobility. As the envelope stretches with technology, so will the learning modalities and capabilities to fit it. Your success will necessitate nimbleness to deliver programs and services in desired formats. Be prepared for some pretty rapid changes in how and with what you go to market.

What It Will Take to Get What You Want: Entrepreneurial Spirit

Many lessons can be gleaned from this book. Prime among them should be the lessons about yourself. What do you want? How much are you willing to put in to get it? What price are you willing to pay? What sacrifices are you willing to make?

Building and growing a talent development firm is not for the faint of heart. But it can also offer unparalleled excitement and rewards. You will face many bumps in the road, many hurdles, and many walls to break down. The key to navigating this is to focus on your wants and wishes, however you define them. Whether you are starting a firm or growing one, there are some key things to keep in mind. Based on the topics presented in this book, here are 30 tips for building and growing a successful talent development firm, to help you manage and integrate your personal and professional lives to your ultimate satisfaction.

Personal

1. Maintain an owner's mentality whether you are one or not.
2. Be realistically optimistic, remembering even a glass half-full has another half to fill.
3. Demonstrate honesty and integrity in everything you do.
4. Ensure a spotless reputation by doing what you say you will do.
5. Create a culture and value system you are passionate about.
6. Hire and surround yourself with people better than you and surround yourself with them.
7. Demonstrate an enduring positive attitude—your attitude always determines your altitude in life.
8. Be open to change by embracing the challenges that come with it.
9. Take care of yourself both physically and mentally.
10. Leave on your own terms when and how you want to.

Professional

1. Have a vision of where you and your business will be and when.
2. Ask "why" first, then "how" and "what."
3. Respect and honor the legalities of the industry.
4. Don't make false promises you cannot keep.
5. Stay competitive and hungry.
6. Be relevant by engaging a variety of sources and people.
7. Hire coaches and advisers whose experience and expertise close your gaps.
8. Learn from the lessons of failure and fail gracefully.
9. Avoid taking shortcuts by being overly thorough in your actions.
10. Grow or die—there are no other options.

Practical

1. Develop a playbook for moving forward with discipline.
2. Create boundaries around your strategy but keep it lean and flexible.
3. Scale the business however you can because this is where your margins will reside.
4. Always look for improvements in everything you do.
5. Develop a management structure, processes, and systems aligned with the culture of your business.
6. Monitor and track performance of both individuals and your business.
7. Reduce complexity by keeping it as simple as possible.

8. Know where your sales come from and their future sources.
9. Manage your margins to the percentage point, as every little bit helps.
10. Know your customers like the back of your hand.

As you reflect on these suggestions, there is one big question you must ask yourself: What are you doing to plan to meet the new demands of the talent development industry?

Conclusion

As you near the end of this book, I very much hope you take some of the ideas and apply them when building and growing your talent development firm. Undoubtedly, workers, workplaces, learners, learning, and technology will change. You have to decide whether to fully embrace these changes by adapting your business to their demands or stay the course. Change offers countless opportunities to start fresh, to serve new and exciting needs that matter to talent development. The fragmented state of the industry is enough that you can be successful by finding your niche without making wholesale changes. The key to this decision, however, is to understand your choices and why you have made them.

In writing this book, I wanted to highlight a number of topics and present different perspectives to help you think through your own individual and business situation. I hope you can put the action planning forms in Appendix D to good use to help you capture your thoughts on how you will act on them.

SAMPLE BUSINESS PLAN TABLE OF CONTENTS

Creating a business plan is an excellent way to capture and clarify your thoughts, and then lay out your plan for your business, regardless of its size. While you might want to ask some of your trusted advisers to review the plan, it isn't necessary to share it with anyone unless you are interested in securing financial investors. Its purpose is to help guide your thinking about the type of business you want to build and the various factors that will contribute to your success. The following is a sample table of contents that lists the various topics you will want to include.

Executive Summary
Business Overview
- Company Ownership
- Business Mission
- Business Objectives
- Critical Success Factors

Products and Services
Full Offer Description
Competitive Landscape
- Main Competitors
- Competitive Edge
- Service Business Analysis
- Competition and Buying Patterns

Sales and Marketing
- Literature and Collateral
- Market Segmentation
- Addressable market

- Target Market Segment Strategy
- Market Needs and Trends

Overall Business Strategy

- Marketing Strategy
- Promotion Strategy
- Positioning Statement
- Pricing Strategy
- Sales Strategy

Business Start-Up and Implementation Plans

- First Month Start-Up Expenses
- Milestones
- Location and Facilities
- Strategic Alliances
- Staffing
- Advisory Support Team

Financials

- Pro Forma and Assumptions
- Monthly Operating Expenses

Investment Opportunity (if appropriate)

- High-Interest Loan
- Private Equity
- Venture Capital
- Minority Ownership

Contact Information

LIFETIME VALUE
OF A CUSTOMER

Often we fail to realize just how valuable our customers are over the long term. We can be so concerned with keeping them satisfied that we don't realize they have become repeat purchasers of our products and services. Furthermore, they can be an invaluable source of referrals, which you can then convert to more customers. This multiplier effect is illustrated here using a relatively simple calculation that determines the ultimate value you can obtain from a loyal customer.

Name of your best long-term customer	_____
Average amount they spend with you each month	$_____
Multiply by 12 for their annual value as a customer	$_____
Multiply by 20 years (lifetime value)	$_____
Their lifetime value (LTV) as your customer Is:	$_____
1. Now, take your LTV figure of:	_____
2. Insert the number of customers they have referred to your organization:	_____
3. Estimate the number who actually became your customers:	_____

4. Estimate the amount each of these new customers spends, on average, annually with your organization:	_____
5. Multiply the amount in #4 by the number of referrals you listed in # 3:	_____
6. Multiply the amount in #5 by 20 (potential years for each customer):	_____
7. Add the amount in #6 to the amount in #1:	_____

This figure is the potential real lifetime value of that customer.

BOARD MEMBER ROLE ASSESSMENT

You might find the board member roles assessment tool helpful when creating and evaluating your board. The nine areas offered can give you some perspective on which are most important for your specific business needs. Identifying these can help you focus on the type of advisers you might want to select. Once they are on board, the form will allow you to periodically assess performance assessment on how they are contributing to meeting those needs.

Board Member Role Assessment

Following are nine areas board members can contribute to you organization's growth. Use the rating scales provided to assess the extent to which you believe you are getting what you need from each person or as a whole, as well as how important each potential contribution are is for you toward the well-being of your bussiness.

Performance (P)

3 = Better than
   expected contribuiton

2 = Expected Contribution

1 = Less than expected contribution

0 = Not providing
   any contribution at all

Importance (I)

3 = Extremely important

2 = Somewhat important

1 = A little important

0 = Not important at all

P x I scores that are closer to 9 are far better than those closer to 0. But what are their implications for either individual board members, or the Board as a whole? Do changes need to be made? Does feedback need to be given? To whom? Do you need to be clearer with what your expectations are for the boards' contributions?

Contribution Area	P.	I	P X I
Access: providing connections to relevant people and organizations that can provide information conducive to the effective operation and growth of the business.			
Accountability: holding the CEO and senior team learn to do what they say they will do by periodically check on, probing, and challenging progress status.			
Advice: offering strategic inside and perspective on operational, business development, talent management, and overall growth challenges based on varied past experiences that the business hasn't yet entertained or even fathomed.			
Action: encouraging and supporting positive movement toward growth objectives aligned with the business's mission, purpose, values, and central idea.			
Acceleration: challenfing the business to think out of the box by facilitating rapid, yet thoughtful decision making and innovative growth.			
Achievement: challenging the business to not only reach but exceed all of its measurable goals and objectives in a predictably frequent manner.			
Advantage: ensuring the business is continually competitive in its market place by focusing on customer metrics and market data.			
Assessment: evaluating periodically the organization's individual talent, culture, and overall performance.			
Alignment: understanding and monitoring the consistency of the organization's vision, mission, and values with its daily operating activities and decisions.			
Other:			

ACTION PLANNING

After reading this book, there is a lot to consider. The chapter reflection questions gave you the opportunity to ponder the possibilities for your business, whether it's a one-person consulting practice, a larger firm, or an internal L&D function. Now it is time to apply what you have learned to improve your practice, operation, or business. The questions in this appendix will help you take a deeper dive into considering what you have learned and create some specific actions to address the issues and challenges that may emerge. You may have to review the book to reacquaint yourself with many of the topics covered. You will then have an opportunity to summarize your responses and transfer them into specific actions to build and grow your business.

Documenting your plans will help you carry them out. A separate page is provided for your notes on each of the chapters with the summary action planning forms at the end. Best of luck in your future business endeavors?

Chapter 1: Understanding Industry Dynamics and Trends

1. What was the most important idea or lesson you took from this chapter?

2. To what extent do you think you have a good grasp of the issues and challenges presented in this chapter?

    Quite a Bit   Somewhat   Only a Little   Not Much at All

3. What can you do differently that will enhance your understanding and capability in addressing these issues and challenges?

4. What is getting in the way of you addressing these issues and challenges?

5. What is the first action you will take to address how to improve your business's capability in the topics presented in this chapter?

Chapter 2: Deciding What You Want and Need

1. What was the most important idea or lesson you took from this chapter?

2. To what extent do you think you have a good grasp of the issues and challenges presented in this chapter?

   Quite a Bit   Somewhat   Only a Little   Not Much at All

3. What can you do differently that will enhance your understanding and capability in addressing these issues and challenges?

4. What is getting in the way of you addressing these issues and challenges?

5. What is the first action you will take to address how to improve your business's capability in the topics presented in this chapter?

Chapter 3: Setting the Foundation for Success—or Failure

1. What was the most important idea or lesson you took from this chapter?

2. To what extent do you think you have a good grasp of the issues and challenges presented in this chapter?

   Quite a Bit   Somewhat   Only a Little   Not Much at All

3. What can you do differently that will enhance your understanding and capability in addressing these issues and challenges?

4. What is getting in the way of you addressing these issues and challenges?

5. What is the first action you will take to address how to improve your business' scapability in the topics presented in this chapter?

Chapter 4: Understanding What You Own—and Don't

1. What was the most important idea or lesson you took from this chapter?

2. To what extent do you think you have a good grasp of the issues and challenges presented in this chapter?

   Quite a Bit   Somewhat   Only a Little   Not Much at All

3. What can you do differently that will enhance your understanding and capability in addressing these issues and challenges?

4. What is getting in the way of you addressing these issues and challenges?

5. What is the first action you will take to address how to improve your business's capability in the topics presented in this chapter?

Chapter 5: Differentiating Your Offer From Others

1. What was the most important idea or lesson you took from this chapter?

2. To what extent do you think you have a good grasp of the issues and challenges presented in this chapter?

    Quite a Bit   Somewhat   Only a Little   Not Much at All

3. What can you do differently that will enhance your understanding and capability in addressing these issues and challenges?

4. What is getting in the way of you addressing these issues and challenges?

5. What is the first action you will take to address how to improve your business' scapability in the topics presented in this chapter?

Chapter 6: Moving Your Offer off the Shelf

1. What was the most important idea or lesson you took from this chapter?

2. To what extent do you think you have a good grasp of the issues and challenges presented in this chapter?

    Quite a Bit   Somewhat   Only a Little   Not Much at All

3. What can you do differently that will enhance your understanding and capability in addressing these issues and challenges?

4. What is getting in the way of you addressing these issues and challenges?

5. What is the first action you will take to address how to improve your business's capability in the topics presented in this chapter?

Chapter 7: Operating Profitably and Sustainably

1. What was the most important idea or lesson you took from this chapter?

2. To what extent do you think you have a good grasp of the issues and challenges presented in this chapter?

    Quite a Bit   Somewhat   Only a Little   Not Much at All

3. What can you do differently that will enhance your understanding and capability in addressing these issues and challenges?

4. What is getting in the way of you addressing these issues and challenges?

5. What is the first action you will take to address how to improve your business's capability in the topics presented in this chapter?

Chapter 8: Serving Your Customers and Your Needs

1. What was the most important idea or lesson you took from this chapter?

2. To what extent do you think you have a good grasp of the issues and challenges presented in this chapter?

   Quite a Bit   Somewhat   Only a Little   Not Much at All

3. What can you do differently that will enhance your understanding and capability in addressing these issues and challenges?

4. What is getting in the way of you addressing these issues and challenges?

5. What is the first action you will take to address how to improve your business' s capability in the topics presented in this chapter?

Chapter 9: Overcoming Barriers to Growth and Success

1. What was the most important idea or lesson you took from this chapter?

2. To what extent do you think you have a good grasp of the issues and challenges presented in this chapter?

   Quite a Bit   Somewhat   Only a Little   Not Much at All

3. What can you do differently that will enhance your understanding and capability in addressing these issues and challenges?

4. What is getting in the way of you addressing these issues and challenges?

5. What is the first action you will take to address how to improve your business's capability in the topics presented in this chapter?

Chapter 10: Establishing Your Growth Plan and Exiting

1. What was the most important idea or lesson you took from this chapter?

2. To what extent do you think you have a good grasp of the issues and challenges presented in this chapter?

   Quite a Bit   Somewhat   Only a Little   Not Much at All

3. What can you do differently that will enhance your understanding and capability in addressing these issues and challenges?

4. What is getting in the way of you addressing these issues and challenges?

5. What is the first action you will take to address how to improve your business's capability in the topics presented in this chapter?

Your Action Plan

The purpose of the following pages is to summarize and prioritize the previous pages by selecting those actions that provide the most value as you build and grow your business. There are two parts to this action planning process. Part I asks you to summarize your previous responses into a short list of actions you will take to build and grow your business. Part II asks you to include some timelines, milestones, and resources with your plans.

PART I: Action Summaries

Use the chapter summaries to identify one or two actions, activities, or behaviors you are going to *Start* doing that will enable your business to grow; the one or two things you are going to *Stop* doing that are preventing your business from growing; and the one or two things you are going to *Continue* to do that are currently working and enabling your growth. Let this be your initial action plan for building and growing your business.

> Based on your responses on the previous pages, what are the one or two behaviors, actions, and/or activities you will *Start* doing that will enable the growth of your business?
>
> a.
>
>
> b.

> Based on your responses on the previous pages, what are the one or two behaviors, actions, and/or activities you will *Stop* doing that you are preventing your business from growing?
>
> a.
>
>
> b.

> Based on your responses on the previous pages, what are the one or two behaviors, actions, and/or activities you will *Continue* to do that will further your leader effectiveness?
>
> a.
>
>
> b.

PART II: Business Growth Action Plan

Below are some forms for you to establish a timetable for whenyou will accomplish your action plan. In addition, you are asked to record some milestones against which you can monitor your progress and the resources you might need to accomplish these actions.

You are encouraged to work on a number of other actions you and potentially your senior leadership team or partners feel will enable the growth of your business. But research has shown that for real change to occur, working on less rather than more actions is likely to return greater dividends and improvements. Putting too much on your plate, in addition to your normal job duties, can often be overwhelming, resulting in less time spent on your business' improvement. Therefore, you should only work on a few items at a time. You are also encouraged to share the entire process with your senior leadership team and/or partners. First, restate your *Stop, Start,* and *Continue* actions from Part I. Then complete the progress check milestones, timelines, and needed resources for each.

Start doing:

a.

b.

Action	Milestones	Timeline	Resources
a.			
b.			

Stop doing:

a.

b.

Action	Milestones	Timeline	Resources
a.			
b.			

Continue doing:

a.

BIBLIOGRAPHY

Ainsworth-Land, G.T. 1973. *Grow or Die: The Unifying Principle of Transformation.* New York: Random House.

Allen, M. 2012. *Leaving ADDIE for SAM: An Agile Model for Developing the Best Learning Experiences.* Alexandria, VA: ASTD Press.

Almquist, E., J. Senior, and N. Bloch. 2016. "The Elements of Value." *Harvard Business Review,* September.

Anderson, C. 2014. "Do You Have the Right Business Partners?" *Chief Learning Officer,* March, 48-50.

ATD (Association for Talent Development). 2015a. *Building a Talent Development Structure Without Borders.* Alexandria, VA: ATD Press.

———. 2015b. *State of the Industry Report.* Alexandria, VA: ATD Press.

Barsade, S., and O.A. O'Neill. 2016. "Manage Your Emotional Culture." *Harvard Business Review,* January-February, 58-66.

Barton, D., and M. Wiseman. 2015. "Where Boards Fall Short." *Harvard Business Review,* January-February.

Beahm, G., ed. 2013. *Billionaire Boy: Mark Zuckerberg in His Own Words.* New York: Collins Business.

Bellman, G.M. 2002. *The Consultant's Calling,* 2nd ed. San Francisco: Jossey-Bass.

Bennett, D. 2016. "United's Quest to Be Less Awful." *Bloomberg Businessweek,* January 14. www.bloomberg.com/features/2016-united-airlines-struggles.

Berk, J., P DeMarzo, and J. Harford. 2015. *Fundamentals of Corporate Finance,* 3rd ed. London: Pearson.

Bersin, J. 2016. "Wake Up to the New World of Learning." *Chief Learning Officer,* August 10. www.clomedia.com/2016/08/10/wake-up-to-the-new-world-of-learning

Bersin by Deloitte. 2015. *HR Technology for 2016: 10 Big Disruptions on the Horizon.* Oakland, CA: Bersin by Deloitte.

Bertolini, M., D. Duncan, and A. Waldeck. 2015. "Knowing When to Reinvent." *Harvard Business Review,* December, 92-101.

Betts, B., and A. Anderson. 2016. "Diamond in the Rough." *TD,* January. www.td.org/Publications/Magazines/TD/TD-Archive/2016/01/Diamond-in-the-Rough.

Biech, E. 2000. *The Consultant's Legal Guide.* San Francisco: Pfeiffer.

———. 2001. *The Consultant's Quick Start Guide: An Action Plan for Your First Year in Business.* San Francisco: Pfeiffer.

———. 2007. *The Business of Consulting: The Basics and Beyond*, 2nd ed. San Francisco: Pfeiffer.

Bina, S.S. 2016. "Dealing with Decision Rights: Part of Transformational Leadership Development." *Insigniam Quarterly*, Spring. http://quarterly.insigniam.com/leadership/decision-rights-transformational-leadership-development.

Birkinshaw, J., and M. Haas. 2016. "Increase Your Return on Failure." *Harvard Business Review*, May.

Block, P. 2000. *Flawless Consulting*, 2nd ed. San Francisco: Pfeifer.

Block, S.B., G. Hirt, and B. Danielsen. 2014. *Foundations of Financial Management*. New York: McGraw-Hill Education.

Bond, A. 2016. "The Importance of Culture in Accelerating Growth." Instructional Systems Association's Annual Business Retreat, Scottsdale, AZ, March 22.

Bonnstetter, B.J. 2012. "New Research: The Skills That Make an Entrepreneur." *Harvard Business Review*, December 7. https://hbr.org/2012/12/new-research-the-skills-that-m.

Brown, T. 2008. "Design Thinking." *Harvard Business Review*, June, 84-92.

Bunker, K.A., and S.L. Cohen. 1978. "Evaluating Organizational Training Efforts: Is Ignorance Really Bliss?" *Training & Development Journal* 32 (8): 4-11.

Burnison, G. 2013. "Korn-Ferry's CEO on Transforming the Company in Mid-Crisis." *Harvard Business Review*, December, 45-48.

Carroll, K. 2014. "Beating the Odds: Why Most Mergers and Acquisitions Fail." *Talent Management*, February, 20-23.

Chaffey, D. 2016. "Digital Marketing Trends for 2017." Smart Insights, December 15. www.smartinsights.com/managing-digital-marketing/marketing-innovation/digital-marketing-trends-2016-2017/.

Chaffey, D. 2017. "10 Reasons You Need a Digital Marketing Strategy." http://www.smartinsights.com/digital-marketing-strategy/digital-strategy-development/10-reasons-for-digital-marketing-strategy/ January 9.

Chambers, J. 2016. "Cisco's John Chambers on the Digital Era." McKinsey & Co. Interview, March. www.mckinsey.com/industries/high-tech/our-insights/ciscos-john-chambers-on-the-digital-era.

Charan, R., D. Casey, and M. Useem. 2014. *Boards That Lead*. Boston: Harvard Business Review Press.

Christensen, C.M., T. Hall, K. Dillon, and D.S. Duncan. 2016. "Know Your Customers' 'Job to Be Done.'" *Harvard Business Review*, September.

Christensen, C.M., M. Raynor, and R. McDonald. 2015. "What Is Disruptive Innovation?" *Harvard Business Review*, December, 45-53.

Christensen, C.M., D. Wang, and D. van Bever. 2013. "Consulting on the Cusp of Disruption." *Harvard Business Review*, October, 107-113.

Cohen, S.L., and N.K. Backer. 1999. "Making and Mining Intellectual Capital: Method of Madness." *Training & Development*, September, 46-50.

Cohen, S.L. 1993. "The Art, Science and Business of Program Development." *T+D*, May, 49-58.

———. 2002. "Matching the Method to the Message: Strategies for Instruction." *Performance Improvement* 41 (6): 28-33.

———. 2004. "Performance Improvement Through Relationship Building." *T+D*, July, 41-46.

———. 2005. "Controlling Program Evaluation." *Performance Improvement* 44 (8): 23.

Cohen, S.L., A. Deege, and U. Brewer-Frazier. 2006. "Learning Tools: New Tricks for Non-Technical Learners." *Chief Learning Officer*, December, 36-53.

Cohen, S.L., and J. Jurkovic. 1997. "Learning From a Masterpiece." *T+D*, November, 66-70.

Cohen, S.L., J.J. L'Allier, and D. Stewart. 1987. "Interactive Videodisc—Then, Now, and Minutes From Now." *Training & Development Journal*, October, 31-38.

Cohen, S.L., and D. Payiatakis. 2002. "E-Learning: Harnessing the Hype." *Performance Improvement* 41 (2): 7-15.

Cohen, S.L., and J.P. Pine, III. 2007. "Mass Customizing the Training Industry." *T+D*, June.

Cohen, S.L., and C. Reinhart. 2000. "50 Ways (More or Less) to Leave Your Client." *T+D*, May, 86-89.

Cohen, S.L., and R. Whiteley. 2014. "How to Effectively Create, Manage and Leverage a Company Board." Instructional Systems Association's Annual Business Retreat, Scottsdale, AZ, March.

Cohn & Wolfe. 2014. "Authentic Brands 2014: Key Findings." www.cohnwolfe.com/en/authenticbrands/keyfindings.

Cooper, R.G. 1990. "Stage-Gate Systems: A New Tool for Managing New Product Development." *Business Horizons* 33 (3): 44-55.

Collins, J.C., and M.T. Hansen. 2011. *Great by Choice*. New York: Harper Collins.

Covey, S. 2004. *The 7 Habits of Highly Effective People*. New York: Simon & Schuster.

Del Prado, G.M. 2015. "Mark Zuckerberg's Vision of the Future Is Full of Artificial Intelligence, Telepathy, and Virtual Reality." *Business Insider*, July 2. www.businessinsider.com/facebooks-mark-zuckerberg-predictions-about-the-future-2015-7.

DeMers, J. 2013. "The Top 7 Online Marketing Trends That Will Dominate 2014." Forbes.com, September 17. www.forbes.com/sites/jaysondemers/2013/09/17/the-top-7-online-marketing-trends-that-will-dominate-2014.

———. 2015. "The Top 7 Online Marketing Trends That Will Dominate 2016." Forbes.com, September 29. www.forbes.com/sites/jaysondemers/2015/09/29/the-top-7-online-marketing-trends-that-will-dominate-2016.

Devine, J. 2009. "The Four Types of Intellectual Property." Ezine Articles, March 13. http://ezinearticles.com/?The-Four-Types-of-Intellectual-Property&id=2098198.

Dillow, C., and A. Nusca. 2016. "This Is What Your Company Should Look Like." *Fortune*, June 10. http://fortune.com/21st-century-corporation-office.

Dobbs, P., J. Manyika, and J. Woetzel. 2015. *No Ordinary Disruption: The Four Global Forces Breaking All Trends*. New York: Public Affairs.

Equiteq. 2013. *100 Tips for Consulting Firms to Accelerate Profit and Value Growth*. New York: Equiteq. www.equiteq.com/media/9257/100%20Growth%20Tips.pdf.

Fortune. 2016. "World's Most Admired Companies: 7. Southwest Airlines." January 1. http://fortune.com/worlds-most-admired-companies/southwest-airlines-7.

Freeman, D. 2013. "New Customer-Rage Study Out for Holiday Shopping Season." Press Release. Arizona State University, W.P. Carey School of Business, November 26. https://wpcarey.asu.edu/news-releases/2013-11-26/new-customer-rage-study-out-holiday-shopping-season.

Galagan, P. 2015. "Trends and Tides in Talent Development." *TD*, October, 28-33.

Gartner and Pemberton Levy, H. 2015. "Gartner Predicts Our Digital Future," October 6. http://www.gartner.com/smarterwithgartner/gartner-predicts-our-digital-future/

Grove, A. 1996. *Only the Paranoid Survive: How to Exploit the Crisis Points That Challenge Every Company*. New York: Currency Books.

Gwin, B.W., and C. Vavrek. 2011. "Three Critical Questions You Should Ask Yourself About Your Board Evaluation." *Directors & Boards*, Heidrick & Struggles Governance Letter, Fourth Quarter, 68-69.

Hamel, G., and C.K. Prahalad. 1994. *Competing for the Future*. Boston, MA: Harvard Business School Press.

Hart, C.W., J.L. Heskett, and W.E. Sasser Jr. 1990. "The Profitable Art of Service Recovery." *Harvard Business Review*, July-August.

Heskett, J.J., W. Sasser Jr., and L.A. Schlesinger. 1997. *The Service Profit Chain*. New York: The Free Press.

Informa. 2013. "Informa PLC: Disposal of Its Five Corporate Training Businesses." Press Release, July 19. www.informa.com/media/press-releases-news/latest-news/disposal-of-its-five-corporate-training-businesses.

ISA (Instructional Systems Association). 2016. "Like Size Company Session Survey Results." Instructional Systems Association's Annual Business Retreat, Scottsdale, AZ, March.

Jones, J.M. 2015. "U.S. Telecommuting for Work Climbs to 37%." Workplace, August 19. http://www.gallup.com/poll/184649/telecommuting-work-climbs.aspx.

Jones, K., and W. Wang-Audia. 2014. *The Market for Talent Management Systems 2014: Talent Optimization for the Global Workforce*. Oakland, CA: Bersin by Deloitte.

Kaplan, R.S., and D.P. Norton. 1992. "The Balanced Scorecard: Measures That Drive Performance." *Harvard Business Review*, January-February.

Kim, W.C., and R. Mauborgne. 2005. *Blue Ocean Strategy: How to Create Uncontested Market Space and Make Competition Irrelevant*. Boston: Harvard Business School Press.

Kiss Metrics. 2016. "Customer Acquisition Cost: The One Metric That Can Determine Your Company's Fate." Kissmetrics Blog, https://blog.kissmetrics.com/customer-acquisition-cost.

Knowles, M.S., and Associates. 1984. *Andragogy in Action: Applying Modern Principles of Adult Learning*. San Francisco: Jossey-Bass.

Ko, I., L. Nieminen, S. Patrick, and A. Wastag. 2016. "Culture Can't Wait to Be King." *Chief Learning Officer*, January, 18-20.

Kotter, J. 2016. "Thought Leader Award." Presented at the Instructional Systems Association's Annual Business Retreat, Scottsdale, AZ, March 21.

Kriegel, R.J., and L. Patler. 1991. *If It Ain't Broke, Break It.* New York: Warner Books.

Krishna, A., G. Dangayach, and S. Sharma. 2014. "Service Recovery Paradox: The Success Parameters." *Global Business Review* 15 (2): 263-277.

Kübler-Ross, E. 1969. *On Death and Dying.* New York: Simon & Schuster.

Lafley, A.G., R.L. Martin, J.W. Rivkin, and N. Siggelkow. 2012. "Bringing Science to the Art of Strategy." *Harvard Business Review,* September, 57-66.

Lamp, A. 2014. "The Value of Balancing Desirability, Feasibility, and Viability." Crowd Favorite Insights. https://crowdfavorite.com/the-value-of-balancing-desirability-feasibility-and-viability/.

Lindsey, E. H., V. Homes, and M.W. McCall Jr. 1987. *Key Events in Executives' Lives.* Greensboro, NC: Center for Creative Leadership.

Lippett, M. 2007. "Fix the Disconnect Between Strategy and Execution." *T+D,* August, 54-57.

Maddocks, J., and M. Beaney. 2002. "See the Invisible and Intangible." *Journal of Knowledge Management,* March, 16.

Markidan, L. 2014. "Why It's Okay to Fire Your Bad Customers." Groove blog, November 18. www.groovehq.com/support/how-to-fire-a-bad-customer.

Martin, R.L. 2016. "M&A: The One Thing You Need to Get Right." *Harvard Business Review*, June, 43-46.

Maynila, D., M. Chui, J. Bughin, R. Dobbs, P. Bisson, and A. Marrs. 2013. *Disruptive Technologies: Advances That Will Transform Life, Business and the Global Economy.* New York: McKinsey Global Institute.

McCall, M.W., Jr. 2010. "Recasting Leadership Development." *Industrial Organizational Psychology: Perspectives on Science and Practice* 3 (1): 3-19.

McCall, M.W., Jr., M.M. Lombardo, and A.M. Morrison. 1988. *The Lessons of Experience: How Successful Executives Develop on the Job.* Lexington, MA: Lexington Books.

Miller, D. 2016. "Story Brand." Presented at the Instructional Systems Association's Annual Business Retreat, Scottsdale, AZ, March 23.

Mindshare. 2016. "Brand Badges and the New Millennial Identity." www.scribd.com/document/245726568/Brand-Badges-and-the-New-Millennial-Identity.

Morin, C. 2016. "Mobile Neuromarketing: The Future of Customer Engagement." Presented at the Riverside Leadership Summit, Woodlands Conference Center, Houston TX, February 23.

Mosher, B. 2016. "I Don't Hate the Classroom." *Chief Learning Officer,* July.

Murray, A. 2016a. "The Pinnacles and Pitfalls of Corporate Culture." *Fortune,* March 3. http://fortune.com/2016/03/03/best-companies-to-work-for-editors-desk.

———. 2016b. "Oracles of Davos: CEOs See Sweeping Changes in the World of Work." *Fortune,* March 1. http://fortune.com/2016/03/08/davos-new-industrial-revolution.

Neal, A., and D. Sonsino. 2015. "Talent Management Disrupted." *TD,* September, 30-35.

Neilson, G.L., K.L. Martin, and E. Powers. 2008. "The Secrets to Successful Strategy Execution." *Harvard Business Review*, June.

Nichols, F., and H. Bergholz. 2013. "The Consultant's Competency Circle: A Tool for Gauging Your Success Potential as an Independent Consultant." *Performance Improvement* 52 (2): 37-41.

Nowack, K.M. 2015. "Urban Talent Myths Exposed." *Talent Management*, June, 35-47.

Otalcan, O. 2016. "The E-Marketing Plan." Professional Education Organization International course. www.peoi.org/Courses/Coursesen/emarket/emarket7.html.

Patler, L. 2016. *Make Your Own Waves: The Surfer's Rules for Innovators and Entrepreneurs*. New York: AMACOM.

Porter, M. 1985. *Competitive Advantage*. New York: The Free Press.

Raynor, M.E., and M. Ahmed. 2013. *The Three Rules: How Exceptional Companies Think*. New York: Penguin.

Reeves, M., S. Levin, and D. Ueda. 2014. "The Biology of Corporate Survival." *Harvard Business Review*, January-February, 47-55.

Reichheld, F.F. 1996. *The Loyalty Effect*. Boston: Harvard Business School Press.

———. 2003. "The One Number You Need to Grow." *Harvard Business Review*, December.

———. 2006. *The Ultimate Question: Driving Good Profits and True Growth*. Boston: Harvard Business School Press.

Sanders, T. 2016. "Genius Is a Team Sport." Presented at the Instructional Systems Association's Annual Business Retreat, Scottsdale, AZ, March 20.

Sawhney, M. 2016. "Putting Products Into Services: A Revenue-Growth Playbook for Consultants and Law Firms." *Harvard Business Review*, September, 84-88.

Scafario, C. 2011. "Building a Value Proposition; Your Strategy, Your Brand and Your Business." September 8. www.slideshare.net/cscafario/building-a-value-proposition-your-strategy-your-brand-and-your-business.

Schwab, K. 2015. "The Fourth Industrial Revolution." *Foreign Affairs*, December 12. www.foreginaffairs.com/articles/2015-12-12/fourth-industrial-revolution.

Shaw, D.R. 2013. "Why Does My Private Company Need a Board of Directors?" *Director Journal*, January, 165.

Sheppeck, M.A., and S.L. Cohen. 1985. "Put a Dollar Value on Your Training Programs." *Training & Development Journal* 39 (11): 59-62.

Silverberg, T. 2015. "Mission vs Vision." Blog, May 19. http://tiffanysilverberg.com/mission-vs-vision.

Simons, R. 2014. "Choosing the Right Customer." *Harvard Business Review*, March.

Sinek, S. 2009. "How Great Leaders Inspire Action." TED Talk, September. www.ted.com/talks/simon_sinek_how_great_leaders_inspire_action?.

Smith, G. 2016. "Mission vs. Vision: What's the Difference?" Blog, April 12. www.thegrowthcoachhouston.com/mission-vs-vision-whats-the-difference.

Sonnenfeld, J. 2002. "What Makes Great Boards Great." *Harvard Business Review*, September.

Sonnenfeld, J., K. Kusin, and E. Walton. 2013. "What CEOs Really Think of Their Boards." *Harvard Business Review*, April.

StratGo Marketing. 2013. "How to Get Rid of Innovation-itis." Blog, April 3. https://stratgomarketing.com/tag/innovation-types/2013.

Sull, D., R. Homkes, and C. Sull. 2015. "Why Strategy Execution Unravels—and What to Do About It." *Harvard Business Review*, March.

Taleb, N.N. 2007. *The Black Swan*. New York: Random House.

Tom, J. 2016. "Inbound Marketing and Demand Generation." ISA Webinar Series, January 13.

Training. 2016. *2016 Training Industry Report*. November/December. https://trainingmag.com/sites/default/files/images/Training_Industry_Report_2016.pdf.

Treacy, M., and F. Wiersema. 1997. *The Discipline of Market Leaders*. New York: Perseus Books.

Tulgan, B. 2016. "The Great Generational Shift: The Emerging Post-Boomer Workforce." Rainmaker Thinking, Whitepaper. http://rainmakerthinking.com/assets/uploads/2016/06/Gen-Shift-White-Paper-2016_June.2016.pdf.

van Opzeeland, P. 2015. "9 Ways to Identify a Bad Customer." Userlike blog, May 28. www.userlike.com/en/blog/2015/05/28/9-ways-identify-bad-customer.

Vukotich, G. 2016. "Failing Fast Is Good for Business." *Chief Learning Officer*, January, 27-29.

Walker. 2016. "The Walker Loyalty Matrix." www.walkerinfo.com/knowledge-center/white-papers/the-walker-loyalty-matrix.asp.

Welles, E. 2002. "Rolled Up and Rolled Over." *Fortune Small Business*, February.

Wilkinson, M. 2016. "Accelerated Growth Strategies." Presented at the Instructional Systems Association's Annual Business Retreat, Scottsdale, AZ, March 22.

Zenger, T. 2013. "What Is the Theory of Your Firm?" *Harvard Business Review*, June, 75-77.

Personal Communication

Aldersea, R. (Partner, Equiteq). 2016. Interview With the Author. February.

DeVito, L. (Associate Director, Lead for HR Consulting Research, ALM Intelligence). 2016. Interview With the Author. March.

Jace, T. (CEO, Crisis Prevention Institute). 2016. Interview With the Author. May.

Rosen, B. (CEO, Interaction Associates). 2016. Interview With the Author. February.

Russo, C. (President and Founder, RussoRights). 2015. Interview With the Author. July.

Schmidt, P. (Executive Director, Instructional Systems Association). 2016. Interview With the Author. February.

Zenger, J. (CEO and Co-Founder, Zenger Folkman). 2013. Interview With the Author. September 3.

ABOUT THE AUTHOR

 Steve Cohen is founder and principal of the Strategic Leadership Collaborative, a private consulting practice focused on business strategy and leadership development. He has more than 40 years of experience in the talent development industry, having earned worldwide recognition for his accomplishments when named one of the industry's "thought leaders" by ATD. During his career, he has advanced the strategies of corporations around the globe, creating hundreds of groundbreaking consulting engagements for Fortune 500 as well as training supplier companies. He has also demonstrated a proven track record for building equity by growing top- and bottom-line performance for eight consulting enterprises in the education and training industry he has either founded, led, and/or sold. Thanks to this experience and expertise, he has been called upon to consult with approximately 30 talent development supplier firms needing strategic guidance and board advisory services. He has served on more than 15 advisory boards in the training and education industry, preparing many of them for eventual sale and/or merger, and has facilitated strategic growth planning projects for numerous others.

Cohen has a master's and a doctoral degree in industrial/organizational psychology from the University of Tennessee, a bachelor's in psychology from Hobart and William Smith Colleges, and is a certified performance technologist. He has authored and delivered more than 150 refereed articles, chapters, and presentations on a wide spectrum of talent development topics, including leadership and organizational assessment, development, delivery, and evaluation. He was invited by ATD to author a monthly blog on leading and growing talent development consulting businesses, which has served as the basis for this book. He can be reached at Steve@strategicleadershipcollaborative.com.

INDEX